About *The Way Into...*

The Way Into... is a major series that provides an accessible and highly usable "guided tour" of the Jewish faith and people, its history and beliefs—in total, a basic introduction to Judaism for adults that will enable them to understand and interact with sacred texts.

The Authors

Each book in the series is written by a leading contemporary teacher and thinker. While each of the authors brings his or her own individual style of teaching to the series, every volume's approach is the same: to help you to learn, in a life-affecting way, about important concepts in Judaism.

The Concepts

Each volume in *The Way Into...* Series explores one important concept in Judaism, including its history, its basic vocabulary, and what it means to Judaism and to us. In the Jewish tradition of study, the reader is helped to interact directly with sacred texts.

The topics to be covered in *The Way Into...* Series:

Torah
Jewish Prayer
Encountering God in Judaism
Jewish Mystical Tradition
Covenant and Commandment
Holiness and Chosenness (Kedushah)
Time
The Natural World
Zion
Tikkun Olam (Repairing the World)
Money and Ownership
Women and Men
Jews and Non-Jews
Varieties of Jewishness

The Way Into

Encountering God in Judaism

Neil Gillman

דרך למוד דרך למוד דרך למוד
דרך למוד

JEWISH LIGHTS Publishing

Woodstock, Vermont

The Way Into Encountering God in Judaism

© 2000 by Neil Gillman

Library of Congress Cataloging-in-Publication Data

Gillman, Neil.
The way into encountering God in Judaism / Neil Gillman.
p. cm. — (The way into—)
Includes bibliographical references and index.
ISBN 1-58023-025-3 (hc.)
1. God (Judaism) 2. God (Judaism)—History of doctrines.
I. Title: Encountering God in Judaism. II. Title. III. Series.
BM610 .G53 2000
296.3'11—dc21
00-011769

10 9 8 7 6 5 4 3 2 1

Manufactured in the United States of America
Jacket design by Glenn Suokko
Text design by Glenn Suokko

Published by Jewish Lights Publishing
A Division of LongHill Partners, Inc.
Sunset Farm Offices, Route 4, P.O. Box 237
Woodstock, VT 05091
Tel: (802) 457-4000   Fax: (802) 457-4004
www.jewishlights.com

The publisher gratefully acknowledges the contribution of Rabbi Sheldon Zimmerman to the creation of this series. In his lifelong work of bringing a greater appreciation of Judaism to all people, he saw the need for *The Way Into...* and inspired us to act on it.

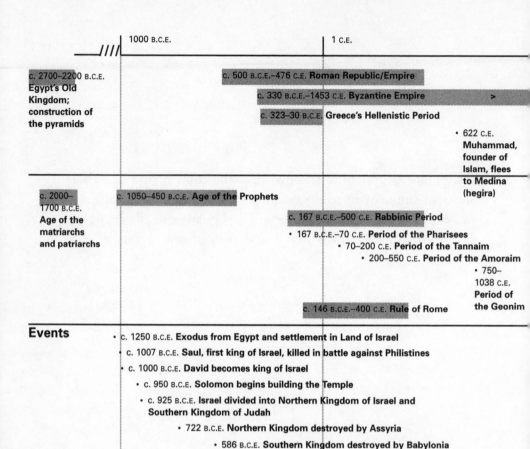

1000 B.C.E.　　　　　　　　　1 C.E.

c. 2700–2200 B.C.E.
Egypt's Old Kingdom; construction of the pyramids

c. 500 B.C.E.–476 C.E. **Roman Republic/Empire**

c. 330 B.C.E.–1453 C.E. **Byzantine Empire** >

c. 323–30 B.C.E. **Greece's Hellenistic Period**

• 622 C.E. **Muhammad, founder of Islam, flees to Medina (hegira)**

c. 2000–1700 B.C.E.
Age of the matriarchs and patriarchs

c. 1050–450 B.C.E. **Age of the Prophets**

c. 167 B.C.E.–500 C.E. **Rabbinic Period**

• 167 B.C.E.–70 C.E. **Period of the Pharisees**

• 70–200 C.E. **Period of the Tannaim**

• 200–550 C.E. **Period of the Amoraim**

• 750–1038 C.E. **Period of the Geonim**

c. 146 B.C.E.–400 C.E. **Rule of Rome**

Events

• c. 1250 B.C.E. **Exodus from Egypt and settlement in Land of Israel**

• c. 1007 B.C.E. **Saul, first king of Israel, killed in battle against Philistines**

• c. 1000 B.C.E. **David becomes king of Israel**

• c. 950 B.C.E. **Solomon begins building the Temple**

• c. 925 B.C.E. **Israel divided into Northern Kingdom of Israel and Southern Kingdom of Judah**

• 722 B.C.E. **Northern Kingdom destroyed by Assyria**

• 586 B.C.E. **Southern Kingdom destroyed by Babylonia**

• 538 B.C.E. **Return from Babylonian exile; Jerusalem ("Second") Temple rebuilt**

• c. 500–400 B.C.E. **The Torah, Five Books of Moses, is compiled/edited, according to biblical scholarship**

• c. 250 B.C.E. **"Septuagint" translation of Torah into Greek**

• 167 B.C.E. **Hasmonean (Maccabean) Revolt**

• 70 C.E. **Rome destroys Second Temple**

• c. 200 **The Mishnah compiled/edited by Rabbi Judah ha-Nasi**

• c. 300–600 **The Babylonian and Palestinian Talmuds are compiled/edited**

1000 C.E.   2000 C.E.

• c. 1040–1105 **Rashi, French Bible and Talmud scholar and creator of line-by-line commentary on the Torah**

   • 1178 **Maimonides (1135–1204) completes his code of Jewish law, the *Mishneh Torah***

      • c. 1295 ***The Zohar,* Kabbalistic work of mystical teaching, composed**

         • 1492 **Jews expelled from Spain**

            • 1565 **Joseph Caro publishes *Shulchan Arukh*, the standard code of Jewish law and practice**

               • 1654 **First Jewish settlement in North America at New Amsterdam**

                  • 1700–1760 **Israel Baal Shem Tov, founder of Hasidism**

                     • 1729–1786 **Moses Mendelssohn, "Father of the Jewish Enlightenment"**

                        • 1801–1888 **Samson Raphael Hirsch, founder of "modern Orthodoxy"**

                           • 1836 **Yeshiva University founded**

                              • 1873; 1875 **Reform Judaism in U.S. establishes
                              Union of American Hebrew Congregations and Hebrew Union College**

                                 • 1887 **Conservative Judaism's Jewish Theological Seminary founded**

                                    • 1897 **Theodor Herzl convenes first Zionist Congress**

                                       • 1933–1945 **The Holocaust (Shoah)**

                                          • 1935 **Mordecai Kaplan establishes the Jewish Reconstructionist Foundation**

                                             • 1948 **Birth of the State of Israel**

For
Jacob Samuel
and
Ellen Shoshana

*But take utmost care and watch yourselves scrupulously
that you do not forget the things that you saw with your
own eyes.... And make them known to your children
and your children's children.* (Deuteronomy 4:9)

How do I fulfill this? It is as if to say that whoever teaches his
children Torah, Scripture considers him to have taught
his children, his children's children, and their children to the
end of all generations. (Babylonian Talmud, *Kiddushin* 30a)

Contents

About *The Way Into...*   **i**
Timeline   **vi**
Acknowledgments   **xv**
A Note on the Text   **xix**

Introduction   1

Can people know anything about God? Can people say anything about God? Worshipful silence or metaphorical language? The sin of idolatry: worshiping the image instead of God. We discover God and create the metaphors. Can we be sure that it is God that we discover?

1. God Is *Echad*   17

The *Shema*: What does it mean? One and not two, or unique? Maimonides on God's integrity. Can love be commanded? Israel loves God, and God loves Israel. Living in a world under one God. God is not yet *Echad*. God is lonely.

2. God Is Power   33

God's power is unchallenged. God even creates evil and reverses the course of nature. There are restraints on God's power: human freedom and the possibilities of repentance. God's power in nature and God's power in history. God's eventual defeat of death.

3. God Is Person   51

Two questions: "Where are you?" and "Where is your brother?" God searches for us as we search for God. God's vulnerability. The hidden face of God. God as spouse, parent, and lover. The wrath of God. Anger versus abandonment. God weeps. God as person or God as process. God can be moved.

4. God Is Nice (Sometimes)   71

Tensions in the Jewish image of God. How Psalms shaped the Jewish consciousness. God as nurturing, as refuge, and as rock. God heals what ails us. The issue of feminist God-language. God is a teacher.

5. God Is Not Nice (Sometimes)   89

The "down" images of God. From feelings to metaphors. The challenge of the Book of Job. Is God ethical? The death of Rabbi Akiva. The problem of human suffering. Holocaust theology. The legitimacy of unbelief. The death of God. A liturgical challenge to God.

6. God Can Change   109

Can God really change? What changes? How God deals with human sinfulness: the evolution of a doctrine. Sin is punished immediately, but the punishment must be just and it may be deferred. Repentance enters the picture. The message of the Book of Jonah. The Thirteen Attributes of God in the Bible and in the liturgy. *Unetaneh Tokef:* the development of a metaphor.

7. God Creates   127

The triad: creation, revelation, redemption. We are partners with God in all three. Four understandings of creation:

as order out of anarchy, as anthropocentric, as the result of a primordial combat, as renewed daily and perpetually. From the Bible to the liturgy. Why four accounts? God is not the conclusion but the point of departure.

8. God Reveals   **145**
The principle of revelation and the fact of revelation. Does God choose Israel? The content of revelation: the traditional position and three liberal interpretations. The image of God in each of these. We are partners with God in revelation. God in Exodus and God in the Joseph narrative. Heteronomy versus autonomy.

9. God Redeems   **165**
To redeem is to save. From history to eschatology. The eschatological impulse. Three dimensions of Jewish eschatology: the universal, the national, and the individual. God's triumph over death. The world as not yet redeemed. We are partners with God in redemption. Repairing the world. God as the power that makes for salvation.

Epilogue   **185**

Notes   **187**
Glossary   **191**
Suggestions for Further Reading   **199**
Index   **201**
About Jewish Lights Publishing   **206**

Acknowledgments

In retrospect, much of my writing on the central issues of Jewish theology over the past decade can be viewed as an extension of the thinking reflected in my *Sacred Fragments: Recovering Theology for the Modern Jew* (Jewish Publication Society, 1991). *The Death of Death: Resurrection and Immortality in Jewish Thought* (Jewish Lights Publishing, 1997) evolved out of the final chapter of the earlier book, and this volume elaborates on what I wrote then on how human beings can think or speak of God. The reader who seeks a more comprehensive statement of my theological assumptions should consult the first book.

I continue to believe that scholarly inquiry takes place primarily in the give-and-take of the classroom. I acknowledge my boundless gratitude to my students, both at The Jewish Theological Seminary and in adult education classes around the country, for helping to clarify my thinking on all the issues dealt with in this book. Their readiness to engage with me in serious theological inquiry, their challenges—usually gentle but often quite sharp—and their unfailing encouragement have meant more to me than I can ever express. My colleagues on the Seminary faculty have always been available to help me deal with questions regarding the interpretation of biblical and rabbinic texts. I thank them all, but I hasten to add that I alone am responsible for my conclusions. The staff of the Seminary library could not have been more gracious in helping me to track obscure bibliographical data. Last but certainly not least, Chancellor Ismar

Schorsch has been unfailingly generous in his support of my research and my teaching.

For some time, I had contemplated writing a book on the various images of God reflected in Jewish texts when Stuart Matlins, the founder and publisher of Jewish Lights Publishing, called on me to contribute a book on God to *The Way Into...* series. Stuart has been a friend and advisor ever since he asked me to serve as a consultant for his new publishing venture, and he was singularly responsible for encouraging me to write *The Death of Death*. Fortunately, the book that I had contemplated writing and the book he wanted me to write turned out to be the same. I cherish his friendship and look forward to many more years of association with Stuart and with Jewish Lights. Beyond this, the entire staff of Jewish Lights has been an absolute pleasure to work with. I am grateful to Sandra Korinchak and Emily Wichland for guiding the preparation of the manuscript for publication and to my editors, Elisheva S. Urbas, whose vision of the series as a whole informed my research at the outset, and Alys R. Yablon, whose meticulous editing of the final versions of the book have made it far superior to what it would have been otherwise.

My long-time research assistant, Rabbi Lea Gavrieli, was unstinting in the time and energy she devoted to helping me with stylistic and bibliographical issues and with the mysteries of word processing. Her support has been indispensable. Rabbi Amy Levin, friend and colleague of many years, has guided me through critical decisions in each of my previous books. She was available to do the same this time.

My wife, Sarah, my daughters, Abby and Debby, my son-in-law, Michael, my future son-in-law, Danny, and my grandchildren, Jacob and Ellen, are a constant source of joy and inspiration. I do not have the words to express my gratitude to them all.

Finally, as we approach the season of forgiveness, I am acutely conscious of having been presumptuous enough to have written an entire book about God, whose nature, I confess, neither I nor any human being can know. That same God, I pray, will be generous with me, forgive me, and continue to grant me the health and curiosity to pursue the work that has given me such unqualified fulfillment so far.

A Note on the Text

Some notes on format: For quotations from Hebrew Scriptures, except for a few instances recorded in the endnotes, I have used the translation in *Tanakh* (Jewish Publication Society, 1985). Citations of biblical texts are added to the body of the text; more extended bibliographical references are in the endnotes. Although I consulted all the standard translations of rabbinic and liturgical texts, again, unless noted, I have felt free to adapt these for my own purposes.

Ever since the publication of *Sacred Fragments*, I have avoided using masculine pronouns for references both to God and to people. Even though this practice has frequently led to cumbersome circumlocutions, I continue this practice here. The one exception to this rule is in my use of biblical texts. Here, I simply reproduce the Jewish Publication Society translation. Also, although it is my hope that this book will also be read by non-Jews, I have also used terms such as "our ancestors" to refer to previous generations of Jews, or "we" to refer to current Jewish thinking and practice, on the assumption that my primary audience will be Jewish. I trust that my non-Jewish readers will understand and forgive this less-than-inclusive practice.

Introduction

Who Is God?

Some thirty years ago I was walking through the corridors of the
school where I teach, and I encountered my teacher, Abraham
Joshua Heschel. For the budding theologian that I was in those
days, Heschel was an intimidating figure: How could I ever know
what he knew, write as he wrote, and have the impact that he had?
Somewhat nervously, I attempted to engage him in a conversation
and I asked him about his new book, *What Is Man?* He turned
sharply and replied, "It's not *What Is Man?* It's *Who Is Man?*"[1]

My error was well intentioned. The formula "What is man?"
is familiar to any worshiping Jew. It appears twice in the Psalms
and is recited four times a year in our *Yizkor* (Memorial) service:

> When I behold Your heavens, the work of Your fingers,
> the moon and stars that You set in place,
> what is man that You have been mindful of him,
> mortal man that You have taken note of him?
> —*Psalm 8:4–5*

> O Lord, what is man that You should care about him
> mortal man, that You should think of him?
> —*Psalm 144:3*

In both of these texts, the question is clearly rhetorical. In fact,
despite the punctuation, the psalmist is not really asking a question,

not asking for information about the nature or essence of a human being. If anything, the statement is an exclamation, an outburst of astonishment at the place of the human being against the backdrop of God's creation, as evidenced by the two responses. In the first, humanity is "little less than divine"; in the second, humanity's days are "like a passing shadow." Of course, both responses are profoundly true. However, my teacher wanted to accentuate the fact that human beings are precisely persons, not inanimate objects. His question was then "Who?" not "What?"

Whatever the thrust of the biblical passages, nowhere in the Bible can we find the alternative question, "Who [or what] is God?" Yet, if the Bible is the story of the complex interpersonal relationship between humanity and God, then the relationship itself demands that both parties to the relationship be persons, and that both "know" something of the nature of the other partner.

That question remains unasked in the Bible because the biblical communities already knew the answer. First, they perceived God's presence everywhere—in nature, in history, and in the range of human experiences. For them, God was an active presence in their lives. The entire biblical narrative bears witness to the authors' perception of God's active presence in the world. Second, they believed that the entire Torah was verbally handed down by God to Moses at Mount Sinai (as narrated in Exodus 19–20). In some biblical texts, God even indulges in explicit self-characterization:

> The Lord! the Lord! A God compassionate and gracious, slow to anger, abounding in kindness and faithfulness, extending kindness to the thousandth generation, forgiving iniquity, transgression and sin; yet [God] does not remit all punishment, but visits the iniquity of the parents, upon children and children's children, upon the third and fourth generation.
>
> —*Exodus 34:6–7*

In its original context, this passage follows the sin of the golden calf (Exodus 32–34). Moses pleads with God to forgive the people and asks God to "let me know Your ways, that I may know you and continue in Your favor." To know God's "ways" is to know something of God's nature, how God deals with human beings. In the context of the story of the golden calf, what Moses wants to know about God's nature is how God deals with human sinfulness. Our text constitutes God's own answer: despite God's infinite patience, sin must eventually be requited. Both this text and its image of God will be radically transformed in the later tradition, but for the present, this is one of God's answers to the question "Who is God?"

Can God Be Known?

There is an additional way of accounting for the unasked question. How, in principle, is it even possible for human beings to capture the nature of God? The anonymous prophet who authored the book we call Second Isaiah (chapters 40–55 of the Book of Isaiah) put it this way:

> To whom can you compare Me
> Or declare me similar?
> To whom can you liken Me,
> So that we seem comparable?
> —Isaiah 46:5

This prophet was a member of the community of Israelites who had been exiled to Babylonia after the destruction of Jerusalem and the First Temple in 586 B.C.E. His question, equally rhetorical, is also derisive, for as the passage continues, he sharply condemns the gods of the surrounding pagan community, gods that are made "of silver and gold," that they "carry on their backs," "that do not budge from their place," and, preeminently, a god that "if they cry out to it, it does not answer."

How can the prophet's God be compared with any of these idols? If that's what people mean by *god,* then indeed there is no comparison. However, the prophet's question has another layer of meaning. He is not only comparing God with idols, he is also asserting the principle that his God is beyond any form of human comprehension or expression. Yet, there is not a passage in the entire Bible that does not speak voluminously about just what this God is like.

That's precisely the paradox about the biblical God. This God cannot be compared with anything else in the world. We call this quality God's absolute transcendence. God is the utter "beyond"— beyond anything that we can experience, know, and describe in human language. That's precisely what makes God God, and that's the difference between any object in the created world and God. We can directly experience, hence know, and hence describe all of creation; we cannot experience, know, and describe God. Nevertheless, the authors of the biblical texts seem to know and say a great deal about what God is like, what God does in nature and history, and what God wants from humanity.

The Sin of Idolatry

The expectation that we humans can capture the nature of God is a good preliminary definition of what the Bible calls the sin of idolatry. In Second Isaiah, the idol is a material object that reflects the prophet's experience in a pagan society. According to the second of the ten commandments:

> You shall not make for yourself a sculptured image, or any likeness of what is in the heavens above, or on the earth below, or in the waters under the earth. You shall not bow down to them or serve them.
>
> —*Exodus 20:4–5*

That text, too, refers to the attempt to worship a material object as a god. By extension, and as the post-biblical tradition understood idolatry, any time we install a feature of creation and call it God, we are committing the sin of idolatry, the cardinal Jewish sin. It need not be a material object; it can be something much more abstract or elusive: a nation, history itself (as in Marxism), financial reward, or another human being. Whenever we take something that is relative and install it as our ultimate value, we have committed the sin of idolatry. We have reduced God to something that cannot bear the burden of ultimacy, of transcendence. That's idolatry.

The Issue of God-Talk

Where does that leave those of us who do need to talk of God? How then are we to understand the multiple characterizations of God that crowd the classical Jewish texts?

There are two possible answers to these questions. One is to slip into worshipful silence, to acknowledge that since God cannot be grasped by the human mind or described in human language, we must simply fall silent, worship only through song and dance, or just acknowledge God's intrinsically unknowable quality. This strategy is reflected in one of the terms Jewish mystics use to refer to God. God is *Ein Sof*, or Infinity—not the Infinite One, but simply Infinity itself in its literal meaning of "beyond anything finite." This is more a confession of ignorance than a description of God.

It is also the approach of Maimonides' doctrine of negative attributes. Maimonides (1135–1204) is universally acknowledged to be the most accomplished Jewish philosopher of all time. He made monumental contributions to every form of Jewish expression, both in philosophy *(The Guide to the Perplexed)* and in law (his *Mishneh Torah*, or Code of Jewish Law), both of which are studied to this day. In his doctrine of negative attributes, Maimonides claims that God can only be described by what God is not—not personal, not ignorant, not wise, not weak, not strong—because any positive identification of God would be too limiting. To claim, for example, that God is omniscient would imply that omniscience exhausts God's nature. However, God is beyond omniscient, which is to say that God surpasses whatever we say about God. Paradoxically, this accumulation of negative characteristics leaves us with an image of God as the sum total of all positive qualities, even though Maimonides' ultimate conclusion is that no human being can grasp the essential nature of God.

The second answer is to concede that although we cannot know God's essence, we must still speak of God, all the while fully realizing that everything we say about God is only marginally accurate, partial, impressionistic, imaginative, and intrinsically subjective. These characterizations become utterly false and idolatrous if and when we understand them to be literally true, objective, and accurate. We have no photographs of God.

Theological Metaphors

Theologians use different terms to clarify the status of our human representations of God; they can be called *analogies, symbols,* or, more popularly, *metaphors,* in the literal sense of that term, which comes from the Greek for "transfer" or "carry over." A metaphor is a figure of speech in which a term is carried over from its familiar use to characterize some other reality that is more elusive and can be captured only implicitly.

Metaphors abound in our everyday talk. We speak of the lion as "the king of the beasts"; we complain that our heart is "heavy" or that we are entering "the evening of our lives." T. S. Eliot speaks of April as "the cruelest month." We conclude that the stock market "shrugged off" General Motors' lowered earnings for the past quarter, or that a bank was guilty of "money laundering." In order to transplant an organ, physicians must first "harvest" it from its original body. We do not weigh a heart, nor does the lion wear a crown. The market does not really shrug off any information, nor is money placed in a washing machine to be cleansed. However, these metaphors serve to capture, in a sharp and vivid way, an elusive and complex piece of information that escapes clear and concise expression. To describe the reaction of the stock market to the lowered earnings of a major corporation would require at least a paragraph; the metaphor captures it in a single phrase.

That all of our God-talk is metaphorical is another cardinal principle of Maimonides' philosophy:

> [W]hat is the meaning of the following expressions found in the Torah: "Beneath His feet" [Exodus 24:10]; "Written with the finger of God" [Exodus 31:18];..."The eyes of God" [Genesis 38:7].... All these expressions are adapted to the mental capacity of the majority of mankind who have a clear perception of physical bodies only. The Torah speaks in the language of men. All these phrases are metaphorical....
> —Mishneh Torah, *Basic Principles of the Torah 1:9*[2]

What Maimonides is addressing here is our tendency to anthropomorphism—literally, the attempt to conceive of God in human form. Maimonides acknowledges that we may need to pursue this way of conceiving God, simply because to conceive God in objective terms is beyond human ability. Nevertheless, we should remain aware that when applied to God, these descriptions must never be taken as literally accurate. This principle applies not only to physical metaphors but also to descriptions of God's inner life; it too can be described only metaphorically.

> The expressions in the Pentateuch and books of Prophets...
> are all of them metaphorical and rhetorical, as for example,
> "He that sits in the heavens shall laugh," (Psalm 2:4)...."Do
> they provoke Me to anger?" (Jeremiah 7:19)
> —Mishneh Torah, *Basic Principles of the Torah 1:12*

Maimonides, the ultimate rationalist, spent the better part of his writing denouncing the popular idea that God is corporeal, has feelings, and works in human ways. These notions were heretical for Maimonides, who believed, as befits a good rationalist, that God was pure Mind.

Most of us would agree with Maimonides that nothing that we human beings say about God or God's activities in the world is literally true. Our description of God is littered with "not really"s. God is not really above or below, or inside or outside, for God is not in space. Nor is God in time—there is no past or future for God. God is not really personal or impersonal, male or female, a shepherd or a warrior, a parent or a lover. God does not really hear prayer, speak at Sinai, or see human behavior. God is never really angry or pleased. All these impressions are human ways of talking about a reality that transcends all human cognition.

The Song of Glory

A strikingly similar spin on this complex of issues appears in a text that stems from a radically different school than that of Maimonides. The "Song of Glory" is ascribed to the thirteenth-century German mystic and saint Rabbi Judah the Pious. For reasons that will soon become clear, this mystical poem has had a contentious history, but it is still recited in traditional synagogues at the conclusion of the morning service on the Sabbath and festivals.

The poem begins by expressing the author's mystical longing for God:

I sing hymns and compose songs
Because my soul longs for You....
When I speak of Your glory,
My heart yearns after Your love.

He concedes that despite this yearning, he knows nothing of this God:

I tell your praise, though I have not seen You;
I describe You, though I have not known You....
They [the prophets] imaged You, not as You are really;
They described You by Your acts only.
They depicted You in countless visions;
Despite all comparisons You are One.

Thus far, we are on familiar ground. Maimonides would have heartily agreed that no human being knows God and that despite all the human characterizations of God, God remains the same. However, after this disclaimer and to our astonishment, the poet adopts the boldest possible images of God, using vividly anthropomorphic language:

They saw in You both old age and young age,
With the hair of Your head now grey, now black:
Age in judgement day, youth in time of war,...
A helmet of triumph tied on His head,...
As though His head is drenched with dew of light,
And His locks are filled with drops of the night....
The locks of His head are such as in youth;
His curls, forming countless ringlets, are black.[3]

By this point, Maimonides would surely have thrown up his hands! However, note the poet's message: No human being has ever seen you, God; no one, not even the prophets, knows what you are like, but still they have imagined you in vividly physical ways. Despite these contrasting images, you remain what you are. This combination of total ignorance of God's true nature and the most vivid of images of this unknown, unseen God captures perfectly the tension we confront: we experience God, we need to speak of this God, but we remain ignorant of what it is we are speaking of, and we portray this unseen God in images that we create.

When we pause, look into ourselves, and ask what we envision in our mind's eye when we think of God, we might not go as far as Rabbi Judah, but we might begin with the familiar "old man with a white beard wrapped in a caftan and sitting among the clouds." Then most of us would quickly add, "But not really," and we might move toward more abstract images such as a "soul of the whole world" or a power that impels us to act morally. Again, the "not really"s will accumulate. We might add the word *like* so that God is "like" any of these images, but that turns them into similes, which are just another kind of metaphor.

To think and talk of God, then, is to think and talk metaphorically. We must make our peace with that conclusion and then trace its implications.

The Inevitability of Agnosticism

The first implication is that in regard to God's intrinsic nature, we are all agnostics. We know nothing. Some of us would extend the agnostic perspective to how God acts or what God wants of us. The latter takes a decisive step out of the Jewish religious tradition, because it is the overwhelming consensus of Jewish thinkers until the dawn of the Jewish Enlightenment (the end of the eighteenth century) that we do know precisely what God wants us to do and not do. That is recorded in the body of traditional Jewish law, what we call *halakhah* (from the Hebrew for "to walk" or "to go").

However, if the Torah as a whole is not the "word" of God, if God does not really speak, then the words of Torah must be human words. However controversial that conclusion may be, it seems to be inevitable. Torah is how our ancestors *understood* God's will, not God's will per se.

The second implication is that the image of God in the Bible and, even more so, in the later tradition is a complex metaphorical system. The primary characteristics of this system are its pluralism and its fluidity. It is pluralistic because it is composed of images formed by countless human beings who, over centuries, experienced God's presence in their lives in an infinite number of ways and then translated their experiences into metaphors that captured what they felt. It is fluid because as we study Judaism's classical texts, certain metaphors disappear, presumably because they no longer capture our ancestors' sense of God's presence in their lives; other ones are added—again presumably because these new metaphors more effectively capture experiences that our ancestors did not share; still others are transformed before our eyes so that the later image, though clearly emerging out of an earlier one, completely subverts the original meaning.

Theological metaphors exist in a state of constant tension; they are true and not true, necessary but dangerous. We need them, but we are constantly tempted to take them as photographs, and then we slip into idolatry.

Contemporary Reformulations

We will see many examples of each of these processes as we pursue our inquiry. In a preliminary way, let us take two examples from contemporary theological writing: the reformulations of the God-image by Jewish feminists and by post-Holocaust theologians.

A Jewish feminist finds it difficult or undesirable to respond positively to the traditional image of God as a "father" or "king."

These metaphors are perceived to exclude the distinctive religious experience of a Jewish woman. They do not "reveal" God to these women; rather, they become obstacles. Jewish feminists have pursued two different strategies. The first is to reappropriate some traditional feminine images of God, such as *Shekhinah* (the term used by Jewish mystics for God's presence in the world, and a feminine noun). The second is to create entirely new images, such as *Mekor HaChayim* ("Source of Life"), that more directly reflect their experiences.

What is a post-Holocaust Jew to do with the traditional image of God who loves Israel—who is beneficent, caring, all-powerful, and, above all, just? This dilemma has led some modern thinkers to notions of God as limited, vulnerable, and not quite capable of controlling the chaotic forces that seem to compete with God in ruling the world.

Both of these examples catch the metaphorical system in the very process of evolution.

The third implication of this approach, then, is that the process of creating new images of God never ends as long as there are people who continue to experience God's presence in their lives and to reflect on that experience. Every generation encounters the classic system, sifts the useful exemplars from those that no longer work, and substitutes its own novel ones—and the chain continues.

It continues because despite what we might have concluded, the fact that no human being can capture God's essence never inhibited our ancestors from describing what God must be like. If anything, the opposite is the case. God's intrinsic unknowability was liberating. It freed them, as it can free us to reach into the core of our own experiences of God and to fashion the widest possible range of images to capture our experiences as it captured theirs. To them, God was parent, judge, lover, spouse, rock, military hero, and teacher. God was sometimes nurturing, sometimes abusive. God visited them when they were ill, comforted them when they mourned, clothed the naked, freed the bound, listened to their prayers, and spoke at Sinai. The liturgical year brought specific images into their consciousness. The judging God of Rosh Hashanah was different from the liberating God of Passover or the victorious God of Chanukah. The God of my adolescence was different from the God of my middle years or the God of my old age. The range of possibilities is limitless. One can travel very far along that range before encountering an image that is inherently outside the boundaries of legitimacy.

When I once asked a student of mine to put her personal metaphor for God on paper, she wrote that for her, God was Fred Astaire to her Ginger Rogers. She explained:

> When we miss a step, it's always my fault. He dances in flats; I have to dance in heels; he's on the ceiling, I'm on the floor; he can be late, I can't. He pinches me in the clinches; I mustn't. And Cyd Charisse is waiting for me to fail. But when we get it together, it's sheer ecstasy.

This is one of the most fascinating pieces of theological writing I've seen in decades of teaching.

Seeing the Invisible

The notion that all of our talk of God is composed of metaphors created by human beings leads inevitably to the charge that human beings "invent" God. The only appropriate response to this charge is that no, human beings *discover* God and then invent metaphors to characterize the God they experience. Sometimes the metaphors come first; they make it possible for us to feel God's presence in our lives in certain distinctive ways. However, these metaphors also originate in an act of discovery, a genuine experience of a reality that infinitely transcends us.

How do we know that these experiences are genuine? How do we respond to the charge that these experiences of a God who is "out there" are simply wishes, projections, or illusions? This question touches upon the central issue in the philosophy of religion, an issue that has agitated philosophers for centuries and that is clearly beyond the scope of this inquiry. It must be addressed here in a preliminary way, however.

One way of addressing it is to show that religion is not the only instance in which we speak at great length about realities that are not clearly visible, and that we do so in ways that remain quite indispensable and meaningful. For example, suppose I am sitting next to a clinical psychologist who is observing the behavior of a child through a one-way mirror. Suddenly the psychologist turns to me and exclaims, "Neil, look at this child's ego!"

I look. What do I literally see? A child playing with dolls, blocks, and a tricycle. The psychologist sees all this but also something more—the child's ego, which he clearly admires. Yet, where is this ego? In some sense, it is "in" the child—not as an object like the child's heart or brain, but still very much "within" the child, more as a pattern that suffuses the child and her behavior, the way she plays with her dolls and her tricycle. The child's ego is then both invisible and visible—invisible because it is not explicitly seen, but very much visible to someone who is trained to observe and evaluate human behavior and, most important, to someone who believes that human beings have egos in the first place. Were this psychologist to work with a theory of human behavior that does not include the ego, he would not be looking for an ego and would never see one.

The ego functions within a complex theory that seeks to explain human behavior. Psychologists who accept this theory believe that in order to explain what they do explicitly see—the way human beings behave—they need to construct an inner world that they don't explicitly see but that has to be there.

However, no psychologist who works within this theory would deny that there is an "out-thereness" to the ego. None would claim that the ego is a pure fabrication or fiction. Two assumptions are required for seeing the ego: a belief that there is an ego out there to be seen, and that one has been sufficiently well trained in the observation of human behavior to know what to look for when looking for the egos.

Believers in God are like psychologists: they too want to explain what they do explicitly see—in this case the ultimate canvas, the entire complex of nature, history, and human experience viewed as one integrated whole. To explain all this, believers have to posit that beyond what they do see, there is an invisible world that must be there if what they see is to make sense. Part of this invisible world includes a reality they call God.

There is no way of proving objectively and conclusively that God exists. For centuries philosophers have tried to devise such proofs, but with little success. To perceive God, then, one has to (1) want to make sense of the world, (2) believe that this ultimate canvas is in fact one integrated whole, (3) believe that the world does cohere and make sense, and (4) believe that the reason it does cohere—in fact, the very principle of its coherence—is the existence of a reality we call God, and that this God can be "seen" in and through our experience of the world. This God may not be directly seen, but it can be "seen" as the ego is seen by the psychologist. Like the ego, God is not an object but more like a pattern that suffuses all things. Just as the ego is elusive, so is God; that's precisely why we need the range of metaphors to bring this God sharply into our consciousness, just as we use metaphors to bring the ego to life. A friend of mine once referred somewhat disparagingly to a mutual acquaintance of ours as having "the ego of a feather." That metaphor captured him perfectly!

Finally, like the psychologist, the believer must have a certain refinement, some education or training, a knowledge of what to look for. Without this training, all the looking in the world would not help. The entire task of religious education can be summed up this way: it is the attempt to train people to see the world as suffused with the presence of God, just as the psychologist is trained to see the ego in the behavior of a child. Believers, like psychologists, are members of a community that sees the world in a certain way. The community of believers has endured infinitely longer than that of psychologists, and—to use an admittedly pragmatic criterion—their way of seeing the world has worked remarkably well to help people in widely different ages and cultures make sense of the world and of their human experience. That conclusion may not be objectively true, but it is true enough to dispel any notion that God is a total human fabrication. That may be as much "proof" as we can ever attain in this matter.

To answer the question "Who is God?" is to study the twists and turns of the complex metaphorical system that Jews have used to try to make sense of the world and their lives, as this system winds its way through the generations.

1

God Is *Echad*

The *Shema*

By any measure, the one passage in all of Scripture that every Jew, whatever his or her identification with Judaism, will recognize is Deuteronomy 6:4, commonly known as "the *Shema*." It appears more frequently in the traditional liturgy than any other single passage in the entire Bible. Worshiping Jews recite it daily, morning and evening, and more frequently on the Sabbath and festivals. It is also the most ancient biblical passage to be incorporated into our liturgy, dating at least from the days of the Second Temple (before 70 C.E.). It has been the traditional "last word" of Jewish martyrs throughout the ages, and to this day pious Jews pray that they may be able to recite this verse as death approaches. Their model for this practice was the second-century C.E. talmudic sage and martyr Rabbi Akiva, of whom, legend recounts, "his soul left him as he was saying the word *echad*," the final word of the passage (Babylonian Talmud, *Berakhot* 61b).

In its original context, the verse is part of Moses' extended sermon to the Israelites prior to his death and to their entering the Promised Land. Moses begins by exhorting the people to revere God and to observe and obey God's Torah (literally, "Instruction"), so that they may increase and prosper in the land that God has promised to them. Then comes the *Shema*, followed immediately by the almost equally familiar exhortation to "love the Lord your God with all your heart and with all your soul and with all your might."

The *Shema* verse has suffered the fate of other familiar texts: it has come to be recited almost mindlessly, with little attention to what it really means. In fact, its meaning is not all that obvious. The translation of the verse in the English edition published by the Jewish Publication Society in 1985 reads "Hear O Israel! The Lord is our God, the Lord alone." A footnote in the text adds the more familiar "the Lord our God, the Lord is One." That latter reading—sometimes with a minor variation in the first phrase, "the Lord *is* our God, the Lord is One"—is omnipresent in traditional prayer books. A further variation is to translate the first word as "Hearken" or "Take heed" rather than "Hear."

"The Lord is One" is by far the more conventional translation because the Hebrew word *echad* is usually translated as "one," the first in the chain of integers. However, that translation has been subject to much criticism. It is not at all clear what it means to claim that any single being is in fact "one." Is this a mathematical statement? God is one, not two or three? Hearing this, one might be tempted to add, "One what?" The word is an adjective, but here there is no noun for it to modify. God may be "one," but so is this apple in my hand. To refer to this apple as "one" implies that there are other apples around but that I am holding one apple, not two or three. Does this also apply to God?

That is why the translation "the Lord alone" has much to commend it. It indicates that Israel's God alone is Israel's Lord; God is the only Lord. The other putative gods do not qualify to be Israel's Lord. The claim that God is *echad* is now a statement about the exclusivity of this God to Israel. That understanding is borne out by the use of the word *our* in the verse. For Israel, God alone is God. The statement expresses Israel's relationship to God. Thus, the verse probably means something along these lines: "Take heed, O Israel! The Lord our God alone is God."

If this is the literal meaning of the verse, then it is echoed elsewhere in the Bible—for example, in the first two of the ten commandments (Exodus 20:2; Deuteronomy 5:6): "I am the Lord your God.... You shall have no other gods besides Me...in the heavens above, or on earth below, or in the waters under the earth." That formulation accentuates the relational nature of the claim that God alone is *our* God. For *Israel*, God alone is God. *Israel* shall have no other gods besides this one. That is why we are to love this God with all our heart and with all our soul and with all our might.

Loving God

How can we be commanded to love anything? Can feelings be commanded? The Bible does in fact suggest that people can be commanded to have certain feelings. The last of the ten commandments, for example, instructs us not to covet. Elsewhere, we are told not to bear hatred to our kinfolk in our hearts. In the Bible there is no clear distinction between a feeling itself and the expression of that feeling in action or behavior. In this context, then, the command to love God includes the command that we are to act lovingly toward God. Even more, we are to act lovingly with all our heart and with all our soul and with all our might. This threefold formula lends a note of urgency or emphasis to the command. How are we to act lovingly toward God? Exceedingly! Emphatically! Exclusively! We are to take God's instructions to heart, the passage continues. We are to impress them on our children, recite them morning and evening, bind them on our hands and foreheads, and inscribe them on the doorposts of our houses and our gates. (The latter two references account for *tefillin,* the black leather boxes worn on the upper arm and the forehead when worshiping in the morning, and the *mezuzah* affixed to our doorposts. Both contain this passage inscribed on parchment.)

The juxtaposition of God being *echad* with the obligation to love God "with all your heart and with all your soul and with all your might" implies that because this God is exclusively our God, we are to grant this God exclusive loyalty. The claim is twofold: a statement about the nature of God and, at the same time, a statement about how we are to relate to this God. Because God alone is God, we should worship this God exclusively and totally.

The notion that God alone is exclusively Israel's God is also borne out by the practice, when writing a Torah scroll, of inscribing the last letter of the first Hebrew word of the verse (an *ayin*) and the last letter of its last word (a *dalet*) in large boldface. Put together, the letters form the Hebrew word *eid*, or "witness." By reciting the passage, Israel becomes witness to God's absolute sovereignty.

Mutuality

In another homiletical extension of this notion, the Rabbis of the Talmud note a second biblical use of the word *echad*, this time applied to Israel, and, typically, they find a common thread between the two uses. 1 Chronicles 17:20–22 reads:

> O Lord, there is none like You, and there is no other God but You.... And who is like Your people Israel, a unique nation on earth, whom God went and redeemed as His people.... You have established Your people Israel as Your very own people forever; and You, O Lord, have become their God.

In this passage, the Hebrew term for "unique" is also *echad*. God and Israel share the quality of being unique to each other; these two "uniquenesses" are mutually dependent. As Israel proclaims God's uniqueness (by wearing *tefillin* and reciting the *Shema*), so does God establish Israel's uniqueness—in a stunning image that has God wearing *tefillin* in which is inscribed this verse from

Chronicles, just as human *tefillin* contain the *Shema* (Babylonian Talmud, *Berakhot* 6a).

This interdependence of God's and Israel's uniqueness is captured in the liturgical passage of rabbinic origin that immediately precedes the recitation of the *Shema* in the morning service. The conclusion of the passage reads:

> You have chosen us from among every people and tongue, and you have brought us close to Your great name forever in truth, to offer praiseful thanks to You, and to proclaim Your uniqueness with love. Blessed are you, God, who chooses His people Israel with love.

This segues into the *Shema* verse and then the continuation of the biblical passage, "And you shall love the Lord your God..."

In this passage, to "love" and to "choose" are synonyms, and both are also synonymous with proclaiming someone as unique, as singled out. The relation is between two exclusivities, and this mutuality of exclusivities implies a mutuality of loyalties. As we proclaim God's uniqueness, so does God proclaim Israel's uniqueness by "choosing" Israel from among the peoples. As God loves Israel, so Israel is to love God "with all your heart," etc. What else does "love" mean than that I and the one I love are exclusively loyal to each other, to the exclusion of anyone else—especially one I love "with all my heart"?

In a more modern idiom, the theme of mutual exclusivity is best captured by Martin Buber's notion of an I-Thou relationship. The difference between an I-Thou relationship and an I-It relationship is that the latter tolerates any number of different "It"s and "I"s; I have multiple I-It relationships—with bus drivers, store clerks, the maintenance workers in my apartment building—none of which is exclusive; they can all be easily replaced. But in my I-Thou relationships—with my wife and daughters—both the I and the Thou are unique and exclusive to each other. Of course, I can also have multiple I-Thou relationships, but in each of these the I and the Thou acknowledge the uniqueness and personhood of the Thou.

The notion that the *Shema* is a statement about God's exclusivity and our corresponding responsibility to be loyal only to God is captured by the claim of the rabbinic tradition that the very recitation of this passage with inner focus and full attention constitutes a Jew's "acceptance of the yoke of the kingdom of heaven." It is an example of "performative language," in which saying certain words is an activity, a deed. As in the similar "*Harai at mekudeshet li betaba'at zu kedat moshe veyisrael*," or "Behold, you are sanctified unto me with this ring according to the law of Moses and Israel," the recitation of the words has a substantive effect; it is our human way of accepting God as the absolute in our lives. Just as the recitation of those words establishes the couple as husband and wife, so the recitation of these words establishes God as exclusively our God.

God's Integrity

Maimonides' interpretation of the *Shema* takes our understanding of this passage in a very different direction. As the heir to two ancient traditions—the biblical-talmudic readings of Judaism and the Greek philosophy of Plato and Aristotle and their successors—his central agenda was to reconcile these two traditions. Since truth is singular, and since he was convinced that both traditions were true, he concluded that they must ultimately be saying the same thing, albeit in different idioms. His goal was to expose the underlying commonalities in the two traditions.

This enterprise inevitably lends a certain abstract, philosophical tone to his discussion of the existence and nature of God. His earliest commentary on the *Shema* verse is in an extended essay included in his first major book, *Commentary on the* Mishnah. The *Mishnah,* compiled about the year 200 C.E., was the earliest comprehensive codification of the entire body of Jewish scriptural and oral legal traditions to that date. The brunt of Maimonides' essay (called "Introduction to *Chelek*," *chelek* being the Hebrew name of the tenth chapter of Tractate *Sanhedrin*) deals with Jewish teachings regarding the end of days, the messianic era, the world to come after the culmination of history. (The association comes from the beginning of the *Mishnah* text, which claims that "All Israel has a share [*chelek*] in the world to come.") The essay as a whole describes the author's understanding of what will transpire in the world to come and how one can qualify to achieve a place in that new age.

At the end of the essay, Maimonides includes a set of Thirteen Principles of Faith that constitute his assertion of the beliefs that he claims all Jews must accept in order to merit a share in the messianic age. The second principle reads as follows:

> We are told to believe that God is one, the cause of all oneness. He is not like a member of a pair, nor a species of a genus, nor a person divided into many discrete elements. Nor is He one in the sense that a simple body is, numerically, one but still infinitely divisible. God, rather, is uniquely one.[1]

He then quotes the *Shema* as a biblical proof-text.

Apart from that last sentence, the statement is familiar. It dismisses most of the more common erroneous interpretations of the verse. However, what is the import of that last sentence? In what sense is God "uniquely one"?

To answer this, we should turn to another statement, this time in Maimonides' *Mishneh Torah,* a fourteen-volume compendium of Jewish law. Legal codes usually prescribe correct behavior, but Maimonides opens his work with an extensive compilation of Jewish philosophical teachings, which he understands to be as binding for the believing Jew as the behavioral laws—a scandalous notion to his contemporaries. Indeed, to this day many Jews would assert that authentic Jewish identity demands observance of the behavioral commandments much more than correct belief. Maimonides would disagree.

In chapter 10, paragraph 2, of the section entitled "Basic Principles of the Torah," he writes:

> The Holy One, blessed be He, realizes His true being, and knows it as it is, not with a knowledge external to Himself, as is our knowledge. For our knowledge and ourselves are separate. But as for the Creator, blessed be He, His knowledge and His life are One, in all aspects, from every point of view, and however we conceive Unity. If the Creator lived as other living creatures live, and His knowledge were external to Himself, there would be a plurality of deities, namely: He Himself, His life, and His knowledge. This, however, is not so. He is One in every aspect, from every angle, and in all ways in which Unity is conceived. Hence the conclusion that God is the One who knows, is known, and is the knowledge [of Himself]—all these being One.[2]

He then concludes this somewhat tortuous exposition as follows: "This is beyond the power of speech to express, beyond the capacity of the ear to hear and of the human mind to apprehend clearly." To which we would surely respond, "Amen."

What is Maimonides trying to say here? His purpose is to emphasize the total integrity of God's essence. When we deal with human beings, we understand that our very selves, our lives, and our knowledge can be separated from each other; they seem to represent aspects of our personality that don't depend on each other. My knowledge is separate from myself in the sense that there was an "I" before I acquired knowledge, and there will continue to be an "I" after I have forgotten what I know. Knowledge, then, is not intrinsic to my essence.

Not so with God. Knowledge is intrinsic to God's nature. God is intrinsically knowledge, and God's essence is knowledge itself. This leads to the claim that God is simultaneously the subject of knowledge (the One who knows), the verb or activity of knowing, and the object of knowledge (that which is known). That knowledge is the supreme value—the very mark of God—Maimonides learned from Greek philosophy. God, then, is the supreme embodiment of the supreme virtue. To claim that God is "one" is to insist that God is not only syntactically but also metaphysically subject, verb, and object, all at the same time, all eternally and without change. To put it another way, God is "knowledge knowing knowledge," or "knowledge knowing itself." For Maimonides, that's what the *Shema* means when it affirms that God is "one."

To put this another way, for Maimonides, God's oneness is a statement about the integrity of God's nature. However, note the effect of Maimonides' transformation of the biblical passage; it is quite characteristic of how he transforms the bulk of biblical and rabbinic teachings in order to achieve his synthesis of Torah and Greek philosophy. The *Shema* is no longer a statement of Israel's relationship to God or of how God and Israel are to be exclusively committed to each other. It now becomes an abstract, philosophically rigorous articulation of God's essential nature. From a biblical statement that bears a rich emotional message, it becomes a philosophical one that satisfies the mind. It embodies much more of Aristotle than of the Bible. It is no small wonder that this thinker's teachings proved to be so controversial to his contemporaries.

Living under One God

In its original context the *Shema* was a statement about Israel's relationship to God, but it is also a statement about how our ancestors viewed the world. What was it in the experience of our ancestors that led them to proclaim that God is indeed the only god? Our ancestors were ordinary human beings, not intrinsically different from you or me. They observed the same world that we do—nature, history, and the entire gamut of human experience. From these observations they reached certain conclusions about how their experience of the world achieved a measure of coherence. The key to that effort was the notion that this experience, taken as a whole, reflected the presence and power of a single, unique, and transcendent Being.

That conviction was not the only one possible. They could have concluded, as their pagan neighbors did, that the world is governed by a multitude of competing deities, each ruling over a portion of the world, or that there are two gods, one personifying the impetus for order in the world and the other the impetus for chaos or anarchy. Either of these conclusions could easily be supported by the evidence that was available to them.

In fact, that dualistic conception of the world seems to make perfect sense even today. The world does seem to manifest both order and anarchy. The sun does rise every morning, and the seasons do seem to follow each other in a totally predictable way, but then there are the earthquakes, the hurricanes, the tornados, and the epidemics that wreak terrible havoc on perfectly innocent people. Airplane crashes take human lives seemingly at random; people die from seemingly unpredictable coronaries; children are born with unexpected genetic defects. Therefore, does the world manifest one integrated system, or is it inherently discordant, ruptured, and ambiguous? Each view has its trade-offs. Accept the view of an ordered world, and then you have to account for the chaos. Accept the view of an anarchic world, and then you have to account for the order that is also manifestly there. Our ancestors opted for the first view. They viewed the world as inherently ordered, and they accounted for this order by positing the presence of one, single, supreme, and transcendent God who is both the cause and the principle of the order. Then they worked mightily to account for the seemingly inexplicable suffering that hovers beneath and around the periphery of the order.

We have explicit evidence that our ancestors were aware of a dualistic view of the world, the possibility that the world is ruled by two warring supreme powers, and that they rejected it. A passage in Second Isaiah reads

So that they may know, from east to west,
That there is none but Me.
I am the Lord, and there is none else,
I form light and create darkness,
I make order and create bad.
I the Lord do all these things.

—*Isaiah 45:6–7*[3]

This prophet lived and prophesied among the exiled Jewish community in Persia in the middle of the sixth century B.C.E., where the reigning religion was Zoroastrianism. Persians believed that there were two warring gods, a god of light and a god of darkness. When the god of light won out, good or order reigned; when the god of darkness won out, bad or chaos reigned. This theological dualism reflected a reading of human experience that still makes perfect sense to us today, but the prophet emphatically rejects it. There is only one God, and this God accounts for both light and darkness, for both the good and the bad in the world. With all the problems that this unified reading of the world raises, that prophet still proclaims the classical, biblical view of the world as unified and, with it, the monotheistic image of God. The world is one and so is God.

The world is not simply given to us. How we view the world is an act of human or cultural construction, and different cultures construct the world in different ways. Our ancestors concluded that the entire world—the broadest possible canvas—manifests one singular, all-encompassing, and coherent order. That assumption could be seen to fly in the face of the evidence provided by earthquakes, hurricanes, and epidemics. Yet, our ancestors insisted on it and made it a cornerstone of their faith. They "saw through" the variegated, often contradictory evidence of their senses to perceive an elusive but strikingly unified order that pervades all things. To borrow a term from contemporary physics, they proposed a "unified field theory"—one formula that explains why all things are as they are. They were making a statement about God, but in the same breath they were making a statement about the world as a whole.

Finally, they were also making a statement that had a powerful psychological subtext. What is it like to live in a world that is ruled by two or more gods? It means that the realm of the divine was marked by a state of perpetual indecision, and perpetual indecision above breeds perpetual insecurity below. One simply never knows who is running things today.[4] The alternative position has its own problems, and we will have to deal with that ensemble of problems—what we call "the problem of evil" or "suffering," why bad things happen to good people—later in this inquiry, but Judaism clearly preferred to tackle those issues than the ones raised by dualism or polytheism.

A talmudic homily suggests a similar conclusion:

[God] appeared [to the Israelites] at the Red Sea as a mighty hero doing battle.... At Sinai [God] appeared to them as an old person full of compassion.... Therefore Scripture would not let the nations of the world have an excuse for saying that there are two powers, but declares: "I am the Lord your God. I am the one who was in Egypt, and I am the one who was at the Sea. I am the one who was at Sinai. I am the one who was in the past, and I will be in the future. I am the one in this world, and I am the one who will be in the world to come."[5]

Is the World Really One?

Our experience of the world is that it is not really one. If it is not one, then is God really *echad*, now, in history, and in our lifetime? One prophetic text suggests that neither is the case now. Zechariah 14 is an extended description of what will take place when "the day of the Lord" arrives. It is an apocalyptic vision of the tumultuous events that will take place at the end of days. All the familiar patterns of nature and history will be overthrown. The world as we know it, together with Israel's enemies, will be destroyed, and in its place God will erect a new world in which all nations will join Israel in worshiping the only true God. In this context, the prophet proclaims: "And the Lord shall be king over all the earth; in that day there shall be one Lord with one name" (14:9).

That text too has entered our daily liturgy as the final note in the prayer that concludes every service of worship, the prayer that begins with the words *Alenu LeShabeach* ("It is our duty to praise..."). That prayer, composed during the talmudic age, proclaims a vision of the end of days when all peoples "will accept the yoke of Your kingship so that You will reign over them soon and eternally." The passage then cites the verse from Zechariah as its proof-text.

Again, as with the *Shema*, what does that verse mean? The original Hebrew uses the term *echad* twice here, to characterize both God and God's name: on that day, God shall be *echad*, and God's name *echad*. The more conventional translation of the verse reads, "on that day, God will be One and His name One." Because of the ambiguity surrounding the notion that God has "one name," the 1985 Jewish Publication Society translation footnotes an interpretation of the verse as follows: "The Lord alone shall be worshiped and shall be invoked by His own name."

Even that interpretation misses the true sense of the passage, however. It should be understood, rather, as an extension of the

Shema, which it so clearly echoes by its own double use of the word *echad*. The *Shema* claims that God is Israel's God, exclusively, but not the God of the nations of the world. The Zechariah passage claims that "on that day"—namely, at the end of days, in the age of the Messiah—God will also be acknowledged by all the nations of the world. Only then will God be truly *echad*—for all of humanity. Only at the culmination of history as we know it will God's sovereignty be ultimate.

The liturgy barely conceals a remarkable tension. In one breath, we affirm that God is now ultimate; in another breath, we affirm that God will become ultimate only in some messianic future. This tension reflects the tension inherent in our experience. Our ancestors were painfully aware of the discordancies, the flaws, and the ruptures that pervade our experience of the world and of human life, all the while insisting that beyond and through these discordancies there is an ultimate unity of impulse and purpose. In history these two visions are in tension, but at the end of days they will be totally resolved. Then God will be truly unique.

Is God Lonely?

We have devoted the bulk of this chapter to discussing the various meanings of the biblical claim that God is *echad*, beginning with the sense that the most accurate translation of the *Shema* verse is that for Israel and in historical time, God "alone" is God. One implication of that claim is that in the here and now, at least, God has one partner, Israel, and, as we know all too painfully, Israel's loyalty to God is often tenuous. A slight homiletical extension of that claim leads to the further suggestion that if God alone is God, then God is also lonely.

This suggestion opens a vast panorama of new possibilities regarding Israel's perception of God. We all too frequently think of God as having it all together. God is omnipotent and omniscient;

God lacks nothing and needs nothing; God is totally invulnerable. Yet, the entire story of God's relationship with the world, with people, and even with Israel is a story of ongoing frustration. Beginning with the story of Adam and Eve in the Garden of Eden, then with Cain and Abel, the generation of the flood, Sodom and Gomorrah, and continuing through Israel's wrestling with God in the desert and thereafter, the biblical account portrays God's persistent disappointment mingled with unflagging yearning. Whatever God hoped to accomplish by creating a world populated with people and by entering into a covenantal relationship with Israel—God's hopes, dreams, and expectations—none of this has come to pass. God continues to hope and to dream. In the meantime, God remains lonely.[6]

We conclude on this note of tension, which will follow us throughout this study. Here, God is both *echad* and not, or not yet, *echad*. Elsewhere we will see that God is both powerful and singularly vulnerable, sometimes kind and nurturing and sometimes cruel and capricious. Our ancestors were not systematic theologians. They spoke out of their living experience of the world, and that experience was ambiguous. That ambiguity could not but be reflected in how they imaged God. Indeed, to different people at different points in history and in their personal lives, God was all of these, all at the same time. People were perfectly content to affirm both of these seemingly contradictory impulses. They lived with the tension. So must we.

2

God Is Power

Unchallenged Power

If God is *echad*, uniquely and exclusively God, then God's power over all of nature and history—the ultimate canvas—is supreme and absolute. To claim that God shares that power with some other deity or force would deny God's uniqueness. The conventional, abstract term for that divine quality is omnipotence. But is the God of Israel in fact omnipotent? Is the claim true?

It is certainly true in theory. The difference between biblical monotheism and its ancient polytheistic competitors is not simply one of mathematics, not simply whether there is one God or two or many, but rather about the nature of the monotheistic God. If there are many gods, then the world is ruled by multiple, competing powers, each limited to a certain realm of influence. The result is the state of indecision above and insecurity below that we referred to in chapter 1. The late eminent Bible scholar E. A. Speiser used that description to explain what might have led our ancestor Abraham to break with his pagan background, leave his home and native land, and travel not only to another land but also toward an alternative spiritual model. Within the pagan model, how could any human being determine which god to please, to obey, or to worship?

The core of the revolution wrought by biblical religion is to insist that there is only one ultimate power in the world, that this

God governs all that is, and that to this God alone do humans owe loyalty. The difference between biblical monotheism and polytheism is not only an abstract theological debate; it has immediate implications for the lives that we live. The monotheistic model allows us to live in a world that forms one coherent, ordered whole. We can then enjoy the security of knowing that the laws that govern the world are stable and that we too have a stable "place" in this ordered world. That sense of place is ultimately what religion is all about.

The God of Israel described in the Bible is absolutely free, not subject to any other primeval realm or law, not dependent on any other power. This God appears fully present and active in the very first verse of Genesis. This God was not born and does not die, has no lineage, and is not engendered. God is prior to all and rules all. All that is was created at this God's will and, literally, word: "God spoke and the world came into being." The Bible knows no divine mythology, no explicit biography of God, although it does tell us a great deal about God's complex relationship with the created world and with human beings. The life story of the god, omnipresent in paganism, is replaced by the story of God's struggle for recognition by the human community. In the Bible, the only serious challenge to God's power comes from human beings.

Maimonides, with his customary bent for abstraction, puts it this way in the very first words of the *Mishneh Torah*:

> The basic principle of all basic principles and the pillar of all sciences is to realize that there is a First Being who brought every existing thing into being. All existing things, whether celestial, terrestrial, or belonging to an intermediate class, exist only through His true existence. If it could be supposed that He did not exist, it would follow that nothing else could possibly exist. If, however, it were supposed that all other

beings were non-existent, He alone would still exist. Their non-existence would not involve His non-existence. For all beings are in need of Him; but He...is not in need of them nor of any one of them.

—Mishneh Torah, *Basic Principles of the Torah 1:1–3*[1]

This is an abstract, philosophical version of the message of Genesis 1. God exists prior to all creation and is responsible for all creation. Before creation, there was God. Were there no creation, there would still be God, and when the created world will be no more, there will still be God.

God Also Creates Evil

The Bible is not given to abstractions like those of Maimonides. It makes the same point far more dramatically in the passage from Second Isaiah that we studied earlier:

> I am the Lord, and there is none else; beside Me there is no
> god....
> So that they may know, from east to west,
> That there is none but Me.
> I am the Lord, and there is none else.
> I form light and create darkness,
> I make order and create bad.
> I the Lord do all these things.
>
> —*Isaiah 45:5–7*[2]

There is only one transcendent God, who alone is responsible for light and darkness, for good (order) and evil. The prophet lists these polarities, but they include everything in between as well. Thus the concluding statement: "I the Lord do all these things."

To anticipate some of the qualifications that this doctrine of divine omnipotence will undergo, it is worth noting that the later tradition felt decidedly uncomfortable with proclaiming that God is also responsible for the creation of evil. When transposed into the later talmudic liturgy, that specific biblical phrase was omitted. The liturgical text that opens the formal, daily *shacharit* (morning) service, and that clearly borrows from Second Isaiah, reads: "I form light and create darkness, I make order and create all things."

Of course, "all things" can also include evil, but that stark statement would be disturbing to the worshiper, so the authors of the liturgy simply sidestep it by substituting "all things" for "bad." Yet, the problem remains: if God is all-powerful, then the bad—the chaos, that is the opposite of order, particularly as it manifests in human suffering—is also God's work. That conclusion remains disturbing to us, but what is the alternative? A return to Persian-style dualism? We see here, in a preliminary way, one significant challenge raised by the doctrine of God's omnipotence: If God is indeed all-powerful, then God must also create evil. How, then, are we to worship this God?

Finally, note that this author introduces a detail that differs from the Genesis 1 account of creation. This prophet has God creating darkness, while in Genesis 1:1, darkness—together with "the deep," "the spirit of God," and the "unformed and void" earth— is part of a primordial, anarchic realm that preexists creation. Out of this anarchic realm, God creates a fully ordered world. The later medieval philosophers would insist that God created the world *ex nihilo*, or out of nothing, but this is not the plain sense of the Genesis creation narrative. It understands creation as God's bringing order out of anarchy, cosmos out of chaos. That view of creation also implies that something else coexisted with God before creation—or, in other words, that at the outset there were two supreme realms. The prophet's inclusion of darkness as part of God's creation, together with the medieval doctrine of creation out of nothing, is designed to warn us against that perception. In Genesis, it is all God's work, but if darkness is created by God, then so is its parallel in the Isaiah verse—namely, evil. So here God creates both darkness and evil, and yet we are to worship this God.

God Reverses the Course of Nature

The doctrine that God is all-powerful is also omnipresent in the later rabbinic tradition. The second benediction in the *amidah,* the central prayer in the daily service, is called *gevurot* (from the Hebrew word *gibor,* "mighty"). It describes God's mighty works.

> Your might, O Lord, is boundless. You give life to the dead; great is Your saving power. You cause the wind to blow and the rain to fall. You sustain the living with compassion, Your great mercies give life to the dead. You support the falling, heal the sick, free the fettered. You keep faith with those who sleep in the dust. Who is like You, master of mighty works, and whose power can compare with Yours, O Sovereign, who brings death and restores life and causes deliverance to flower?

The theme of this passage is reversal. God is so mighty that God can reverse the normal patterns of nature. God is so powerful that the falling stand, the ailing heal, the fettered are freed. Even the dead are brought back to life. Note that the passage does not claim that God actually *does* all of this. What it claims is that God *has the power* to do it all. What God *actually* does is another matter. In fact, God has not, as yet, brought the dead back to life. People who are ailing still die. The claim is a de jure statement, not necessarily a de facto claim. In principle, God is all-powerful; in fact, in historical time, that divine power may not be manifest or, even more seriously, may be hedged in with constraints.

Restraints on God's Power

Other, more striking constraints on God's power abound in the biblical narrative. Take, for example, God's response to the sin of the golden calf. At the outset, God is in a rage: "I see that this is a stiff-necked people. Now, let Me be, that my anger may blaze forth against them and that I may destroy them, and make of you [Moses] a great nation" (Exodus 32:9–10).

There is much to ponder here. First, why does God ask Moses to "let Me be" or, more colloquially, "let Me at them!" Does God need Moses' permission to punish the sinning Israelites? Even more striking is Moses' response. He pleads that God renounce punishment, and he supports that plea with two separate arguments. The first is, astonishingly, "What will the nations say?"

Moses says to God, "Let not the Egyptians say, 'It was with evil intent that He delivered them, only to kill them off in the mountains and annihilate them from the face of the earth'" (Exodus 32:12).

What will the nations say?! God's power should be curtailed because of what the foreign nations—especially the Egyptians, Israel's archoppressors—might think? This is sheer blackmail on Moses' part. His second argument is much more powerful:

> Remember Your servants, Abraham, Isaac, and Jacob, how you swore to them by Your Self and said to them: "I will make your offspring as numerous as the stars of heaven, and I will give to your offspring this whole land of which I spoke, to possess forever."
>
> —*Exodus 32:13*

In other words, God should not destroy this people because of the commitments that God has made to their ancestors. Missing in this argument is the fact that God's promises were always conditional upon Israel's accepting God as their exclusive God—a condition they have just violated by worshiping a golden calf.

God accepts Moses' arguments and renounces the punishment (Exodus 32:14). So much for God's vaunted omnipotence! De jure, God has all the power, but de facto, that power is limited by God's public image and by promises God has freely made. This God seems to be a limited God, not by God's own essence but rather by specific extrinsic factors. This is not an intrinsically limited God but rather a self-limiting God.

God's self-limitation is actually an expression of God's power exercised in a different manner. The episode of the golden calf is not the only time that Moses intercedes with God on behalf of Israel. Numbers 13–14 describes another such incident, this time related to the story of the spies that Moses sent to reconnoiter the land prior to Israel's entry into it. Ten of the twelve spies return with a discouraging report: the cities are fortified and the inhabitants are too powerful. The people rail against Moses and Aaron: "If only we had died in Egypt!" Again God is enraged: "I will strike them with pestilence and disown them," and again Moses intercedes with the same claim: "What will the Egyptians say?"

This time, in pleading that God restrain from punishing the people, Moses sounds a subtly different note. He pleads for God's "forbearance" (Numbers 14:17). The biblical Hebrew term for "forbearance" is *koach,* typically translated as "strength." What Moses seems to be saying is that in this instance, God's "forbearance," God's withholding of punishment, is not an expression of weakness on God's part, but the very opposite: an expression of God's power—in fact, the ultimate expression of God's power. Power does not have to be expressed aggressively; it can also be demonstrated by restraint and self-control. Parents know that the *threat* of parental punishment can serve as a more powerful restraint on their children's behavior than the punishment itself.

The psychology that underlies this insight is beyond dispute. We know from our own self-awareness that, not infrequently, the ultimate expression of our own power over others is self-control. If most of our images of God are metaphors drawn from human experience, then this characterization of God is right on target.

The Power of Repentance

Moses appears here as the paradigmatic intercessor, pleading with God on behalf of his people. That intercessor role is at the heart of the institution of prophecy. In the later prophetic tradition, the prophet's plea has nothing to do with God's public image among the nations. A new factor enters into the complex God-human relationship—namely, the power of *teshuvah,* or repentance, specifically what may be called preemptive repentance, repentance that preempts punishment. That kind of repentance is unknown in the Torah. There, repentance can emerge only after punishment; only then is God prepared to be reconciled with the people who have sinned. Deuteronomy 30:1–6 reflects that stage in the development of the doctrine of repentance. In prophetic literature, repentance has the power to cancel out the punishment before it takes place.

Take the case of Jonah. Jonah is the only successful prophet in the Bible. After many adventures, he eventually does go to Nineveh and preaches a brief sermon, and the entire land, from the king down to the beasts, fasts and mourns. The king orders that everyone should turn back from their evil ways: "Who knows but that God may turn and relent...so that we do not perish" (3:8–9). Whereupon, "God saw...how they were turning back from their evil ways and God renounced the punishment He had planned to bring upon them and did not carry it out" (3:10).

We have now gone well beyond Moses' arguments with God. God's power is not automatic or unbridled; it is, rather, an expression of God's will. God can choose how and when to use that power. *Teshuvah* is God's gift to us, a singular opportunity to reverse God's power from anger to compassion. It also teaches that, ultimately, it is human beings who have the power to determine how God will use that power. That theme is also invoked throughout the liturgy of the High Holidays. We pray that God's compassion should "conquer" God's anger. Note the militaristic term "conquer"; it indicates a power struggle within God. This dynamic interaction between God's power and human power is the core of the prophetic reading of history. Sometimes, God's power to punish bows before the human power to effect a change in God's plan.

One final note on the message of the Book of Jonah: It is conventionally taught that the message of the book is the power of repentance, but if that were the case, the book would end with the third chapter, after God renounces the plan to punish Nineveh. That's not where the book ends, however. Chapter 4 begins with Jonah's astonishing and totally unexpected rage at God. He claims that this was precisely why he didn't want to travel to Nineveh. He knew that God would eagerly welcome Nineveh's repentance and renounce the punishment, and that he, Jonah, would be left looking foolish: all those dire prophecies would have come to naught. This most successful of the prophets seems not to have understood that his prophecy of destruction was entirely conditional upon the people's failure to repent.

The closing verses of the book—the story of that mysterious plant that God creates to shelter Jonah from the sun, the worm that destroys the plant, and Jonah's agony—represent God's attempt to teach the prophet something about the nature of God:

> You cared about the plant, which you did not work for and which you did not grow.... And should not I care about Nineveh, that great city, in which there are more than a hundred and twenty thousand persons who do not yet know their right hand from their left, and many beasts as well!
>
> —*Jonah 4:11*

On that striking note, the book ends. The message of the book is only incidentally about the power of repentance. That repentance can preempt punishment is assumed—at least by everyone except Jonah. The message of the book is purely theological; it is a mini-course on the nature of God, on how God exercises power. The ultimate expression of that power is God's readiness to use that power with compassion rather than with anger.

The Impact of Human Freedom

That struggle within God results from God's own commitment to human freedom. Our freedom is the most significant constraint on God's power, and, again, it was God who set that struggle in motion by creating us free. God could have interfered with Cain's decision to slay his brother, Abel, with the wickedness of the generation of the flood and of the inhabitants of Sodom and Gomorrah, or with the building of the golden calf, but did not do so. Once God created human beings free, God simply had to accept the inevitable implications of that freedom. God may rage over human wickedness, plead for justice and compassion on earth, or choose to punish or to reward, but God has surrendered the power to interfere with the course of human history, even though, as in our day, it leads to phenomena like the Holocaust. This is a self-limiting God—with a vengeance!

If human freedom limits God's power in history, what about God's power over nature? The creation story in Genesis 1 portrays a God whose creative power is absolute and unchallenged; every creation is assigned its proper place in the world. God creates a perfectly ordered world. In this creation story, there is not even a hint of a challenge or resistance to God's creative power.

Not so with the course of human history. Psalm 89 catches the contrast, poignantly beginning with a paean to God's power over nature:

O Lord, God of hosts,
who is mighty like You, O Lord?...
Your faithfulness surrounds You;
You rule the swelling of the sea;
when its waves surge, You still them.
You crushed Rahab; he was like a corpse;
with Your powerful arm You scattered Your enemies.
The heaven is Yours,
the earth too;
the world and all it holds—
You established them.
North and south—
You created them;
Tabor and Hermon sing forth Your name.
Yours is an arm endowed with might;
Your hand is strong;
Your right hand, exalted.
Righteousness and justice are the base of Your throne;
steadfast love and faithfulness stand before You.

—*Psalm 89:9–15*

Note, first, that this passage, like Isaiah's reformulation of the origins of darkness, reflects a creation story that is slightly different from the one recorded in Genesis 1. There, God's power is absolute and unchallenged. This psalm hints that God's creative power had to overcome challenges. Here, the sea swells and the waves surge, although God stills them. Rahab is a mythic, primordial monster who had to be—note the verb—"crushed." Now God has "enemies" whom God had to scatter. The impression here is that God's creation of the world was not unchallenged, that it involved a struggle between God's power and some natural forces that God first had to subdue, whereas in Genesis 1, God simply spoke and the world came into being. The result is much the same, however. There was, and presumably continues to be, some resistance to God's creative power, but God masters that resistance. Hence the psalmist's conclusion: "Righteousness and justice are the base of Your throne; steadfast love and faithfulness stand before You."

That conclusion transposes a statement about God's power into a claim about human life. Precisely because God rules over nature, God can rule over human events as well, according to God's own commitments to justice, mercy, steadfast love, and faithfulness. The first leads to the second. Only a God who controls nature can decree how human beings are to live. To live in God's world, then, implies that God will reward our living in righteousness, justice, steadfast love, and faithfulness.

God's Power in History

As the psalm continues, the author points out that this is not at all the case. In fact, this first portion of the psalm is a setup; it leads to a painful challenge to God's power that emerges out of Israel's historical experience.

> Yet You have rejected, spurned,
> and become enraged at Your anointed.
> You have repudiated the covenant with Your servant;
> You have dragged his dignity in the dust....
> All who pass by plunder him;
> he has become the butt of his neighbors.
> You have exalted the right hand of his adversaries
> and made all his enemies rejoice.
> You have turned back the blade of his sword
> and have not sustained him in battle.
>
> —Psalm 89:39–44

In fact, then, although God's power may control the forces of nature, it is not at all clear that it controls history as well. The conclusion that God's righteousness, justice, steadfast love, and faithfulness govern human affairs is hardly manifest in the world. Otherwise, why would Israel suffer so? The contrast between nature and history is sharp and painful, and the claim that God's righteousness and justice rule history as well emerges as deeply ironic.

> How long, O Lord; will you forever hide Your face,
> Will Your fury blaze like fire?...
> O Lord, where is Your steadfast love of old,
> which You swore to David in Your faithfulness?
> Remember, O Lord, the abuse flung at Your servants....
> How Your enemies, O Lord, have flung abuse,
> abuse at Your anointed at every step.
> *—Psalm 89:47–51*

That same contrast between God's power in nature and in human affairs is echoed in Psalm 104. The first thirty-four verses of this psalm are an extended description of how God rules the natural order, but the thirty-fifth verse, the very last verse in the psalm, pleads, "May sinners disappear from the earth, and the wicked be no more. Clearly, for this psalmist, sinners and wicked people have not as yet disappeared from the earth. Why not, if God's power has created such a splendid natural panorama? This apparently casual postscript to the psalm barely conceals the author's bitterness.[3]

A Holocaust Psalm

Psalm 44 raises a similar charge against God's treatment of Israel. Now the setup for the charge is how God directed Israel's early history.

We have heard, O God,
our fathers have told us
the deeds You performed in their time,
in days of old.
With Your hand You planted them,
displacing nations;
You brought misfortune on peoples
and drove them out.
It was not by their sword that they took the land,
their arm did not give them victory,
but Your right hand, Your arm, and Your goodwill
for You favored them.

—Psalm 44:2–4

With this setup in place, the author devotes the large portion of the psalm to a brutal description of how, in his day, God has abandoned Israel and left them for prey at the hands of the nations. "You let them devour us like sheep; You disperse us among the nations" (44:12). The psalmist understands God's abandonment of Israel as punishment for Israel's sin. In most of the Bible, human suffering in the form of military defeat or natural trauma was accepted as punishment for sin. That tidy package served to maintain the notion of a God who was intrinsically just, but here this simply is not the case. Israel has not sinned, or at least not sinned enough to merit this defeat.

All this has come upon us,
yet we have not forgotten You
or been false to Your covenant.
Our hearts have not gone astray....
If we forgot the name of our God
And spread forth our hands to a foreign god,
God would surely search it out,
For He knows the secrets of the heart.

—Psalm 44:18–22

The truth is even much more painful: "It is for Your sake that we are slain all day long, that we are regarded as sheep to be slaughtered" (44:23).

This passage is arguably the bleakest, most despairing attack on God in the entire Bible. Not only has Israel not sinned, it is precisely because it has remained faithful to God that it is being slaughtered "all day long." There is not a hint of guilt in the psalm, even though the traditional interpretation of human suffering understands pain as God's punishment for sin. But here there is no sin! There is no more obvious biblical anticipation of our generation's Holocaust experience than this single passage. Israel and God had a deal: Israel would be loyal to God, and God would reward that loyalty with peace and prosperity. Israel has kept its side of the bargain, but what about God's side? Then the concluding plea:

Rouse Yourself; why do You sleep, O Lord?
Awaken, do not reject us forever!
Why do You hide Your face,
ignoring our affliction and distress?...
Arise and help us,
redeem us, as befits Your faithfulness.

—*Psalm 44:24–27*

What a startling image! This all-powerful God is asleep! How else to account for God's abandonment of Israel?

The passage is doubly ironic because there is one more instance in the Bible where a god is portrayed as asleep, but there the metaphor is applied to a foreign god, Baal. In 1 Kings 18, the prophet Elijah stages a dramatic confrontation with the priests of Baal, as a decisive test that will prove, once and for all, that the God of Israel is the only true God. Elijah assembles the people and has the priests of Baal construct an altar, prepare sacrifices, and implore their god to consume their sacrifices. He will do the same and implore his God to respond. The priests of Baal prepare their sacrifices and invoke Baal "from morning until noon, shouting, 'O Baal, answer us!'" There is no response. Elijah mocks them: "Shout louder! After all, he is a god. But he may be in conversation, he may be detained, or he may be on a journey, or perhaps he is asleep and will wake up" (1 Kings 18:27). They continue to shout and to gash themselves, but with no response. Whereupon Elijah pleads, "Answer me, O Lord...that these people may know that You, O Lord, are God." Fire descends from God and consumes the sacrifices, and all the people fall upon their faces and proclaim, "The Lord alone is God, the Lord alone is God" (18:39).

So Baal may be asleep, but the God of Israel never sleeps. Hasn't another psalmist assured us, "See, the guardian of Israel neither slumbers nor sleeps!" (Psalm 121:4)? God does seem to be asleep sometimes. In our post-Holocaust age, that challenge to God's power in human affairs seems altogether justified. We moderns might also add that in contrast to the psalmist's perception of the natural order, we have much evidence of God's impotence in nature as well—earthquakes, tornados, diseases, tidal waves, and floods that destroy homes and take many human lives. So much, then, for God's vaunted omnipotence!

God's Power over Death

The Bible, of course, does not represent the final word on any Jewish doctrine. There are numerous instances where the later tradition seems to recognize that biblical teachings on an issue are simply unsatisfactory and then proceeds to rectify those failings. One striking instance of that process deals with God's power over death.

We drew attention above to a liturgical passage of talmudic origin that God has the power to reverse the natural order and to bring the dead back to life. In the Bible itself, death is final. Just about every biblical personality dies. There seem to be only two exceptions to that rule: Genesis 5:21–24 tells us that Enoch "walked with God; then he was no more, for God took him," and 2 Kings 2:11 tells us that Elijah "went up to heaven in a whirlwind." Every other biblical personality dies, and their deaths are final. The people mourn and then move on.

There are only three brief biblical passages (Isaiah 25:18, 26:9, and Daniel 12:2), all dating from the very last stages of the biblical period (third to second centuries B.C.E.), that seem to suggest that God can bring at least some dead people back to life. Based on these three passages, the rabbinic tradition developed a doctrine of the resurrection of the dead that soon became a cardinal doctrine in Judaism, as reflected in the passage from the *amidah* quoted earlier.

That later tradition went even further. It teaches that at the end of days, death itself will die. That teaching appears most explicitly in the sixteenth-century hymn *Chad Gadya*, with which we conclude the Passover seder liturgy. In this song, a Jewish version of "The Farmer in the Dell," the very last stanza has The Holy One slaughtering the angel of death. The death of death at God's hand represents the final manifestation of God's ultimate power, what one of my teachers once called "the final stage in the triumphant march of the monotheistic idea." Now God is even more powerful than death, but that final step will happen only at the end of days. In historical time, death is still the universal, ultimate destiny for human beings, even despite God's vaunted power over human destiny. That God's ultimate power will be realized only at the end of days underlines our earlier conclusion that only at the end of days will God be truly *echad*.

We can speculate on what led the later rabbinic tradition to proclaim God's ultimate victory over death, but one factor would certainly be the sense that if death is final, then God's power would have to be limited by death. Death becomes the ultimate power in the world, and God must bow before death—which is to say that death *is* god, and we should worship death. That conclusion was simply intolerable. If not in historical time, then at the end of days God's power will be supreme, even over death.

De jure, then, God's power is absolute; de facto, it is hedged in with constraints. God has to maintain a public image in the world, remember prior promises to our ancestors, keep the commitment to human freedom, and contend with death, natural disasters, and the persistence of unmitigated evil among human beings. The last of these constraints is particularly pressing. There are only two broad theological responses to the problem of evil in the world. The first maintains the transcendent power of God and then, in various ways, tries to accommodate human suffering within God's rule. The second insists that evil inhabits a realm that is independent of God's rule. Each has its problems. The first has to explain why God could, but apparently refuses to, control evil. The second posits an essentially limited God—not the God who is self-limiting (as implied by human freedom), but a God who is inherently impotent to control this force in nature.

Again, all of this is true now within the framework of history. At the end of days, as God will be totally *echad*, so will God's power be absolute, but for that we have to wait for the end of days. Until then, what about the promise of security and stability that led Abraham to break with his pagan background? Where indeed is the security, if the world is ruled by a supposedly all-powerful God who somehow, for some reason, refuses to exercise, or is incapable of exercising, that power in our lives today?

3

God Is Person

Where Are *You*?

At the very beginning of human history, God goes searching for Adam. Adam and Eve have eaten the forbidden fruit and have hidden among the trees of the garden. God will not let them hide. God wanders through the garden, calling out, "Where are you?" Shortly thereafter, Cain kills Abel, and God calls out to Cain, "Where is your brother, Abel?"

When we read biblical narratives of this kind, we should always ask: Why are the stories written in this way? These same stories could have been narrated in many different ways, but the Bible records these particular versions. In both instances, God uses the second person: "Where are *you*?" and "Where is *your* brother?" In each case the question is directed to an individual human being. These mythic narratives are designed to teach us something about the nature of the human being. They also teach us about the biblical image of God. This God relates to, addresses, commands, and negotiates with individual human beings. More important, this God cares about the destiny of individual human beings, of all human beings. For Adam and Eve and Cain are us. God addresses each of us as well: "Where are *you*?" "Where is *your* brother?"

The image of God in these stories is a "personal" God. God is portrayed as acting with intent, purpose, and concern toward and about individual human beings. God enters into interpersonal relationships. The term *interpersonal relationship* implies the presence to each other of two persons. The only kind of god who would not be a personal god is one who acts blindly, by rote, without focus or intentionality, who mechanically follows a set of laws, whose mind never changes, who does not have a mind to change in the first place, who knows nothing about feelings, who does not have an inner life. The personal God lives in a dynamic, ever-changing relationship with people; the impersonal god knows nothing of relationships. This metaphor of a personal God is concretized in the many more specific biblical metaphors for God: God is a shepherd, a parent, a teacher, a lover, a sovereign, a judge, a spouse. These are all relational qualities: a shepherd needs sheep, a sovereign needs subjects, a lover needs a beloved. They all capture the sense that God is personally and intensely involved in relationships with people.

A striking character sketch of this personal God emerges in the story of Abraham pleading for the wicked inhabitants of Sodom and Gomorrah (Genesis 18:16–33). At the outset, God deliberates whether to reveal to Abraham God's plans to punish the inhabitants of these cities for their sins:

> Shall I hide from Abraham what I am about to do, since Abraham is to become a great and populous nation and all the nations of the earth are to bless themselves by him? For I have singled him out, that he may instruct his children and his posterity to keep the way of the Lord by doing what is just and right, in order that the Lord may bring about for Abraham what He has promised him.
>
> — *Genesis 18:17–19*

First, we are granted a glimpse into God's thought processes: God is conflicted. The conflict is presented as an internal question that reflects a tension within God between two contradictory divine impulses: God's anger and God's concern with doing what is "just and right." God is ambivalent about what to do with these people. To this ambivalence is added a further concern: God cannot act unilaterally without consulting Abraham. After all, Abraham is here in the first place because God commanded him to break with his past and embark on a new relationship with this God. God and Abraham are partners in this new enterprise; they share a commitment to doing what is "just and right." These are the distinctive qualities of the "way of the Lord," to which both God and Abraham are equally committed. That's why God needs Abraham's approval before acting.

The exchange that follows begins with the statement that "Abraham came forward," hardly a physical move on Abraham's part, for this God is not visible in space. To "come forward" to this God is to encounter, to challenge, to share feelings, to engage. Here, it is a challenge: "Will You sweep away the innocent along with the guilty?"

Abraham does not challenge the reality of the people's guilt. What he does challenge is God's moral judgment, God's readiness to obliterate the innocent together with the guilty. Abraham believes that some of the inhabitants of the cities are innocent. The core of his challenge is that God cannot act this way because of God's own commitment, enunciated in God's internal deliberations at the outset, to do what is "just and right." "Far be it from You to do such a thing, to bring about death upon the innocent as well as the guilty.... Shall not the judge of all the earth deal justly?" (18:25). Indeed, it was God's concern for doing what is just and right that led God to invite Abraham's reassurance in the first place, but Abraham does not provide that reassurance. Instead, he claims that for God to destroy the innocent is manifestly unjust. Abraham calls God to account because of everything he knows about his God, because of their relationship, and because of their mutual commitment to justice.

Then follow the negotiations: If there are fifty...forty-five...forty...thirty...twenty...ten innocent people, God cannot destroy the cities. Then the two partners separate: God "departs," and "Abraham returns to his place." The exchange is over. There are no winners or losers here. Both God and Abraham win: God was willing to consider Abraham's argument and, even more, to renounce punishment, but there were no innocent people in Sodom and Gomorrah.

God Cares about People

The complex image of the biblical God that emerges in this passage captures everything we mean when we attribute personhood to God. God cares about society; God does not tolerate wickedness; but God has other commitments here, to do what is just and right. God also has a prior relationship with Abraham; Abraham has been "singled out" because he shares these commitments. These two impulses are in conflict, so God has to deliberate what to do and whether to invite Abraham's reaction. Note that Abraham understands that he has not only the right, but indeed the obligation, to challenge God, which he then proceeds to do. Despite Abraham's self-abnegation throughout—he is but dust and ashes, he fears God's anger—Abraham clearly knows his rights, appreciates his power, and is fully prepared to use it on behalf of innocent people. Even more, God and Abraham share a commitment to the moral law. That, together with their relationship, forms the basis for the entire story. Astonishingly, God welcomes Abraham's challenge.

Consider the image of God portrayed in this story. God deliberates, is conflicted, has feelings, invites consultation, is willing to change the divine plan, is open to negotiation, and needs to be true to previous commitments. Above all, God has an intense relationship with an individual human being. This is what we mean when we attribute personhood to God.

These three stories—God searching for Adam and Eve in the garden, God challenging Cain over his brother's fate, and God's debate with Abraham—all from the earliest Genesis narratives, lead to the conclusion that serves as the title of the late Abraham Joshua Heschel's most comprehensive theological statement, *God in Search of Man.*[1]

Why is God in search of humanity? We "search" for something or someone whom we need, someone who is important to us. Why does God need human beings? For that matter, why does God create a world in the first place, a world populated with erring human beings? Why create them free? Why enter into a relationship first with Abraham, then with his posterity, then with his descendants for all time? Why expose God's deliberations, hopes, frustrations, pride, and anger? We also search for something that we have lost or misplaced. In what sense are people "lost" to God? That may be why God bothers to reveal a Torah. However one understands the story of God's revelation at Sinai, the very fact of that revelation assumes that God cares enough about Israel to want to instruct them on how to live as a people, in loyalty to this God. Torah may be the way that God tries to "find" Israel.

Why does God have such a rich inner life? Isn't God supposed to have it all together? Isn't God supposed to be above all this—transcendent, without needs, all-powerful, beyond feelings, beyond uncertainty, beyond ambivalence? That's the God of the philosophers, but not the God portrayed in the Bible. This God cares profoundly about people. It is the caring quality that Heschel refers to as "the divine pathos."

We are familiar with the word *pathos* as it appears in terms such as *sympathy* or *empathy.* The dictionary defines it as a quality that arouses feelings of pity, tenderness, or sorrow. I sympathize with someone who is suffering, I share that person's pain, and I am sorry for him or her. Heschel's use of the term includes all this, but primarily it denotes something far more basic: God's abiding caring and concern for humanity. This, Heschel claims, is the distinguishing quality of the biblical God; it forms the "ground tone" for all of God's complex interactions with human beings. God cares about people, both the disadvantaged, such as the widows and orphans, and those more fortunate. God searches for people, loves people, needs people. We know all too well that to love someone is to make oneself vulnerable to that person. It gives that person the opportunity to please or to injure us. God undergoes all of this. That's why this God has such a rich inner life, why God merits our pity, tenderness, or sorrow. To speak of God's pathos, then, is to make a statement about how God feels about us and how we feel about God.[2]

God Is Vulnerable

Heschel's character sketch of the biblical God emphasizes God's vulnerability. God may be transcendent and omnipotent, but in the biblical narrative—in fact, throughout history as Judaism understands it—God's hopes and dreams for human society are invariably frustrated. God never gets the kind of world for which God yearns. The biblical narrative is one of constant human rebellion. God expresses frustration, despair, and anger, always mixed with infinite yearning that somehow, sometime, some people will follow God's way.

If God is in search of us, then we too are in search of God; the relationship must be mutual. God can search for us because God assumes that we too need God and that we will respond. God's searching implies God's openness to our response. That mutuality is at the heart of Martin Buber's claim that the divine-human relationship is one of "I and Thou." An "I" can relate only to a "Thou." God's "I" demands a human "Thou," and our "I" demands a divine "Thou." Otherwise there is no relationship. Buber also insists that only in the mutuality of the relationship does each partner become fully a person. In other words, God is personal only when, and to the extent that, God relates to us as persons. Our personhood determines God's personhood, and God's personhood determines ours. That is implied in the rabbinic commentary to Isaiah 43:10: "'You are my witnesses,' declares the Lord," which the Rabbis transform into a conditional statement: "If you are my witnesses, then I am God; if you are not my witnesses, then, so to speak, I am not your God."[3] Or, in God's words to Moses, "I will take you to be My people, and I will be your God" (Exodus 6:7). Implied is "If you are My people, then I will be your God"—and if not?

We Search for God

God's search for us invites our search for God. The psalmist writes:

> Like a hind crying for water,
> my soul cries for You, O God;
> my soul thirsts for God, the living God;
> O when will I come to appear before God!
>
> —*Psalm 42:2*

That desperate yearning for intimacy with God is at the heart of all expressions of mysticism. It is also captured in a poem by the eleventh-century C.E. poet Judah Halevi:

> Lord, where shall I find You?
> Your place is lofty and secret.
> And where shall I not find You?
> The whole earth is full of Your glory!
> I have sought to come near You.
> I have called You with all my heart;
> and when I went out towards You,
> I found You coming towards me.[4]

As with Abraham's "coming forward," the poet's coming near to God is not at all a physical act. We often come near to, or distance ourselves from, another person who is not a physical presence before us. This kind of coming near is an inner movement, an emotional engagement. We can also be emotionally distant from someone who is in the same room as we are.

God's Face Is Hidden

Mysteriously, God is not always accessible. Again and again, psalmists cry out in despair at the realization that despite their search for God, God is not to be found. The relationship is somehow blocked:

> How long, O Lord; will You ignore me, forever?
> How long will You hide Your face from me?
> How long will I have cares on my mind,
> grief in my heart all day?
> Look at me, answer me, O Lord, my God....
> Lest I sleep the sleep of death.
>
> —Psalm 13:2–4

Note the metaphor for God's abandonment: God hides God's own face. That's why the psalmist, in despair, demands that God "look" at him, "answer" him. The metaphor of the hiding of God's face appears many times in Scripture—frequently as punishment, but not always, as in this psalm where there is not a hint of guilt on the part of the author. This metaphor assumes the reality of its opposite—namely, that sometimes God reveals God's face to us, that God is accessible and related to us, that God "looks" at us and "answers" us. Ideally, the relationship is "face to face," thoroughly interpersonal. The metaphor of God's showing God's face in blessing is captured in the Priestly Benediction in Numbers

6:24–26: "The Lord bless you and protect you! The Lord make His face shine upon you and be gracious to you! The Lord lift up His countenance upon you and grant you peace."

A God who can shine God's face upon us is a God whose face can also be hidden. More important for our purposes here, this is a God who *has* a "face" to shine or to hide. The divine-human relationship has a mysterious, unpredictable dynamic of its own, precisely like the dynamic of an intense relationship between two human beings. Sometimes it works; at other times it doesn't. Sometimes we are open to each other; at other times we are blocked, although we persist in working through the hard times.

Spouse, Parent, and Lover

The complex, dynamic interpersonal relationship between God and Israel is captured in a number of vivid metaphors, the most familiar of which are husband and wife, parent and child, and lovers. All of these share the mysterious quality of existing in perpetual flux.

The image of God and Israel linked as husband and wife is omnipresent in the Bible and the later literature. This marital metaphor is portrayed in all the stages that are quite familiar to us today: courtship, engagement, marriage, tension, separation, sometimes divorce, and, more often, reconciliation. The prophet Jeremiah portrays a somewhat idealized picture of God's honeymoon years with Israel following the Exodus:

> I accounted to your favor
> The devotion of your youth,
> Your love as a bride—How you followed Me in the wilderness,
> In a land not sown.
>
> *—Jeremiah 2:2*

The biblical account of that early desert experience portrays it as far more contentious than does Jeremiah's account.

Another prophet, Hosea, portrays the marriage as near dissolution. Israel has now become the adulterous wife who says:

I will go after my lovers,
Who supply my bread and my water,
My wool and my linen,
My oil and my drink.

—*Hosea 2:7*

This unfaithful wife has to be rebuked:

Now I will uncover her shame
In the presence of her lovers...,
And I will end all her rejoicing....
I will lay waste her vines and her fig trees....
Thus will I punish her....

—*Hosea 2:12–15*

In one of the most tender notes in all of prophetic literature, the chapter concludes on a note of marital reconciliation:

I will espouse you forever;
I will espouse you with righteousness and justice,
And with goodness and mercy,
I will espouse you with faithfulness;
Then you shall be devoted to the Lord.

—*Hosea 2:21–22*

For a portion of the Israelite community, however, there was indeed a divorce. Ten of the twelve tribes—commonly called Israel, as opposed to the other two tribes, who were called Judah—were defeated by Assyria in 721 B.C.E., and they subsequently disappeared. God speaks to Jeremiah:

> Have you seen what Rebel Israel did, going to every high mountain and under every leafy tree, and whoring there? I thought: After she has done all of these things, she will come back to Me. But she did not come back; and her sister, Faithless Judah, saw it. I noted: Because Rebel Israel had committed adultery, I cast her off and handed her a bill of divorce; yet her sister, Faithless Judah, was not afraid—she too went and whored.
>
> —Jeremiah 3:6–8

Judah too was to be punished but never divorced. Jerusalem, the city of Judah, and the Temple were to be destroyed by Babylonia, and its population exiled, but later it was all to be restored.

Sometimes, the issue of whether a husband and wife should separate or stay together is much more complicated. Catch God's ambivalence in this remarkable homily:

> It is like a king who became angry at his consort. He wrote her a bill of divorce and gave it to her, but then he returned and grabbed it back. Whenever she wished to marry someone else, the king said to her, "Where is the bill of divorce which I gave you?" And whenever she claimed support from him, he said to her, "I have already divorced you." Similarly, whenever Israel wishes to worship idols, the Holy Blessed One says to her, "Where is the bill of divorce of your mother whom I dismissed?" [Isaiah 50:1]. And whenever Israel asks Him to perform a miracle for her, He tells her, "I have already cast you off," as it is written, "Because Rebel Israel had committed adultery, I cast her off and handed her a bill of divorce" [Jeremiah 3:8].[5]

This is indeed ambivalence, the kind of ambivalence that every spouse would understand quite well. Now place this text into the context in which it was first conceived, probably as a sermon or for some class. This is the way the Rabbis taught theology—not as an abstract discipline, but as emerging out of and responding to the real-life situations of real human beings. The sermon served two purposes: it validated the human experience, and it brought God into the lives of the listening community in a sharp and vivid way. That's what all of these images of God accomplish.

In another poignant biblical passage, Jeremiah turns to the metaphor of Israel as the beloved child. God speaks:

Truly, Ephraim is a dear son to Me,
A child who is dandled!
Whenever I have turned against him,
My thoughts would dwell on him still.
That is why My heart yearns for him;
I will receive him back in love.

—*Jeremiah 31:20*

Israel is God's child, a tot that bounces on God's lap. We are often angry at our children, but in and through the moments of anger, we yearn to reconcile with them. Catch the plaintive *Avinu Malkenu* ("Our Father, our Sovereign") chant that is sounded throughout the High Holiday liturgy, culminating with: "*Avinu Malkenu*, be gracious and answer us, though we are unworthy; treat us with compassion and kindness, and save us." Here the parent metaphor is joined to the sovereign metaphor, reflecting the complex mix of affection and awe, confidence and trembling, with which Jews confront God at that season.

The image of God as lover is best captured in the poetry of Jewish mysticism, as in these opening and concluding lines of the poem *Yedid Nefesh* by the sixteenth-century Palestinian Eleazar Azikri:

> Soul mate, loving God, compassion's gentle source,
> Take my disposition and shape it to Your will.
> Like a darting deer will I rush to You.
> Before Your glorious presence humbly will I bow.
> Let Your sweet love delight me with its thrill.
> Because no other dainty will my hunger still.
>
> The time, my love, is now; rush, be quick, be bold.
> Let Your favor grace me, in the spirit of days of old.[6]

God's Anger

Anger is part of every intense human relationship. Anger is not abandonment; abandonment is much more painful. At the heart of every expression of anger is care and love. The world is filled with people we don't get angry at simply because we don't care enough about them. We only get angry at people we care about. Like all of God's other feelings, anger is reactive; it is prompted by human behavior. It is part of the complex relationship, whereas abandonment implies a breaking off of the relationship. Our ancestors experienced both—as do we—even though the distinction between the two is frequently blurred.

Again, it is Jeremiah who best captures the fury of God's anger:

> Lo, the storm of the Lord goes forth in fury,
> A whirling storm,
> It shall whirl down upon the heads of the wicked.
> The anger of the Lord shall not turn back
> Till it has fulfilled and completed His purposes.
> *—Jeremiah 23:19–20*

But God's anger is fleeting:

For a little while I forsook you
But with vast love I will bring you back.
In slight anger, for a moment,
I hid My face from you;
But with kindness everlasting
I will take you back.

—*Isaiah 54:7–8*

We tend to be embarrassed by the notion that God gets angry. A passage such as Psalm 79:6–7, which appears at the climax of the Passover seder, has occasioned much controversy: "Pour out Your fury on the nations that do not know You, upon the kingdoms that do not invoke Your name, for they have devoured Jacob and desolated his home."

That we should pray for God's anger to flare up at anyone led Mordecai Kaplan, among others, to delete the passage from his edition of the *Haggadah* altogether. That notion, for Kaplan, was seriously offensive. Perhaps it is the term *fury* itself that is troubling. Heschel proposes *righteous indignation* as an alternative.[7] Perhaps it is the attribution to God of what we understand as a destructive emotion. Perhaps it reflects our discomfort with our own anger, or it reflects our problem with the entire notion of attributing any kind of intense emotion to God in the first place. Heschel also addresses that discomfort:

Is it more compatible with our conception of the grandeur of God to claim that He is emotionally blind to the misery of man rather than profoundly moved?...To the biblical mind the conception of God as detached and unemotional is totally alien.[8]

Heschel insists that God's anger is always reactive; it is invariably a divine reaction to human evil. It is also contingent—never blind, unprovoked rage, but rather addressed to specific human failings—and it is never irrevocable. We will address the broader issue of God's emotional life below.

God Weeps

There is no minimizing those passages in which God's rage is expressed clearly and unambiguously. There are still other passages where God's anger seems to turn on itself, where God seems to suffer from the divine anger as much as those to whom it was originally directed.

By any measure, the most horrific result of God's fury at Israel's faithlessness was the destruction of the First Temple at the hands of Babylonia in 586 B.C.E. Whatever the historical factors that led to this traumatic event, both the prophets and the Rabbis of the Talmud understood it as God's punishment for Israel's sin. However, in an elaborate rabbinic commentary on that event,[9] God's rage is transformed into mourning. When the Temple was about to be destroyed, God is portrayed as exclaiming:

> So long as I am within it [the Temple], the peoples of the world will be unable to touch it. However, I will shut My eyes from it and swear that I will have nothing to do with it again till the messianic end of time. Meanwhile, let the enemies come and devastate it.

But after the devastation, God weeps:

> "Woe is Me! What have I done?...I have...become the laughing stock of the nations and an object of derision for mortals." In that instant, Metatron [God's ministering angel] came, fell upon his face, and spoke... "Master of the Universe, let me weep, but You must not weep." God

replied: "If you do not let Me weep, I will go into a place where you have no authority to enter and weep there."

God then calls on Jeremiah and the ministering angels and visits the site of the burnt Temple. God cries out in anguish:

Woe is Me for My house! My children, where are you? My priests, my Levites, where are you? What else might I have done with you, seeing that I kept warning you again and again, but you would not repent?

Abraham, Isaac, Jacob, and Moses join the mourning, while God laments, "Woe to the king who prospered in his youth but did not prosper in his old age."

These are but snippets of a long, extended homily that tries to capture God's complex reactions in this single, most powerful outburst of divine rage. The interweaving of metaphors here is singularly complex and fascinating. Just what is God upset about—Israel's suffering or God's image among the nations? Notice also God's need to justify the punishment: God tried to warn them, but they just didn't listen! God can't suffer alone; Abraham, Isaac, Jacob, and the angels are introduced into the narrative to provide God with a community of mourners. Finally, notice the turn from anger to weeping—or simply, the image of God in tears, refusing to be comforted, even insisting on God's right to weep. This is divine pathos with a vengeance! There is no more powerful testimony to the religious impact of this humanization of God. The mix of emotions is totally familiar to any parent.

God as Process

Contemporary Jewish theologians who are disturbed at the image of God as emotion-ridden must end by denying God's personhood as well. Their alternative is to think of God as an impersonal process, an impulse, a force, or a power operating throughout nature. Mordecai Kaplan, the earliest and still the most influential of Jewish process theologians, defines God as "the power that makes for salvation," where salvation means human fulfillment, the full realization of all those qualities that make us truly human.[10]

Kaplan begins with an assumption that once our physiological needs are satisfied, we start "to experience the need to overcome such traits as self-indulgence, arrogance, envy, exploitation and hatred." Then

> it is natural to arrive at the next step, which requires no blind leap into the dark. The next step is to conclude that the cosmos is so constituted as to enable man to fulfill this highest human need of his nature.

The human need for salvation demands the conviction that the world is constituted so as to enable us to fulfill that need. That power or impulse within the world and within us—for we are part of the cosmos—that impels us to seek, and that enables us to realize our fulfillment as human beings, is what Kaplan calls God. He suggests an illuminating analogy:

> A magnetic needle, hung on a thread or placed on a pivot, assumes of its own accord a position in which one end of the needle points north and the other south. So long as it is free to move about, all attempts to deflect it will not get it to remain away from its normal direction. Likewise, man normally veers in the direction of that which makes for the fulfillment of his destiny as a human being. That fact indicates the functioning of a cosmic Power which influences his behavior. What magnetism is to the magnetic needle, Godhood or God is to man.

The analogy is striking: God is like a magnetic force. What a striking repudiation of the notion of a personal God! It reflects Kaplan's more generalized repudiation of much of the traditional metaphorical image of God: God is not a Being, certainly not a personal Being—not supernatural, not transcendent or omnipotent, not emotion-filled. All these notions strike Kaplan as primitive and anachronistic. The two repudiations go hand in hand: God does not have personality and God does not have feelings. To view God as a power or force operating within nature—and nature is, simply, all there is—is to provide an alternative, possibly more intellectually sophisticated, metaphor. It remains a metaphor, however, just as the image of God as a person is a metaphor. The issue then becomes, which metaphor speaks most meaningfully to us, person or process?

The irony underlying this outline of Kaplan's theology is that I studied midrash in courses that Kaplan taught at The Jewish Theological Seminary. Kaplan fully appreciated the emotional and religious power of the midrashic texts such as the one that describes God's weeping at the destruction of the Temple. He understood that those characterizations of God were metaphorical. He clearly appreciated their homiletical, even their religious, power. He used them in his own preaching, but in constructing his theology he found process theology to be intellectually much more rigorous and satisfying. Heschel, with whom I also studied at the Seminary during some of the Kaplan years, obviously disagreed.

Can God Be Moved?

To give Kaplan's critique its full weight, much of the history of Western philosophical discourse on the nature of God shares his discomfort with attributing emotion to God. Heschel devotes much of *The Prophets* to a rigorous and wide-ranging critique of that tradition. It all goes back, as does much of Western philosophy, to the Greek philosophers. At the heart of that tradition is a sense that emotions are somehow less important, less valued, less intrinsic to the "real me" than is reason.

We have almost intuitively inherited that emphasis. Many of us tend to look down on feelings, to be embarrassed by them, to feel the need to control or suppress them. It emerges in the stereotype that "men don't cry." Women have feelings but men don't, or at least don't exhibit them. Men are "cool," rational, detached, dispassionate, unmoved. Note the term *unmoved*, which shares the same root as *emotion*. To be "moved," in its physical sense, is to be passive; we *are* moved by the impact on us of something or someone else. It also means to change, to go from one stage to another, but this changing quality implies that the original state of affairs is in some way imperfect. Hence we move to another state, or are induced to move by some outside power.

This physical passivity and changeability, now translated into a human being's inner life, is understood by the Greeks to be a weakness that we must overcome by developing our rational powers, our mind. In contrast to emotion, reason is an active, initiating quality; it is stable and universal. It is precisely our reason that is the core of our identity, that which makes us authentically human or, to use the language of Genesis, that which constitutes God's image in us. Human perfection lies in the full realization of our rational powers.

These anthropological assumptions are then projected onto God. God becomes the very principle of reason, the paradigm of rationality, all reason, unchanging and eternal. We have seen a Jewish version of that image in our references to Maimonides, the Jewish philosopher most powerfully influenced by Greek philosophy. To characterize God as emotion-filled is to demean God. God is "unmoved," "apathetic," unchanging, active. We today would recognize Maimonides' male bias here, but that judgment reflects our modern perspective. It is just a short step to the conclusion that God is in no way "personal."

Person and *process,* when applied to God, are both metaphors. They emerge from different human impulses. The process metaphor is driven by the mind; it appeals to our need to understand God, to make what we say about God cohere with everything else we say about the world. In contrast, the person metaphor is driven by the heart, by our emotional life, by our human need to relate to God in some more intimate way. It is an expression of our intuitive search for intimacy and relationship.

Both impulses are legitimate; neither should be denied. Different people exhibit different impulses at different times in their lives or in response to different needs. The God I invoke when I do philosophy is not the God to whom I pray, but we can live with these changing and sometimes contradictory impulses if we remember that all our images of God are metaphors. No human being knows what God is in God's essence; that's what distinguishes God from human beings. Only God knows God's true nature; what we have are impressions, evoked by our variegated experiences of God's presence in our lives. Mordecai Kaplan, the hard-headed rationalist imbued with a scientific, critical temper, seeks above all to understand God. Heschel, the Hasid, the mystic, the poet, needs the intimacy. We need both.

4

God Is Nice (Sometimes)

Tension

Our images of God are in tension. That seems to be one of the conclusions of our work thus far. God is *echad* but not yet. God is all-powerful but not in historical time. We now confront the most striking expression of that tension. Is God caring and loving? Or is God abandoning and even abusive? Again, the answer will be both—sometimes one, sometimes the other. Classical Jewish texts provide ample support for both of these options, but the tension is far from simply textual. These texts emerged out of the life experience of their human authors. Our own experience confirms that tension. We too know moments when God seems near at hand and nurturing. We also know moments when God appears to be distant and even cruel.

Two methodological warnings should be kept in mind. First, here more than ever, we must remember that to attribute positive or negative characteristics to God is to express our human perceptions, not to portray God's essence, which no human being can know. What we try to characterize with these metaphors is how God appears, or feels, to us at one specific moment. None of us has a direct line to God's thinking.

71

Second, it is equally important to note that the distinction between a loving God and a punitive God is also a matter of perspective. One obvious example: a parent who punishes a child for crossing the street against a red light is perceived by the child as punitive. "You're mean!" screams the child, but the parent knows that this punishment is an expression of parental concern. Similarly, that God permits wolves to eat rabbits is perceived as love by the wolf but as cruelty by the rabbit.

On the other hand, we all have friends or acquaintances who seem to be singled out for a life of sheer tragedy. I recall a character in the comic strip "Li'l Abner" whose name was an unpronounceable string of consonants; wherever he stood, there was a cloud over his head and rain was falling. Around and about him the sun shone, but for him it was always raining. We all know people who have suffered this way. Then there are other people who seem to have lived an idyllic existence. Most of us fall somewhere in between. Those of us who do believe that there is a God in the world must try to make sense of this puzzling pattern.

Our discussion throughout is nevertheless permeated with subjectivity. We can never escape our humanness. With these caveats in mind, let us begin with texts in which God appears as "nice."

The Protector

We begin with the hymn that we chant at the conclusion of our morning service on the Sabbath and festivals, the familiar *Adon Olam*. Its last stanza suggests that this poem, of unknown authorship, dating probably from the eleventh century C.E., was originally composed to conclude the private prayers recited immediately before going to sleep at night; it also appears at the conclusion of that service. It begins on a cosmic note:

Master of the universe, Who reigned
Before any form was created,
When at His will, all was brought into being,
Even then was He proclaimed "King."
And after all has ceased to be,
He will reign in awe, alone.

He is One, there is no second
To compare to Him, to serve as His equal,
Without beginning, without end,
His is the power and the dominion.

Here the tone shifts abruptly. This cosmic power becomes
very personal:

He is my God, my living Redeemer,
Rock for my pain in time of distress.
He is my banner, my refuge,
My cup's portion on the day I call.

Finally, the poet's entreaty:

Into His hand I entrust my spirit
When I go to sleep, and I will awaken!
With my spirit, my body as well.
God is with me. I shall not fear.

In reading a text such as this one, we should begin by identifying the metaphor or metaphors expressed in the text and then try
to identify the feelings that prompted the author to craft those
metaphors. Here the metaphors are clear: God is sovereign, eternal,
transcendent, and all-powerful. That's why God can also be the
poet's personal rock, refuge, banner, and portion, in whose "hand"

the poet feels security, absolute trust, serenity, and confidence. There is no tension in the poem, at least not overtly.

The original liturgical context of this poem is important because going to sleep at night can be fraught with anxiety. Falling asleep means losing control over our fate. When I teach this text, I try to reconnect with my own childhood feelings at bedtime and the feelings of my children or, more recently, my grandchildren, when I put them to sleep. Children create elaborate going-to-sleep rituals: we read them stories and sing songs; they hug dolls and teddy bears; some recite prayers. There isn't a culture in the world that hasn't in some way ritualized the process of going to sleep. These rituals are what psychologists might call "transitional objects." They are designed to guide children—and adults as well, for we also ritualize our own going to sleep in other ways—through the threshold from wakefulness to sleep. Thresholds are in-between states, and they are all inherently anxiety producing—like airports for the traveler.

The ancients seem to have understood sleep to be a mini-death experience. Even a cursory glance at the bedtime liturgy will indicate that it is pervaded by references to death, just as the prayers recited immediately upon waking are pervaded by references to resurrection. The subliminal sense that sleep is like death persists in all of us. In the poem, however, that anxiety is concealed, and the poem is permeated with serenity. The author's confidence in God permits him to let go, to welcome sleep, to surrender control over his consciousness and his destiny. Since that cosmically powerful God is there, and since that God is also the poet's personal God, then what is there to fear?

Why Psalms?

This image of God as refuge and protector, with the concomitant feeling of trust in God's power, is omnipresent in Psalms, an anthology

of 150 poems—probably only a trickle of those that were originally composed. Written over many centuries, their authors are anonymous, despite superscriptions such as "a Psalm of David" or "a
Psalm of the sons of Korach" that introduce some of them. We can
only surmise their personal or historical contexts. Psalm 137,
which begins "By the rivers of Babylon, there we sat, sat and wept
as we thought of Zion," was probably written by a member of the
community of exiled Israelites shortly after the destruction of
Jerusalem at the hands of Babylonia in 586 B.C.E. However, that
explicit historical context is a rare exception.

More important to us than the original context in which a
psalm was written and its date of composition are two issues: First,
how was any individual psalm appropriated by the later tradition?
When and why did it come to be recited by later generations in the
post-biblical tradition? Second, what is its pervasive theological
message? What does it tell us about the authors' beliefs about God,
Israel, and the human experience?

On the first question, according to the *Authorized Daily
Prayer Book*,[1] one of the most comprehensive prayer books available to us, approximately seventy-five of the psalms appear some-
place in the liturgy. Many of these psalms appear only once and are
to be recited infrequently. Some appear a number of times; Psalm
91, which we are about to study, appears four times and is recited
daily and weekly by worshiping Jews. Why Psalm 91, and why
were the other half of the psalms in the biblical anthology not
included in the liturgy? We can never be sure of the answers to
these questions, but we can be sure of one conclusion: those psalms
that were recited more or less regularly had a singular impact on
shaping the Jewish religious sensibility. Though women often said
tehillim rather than the male-obligated davening service, most male
Jews encountered the entire biblical Book of Psalms only infrequently, but they encountered the prayer book every single day of
their lives.

If the first question yields only surmises, the second is even more perilous. The biblical psalmists were not systematic theologians. They shared a core set of beliefs learned from their exposure to the rest of the biblical tradition, but that tradition itself was multivocal, and, even more important, they never felt themselves bound to it. Judaism never recognized a supreme theological authority, some committee of priests or rabbis responsible to monitor theological expression. They were probably simple believers who lived and experienced more or less what we experience in the course of our own lives. What distinguishes them, however, is that they were conscious of living under the presence of a transcendent God who, they believed, governed the course of all things. Whatever they experienced, then, was in some way an expression of their beliefs about the nature of this God and this God's governance of nature, history, and their lives. Their compositions were responses to that experience. Even when they were angry at God, they still addressed that anger to God; they never dropped out of the religious community. It is for us to try to surmise what their experience was, how they felt about it, and how they expressed those feelings back to the God who, they believed, was accessible to their prayers, cared about them, and heard them.

Finally, each of the psalms is a poem. The language of poetry is never straightforward. It uses metaphor, allusion, and hyperbole; it suggests a feeling rather than conveying a message or teaching a lesson. That's why the use of a psalm as a theological statement is doubly precarious. We can never get to that message directly. We have to begin by allowing the poem to speak to us, by coming into touch with our own feelings as we read the psalm, by letting our reactions to what the poet is saying seep into our consciousness. Our reaction may then guide us into the poet's feelings. Those feelings are our clue as to how the psalmist dealt with whatever experience was being undergone. Therein lies the clue to the psalm's implicit theology.

Psalm 91 is recited as part of the traditional going-to-sleep liturgy, but it also appears in the selection of psalms that precedes the formal Sabbath and festival morning service (*pesukei de-zimra*—literally, "verses of song"), in the liturgy of the burial service, and at the close of the Sabbath. At the outset, the voice of the poet reassures some other person:

> [God] will save you from the fowler's trap,
> from the destructive plague.
> He will cover you with His pinions;
> you will find refuge under His wings;...
> You need not fear the terror by night
> Or the arrow that flies by day,
> the plague that stalks the darkness,
> or the scourge that ravages at noon.
> A thousand may fall at your left side,
> ten thousand at your right,
> but it shall not reach you....
> For He will order His angels
> To guard you wherever you go,
> They will carry you in their hands
> Lest you hurt your foot on a stone.

At the climax of the psalm, God appears in the first person to add a personal reassurance:

> Because he is devoted to Me I will deliver him;
> I will keep him safe, for he knows My name.
> When he calls upon Me, I will answer him;
> I will be with him in distress;
> I will rescue him and make him honored;
> I will let him live to a ripe old age,
> and show him My salvation.

We know nothing about the original context in which this psalm was composed, but its underlying motif is the peril associated with a journey—either a real journey, or sleep or death, or possibly life itself, all understood as journeys. Journeys are also transitional experiences, in-between states. To this day, it is not unusual for us to feel anxious or vulnerable as we embark on a journey. I travel a great deal, and the hours before I leave home—especially if I am going to fly somewhere—are invariably fraught with anxiety, which persists until I have reached my destination. Many prayer books include the traditional traveler's prayer *(Teffilat HaDerekh),* which addresses that anxiety.

That tension, more muted in the *Adon Olam* poem mentioned above, is explicit in Psalm 91. Note the many forms of danger evoked here: fowlers' traps, plague, disease, arrows, scourge, stones, cubs, vipers, lions, and asps. This sharpened anxiety calls forth equally sharp metaphors of God as protector: God is a refuge and a stronghold, God covers us with God's pinions, God orders the angels to carry us in their hands. The serenity of *Adon Olam* may be missing here, but the confidence and trust in God's protective love remains.

Still a third expression of this theme is the familiar Psalm 23. The opening metaphor here is that God is a shepherd. God does all the things that shepherds do. God

> makes me lie down in green pastures;
> He leads me to still waters;
> He renews my life;
> He guides me in right paths.

Again, as in Psalm 91, God protects the psalmist even though perils abound. The psalmist is walking through "the valley of the shadow of death." Again, we can only guess what experiences inspired this psalm. Is this another journeying psalm? Perhaps, although this journey is more of a metaphor than those of our previous examples. God also sets a table "in full view of my enemies," probably human enemies. Clearly, the psalmist has either experienced, or is in the process of experiencing, or will shortly experience, extreme peril—sufficient peril to endanger his very life. Perhaps this psalmist understands his current life experience as a perilous journey, yet he trusts that God's "goodness and steadfast love shall pursue me all the days of my life."

Is the feeling here closer to that of Psalm 91 than to *Adon Olam*? Is there serenity here, or the tension of the psalm? No two people read a text of this kind in the same way. My own sense is that this psalm abounds with tension; the author is in peril and hopes that God will protect him, but is not quite convinced, even despite that last line. However, many of my students disagree with this reading and see only trust and confidence here. Another of my students was disturbed by the image of God as shepherd because she did not appreciate being viewed as a sheep.

There is no fixed liturgical context for reciting this psalm. It is frequently recited at funerals or at memorial *(Yizkor)* services, and it is chanted late on Sabbath afternoon, before the close of the Sabbath. In each case, the pervasive mood is somewhat nostalgic, elegiac, or even mournful. But of all the psalms, it is the one that is most frequently used to inspire feelings of trust or confidence in the face of some personal crisis. That usage testifies to how it is typically understood.

The Rock and the Healer

A more subtle hint of the pervasive tension between anxiety and trust is in a brief liturgical passage of medieval origin that immediately precedes the recitation of the *amidah* in the morning service. It is the climax of an extended unit that follows the recitation of the *Shema* and that deals with the theme of God as Redeemer. It appears in this precise context with the intent of having the worshiper juxtapose a prayer for redemption with the *amidah*.

> Rock of Israel, rise to Israel's defense.
> Deliver Judah and Israel, as You have promised.
> Our Redeemer is the Holy One of Israel....
> Praised are You, who redeemed Israel.

God is Israel's rock—stable, reliable, trustworthy, powerful, a veritable Gibraltar. But in the same breath, the liturgist appeals to this rocklike God to defend and redeem Israel. This suggests that the historical context of the passage is one in which Israel is in exile and suffering harshly. The promised redemption has not as yet occurred, therefore the psalmist pleads that God should redeem. This rocklike quality of God, then, is more of a hope than a reality. Israel's history suggests that God is in fact a redeeming rock, but that memory is in sharp contrast with the current reality.

A similar tension pervades the use of the God-as-healer metaphor. Psalm 147:3 affirms that God "heals their broken hearts and binds up their wounds," thus attributing both medical and psychological healing powers to God. Psalm 30:3 personalizes God's healing: "O Lord, my God, I cried out to You and You healed me." Sometimes God has not (at least, not yet) healed. "Have mercy on me, O Lord, for I languish; heal me, O Lord, for my bones shake with terror" (Psalm 3:6). The prophet Jeremiah applies this ambiguity to the fate of Israel:

> Is there no balm in Gilead?
> Can no physician be found?
> Why has healing not yet
> Come to my poor people?
>
> —Jeremiah 8:22

In another context, Jeremiah's plaint becomes a prayer for his own healing: "Heal me, O Lord, and let me be healed; save me, and let me saved; for You are my glory" (Jeremiah 17:14). This prayer, in plural form ("Heal us"), was later incorporated into the daily *amidah,* where it is recited three times daily on weekdays. Again, the liturgical use of that metaphor both reflected and then shaped the Jewish sensibility for generations. Every Sabbath morning, during the worship service, the *chazan* (prayer leader) of the congregation recites a prayer for the healing of the sick in the community, who are then identified individually by name. To the Jew, God has the power to heal, even though that power is not as yet manifest in the life of the sufferer or in Jewish history. Again, our human need for healing is fraught with ambiguity; sometimes we are healed, but not always.

The Parent

The image of God as nurturing, protecting, and healing is concretized in the metaphor of parenthood. We have studied some of these parent-metaphor texts above, but we should look at them again, this time from a different, slightly more ambiguous perspective.

The ambiguity is multidimensional. Typically, throughout the classical texts, the parent is a father. Our modern sensitivity to gender issues tempts some of us to substitute "parent" for "father," but the original Hebrew clearly means "father." This gender issue is one reason for the ambiguity that this metaphor evokes. A second, more subtle reason is that like every other metaphor, this one awakens different echoes in different people, depending on our relationships with our own fathers (or mothers), almost always one of our more complicated relationships. Some of us have disturbing feelings about our own parents; others have loving feelings. Most of us have both at different times. Still others are able to distinguish between our human parents and God's parenting: God is the parent that we never had or that we longed to have. God is even described as "the father of orphans" (Psalm 68:6), the father of the fatherless, the idealized father.

In this mode, God seems to appear as the benevolent, loving father. Psalm 103 is a paean to God's eagerness to forgive God's errant children:

> For as the heavens are high above the earth,
> so great is His steadfast love toward those who fear Him.
> As east is far from west,
> so far has He removed our sins from us.
> As a father has compassion for his children,
> So the Lord has compassion for those who fear Him.
>
> —*Psalm 103:11–13*

Fathers are compassionate toward their children, the psalm claims, but note the twice-repeated caveat "to those who fear Him." What about those who do not fear God? God's touted fatherly benevolence is conditional on our "fear" of God. "Fear" may not be the most accurate translation of the Hebrew here; it means something closer to "revere"; yet, the import remains the same: God's compassion is not unconditional.

God's fatherly compassion is conditional because human fatherly compassion is also conditional. Parenting is complicated. Of course parents love their children, but parenting also demands a healthy dose of mentoring, judging, and sometimes punishing. A parent who systematically refuses to punish an errant child has failed as a parent. Divine images that emphasize God's harsh quality are typically ascribed to this punitive dimension of God's parenting.

That same perception is reflected in the first words of the extended liturgical poem, referred to earlier, recited during the High Holiday season. Throughout the poem, God is addressed as *Avinu Malkenu*, "Our Father, our King" (or, in a gender-neutral translation, "our Parent, our Sovereign"). The juxtaposition of the two metaphors suggests that God relates to us simultaneously in two ways: one, with compassion; the other, in judgment. Each tempers the other. The tension persists to the very end of the prayer: "Our Father, our King! Be gracious unto us and answer us, for we have no good works of our own. Deal with us charitably and compassionately, and save us."

The claim is that we come before this Parent-Sovereign empty-handed, but that surely is not the case. In fact, we come before God on the High Holiday season with God's oft-repeated promises of forgiveness, with the merit of our ancestors arguing on our behalf, with the assurance that God is always ready to accept genuine repentance. Here, however, we claim that if God is to deal with us only as a sovereign, we would surely lose our case. Therefore we pray that God should suppress God's kingly nature and relate to us with fatherly compassion.

This raises the gender issue. Some of us tend to stereotype fathers as strict and judgmental and mothers as loving and compassionate. This division of labor in parenting is no longer always the case, however, and sometimes, as we have seen, punishment is an expression of love. But ascribing femininity to God was simply unthinkable to our biblical (and later) ancestors. What they did then was to expand the fatherhood metaphor to include a healthy dose of what appeared to them as motherly attributes as well. It was only some centuries later that Judaism evolved a full-fledged feminine image of God in the mystical concept of God as *Shekhinah*, the immanent divine presence that pervades all of creation and that is a feminine noun.

Feminist God-Language

Many contemporary Jewish feminists have been sharply critical of the dominant masculine, hierarchical images of God in traditional Jewish texts. This attack has taken two complementary tracks: first, an aggressive program for replacing masculine pronouns for God with gender-neutral or even explicitly feminine forms. God is now referred to as "She," as "She/He," as "S/he," by alternating "He" and "She" in different paragraphs, or, as we have done throughout this volume, by simply avoiding the use of any personal pronoun for God. Hebrew second-person pronouns for God, which differ depending on whether one is addressing a male or a female (*atah* for a man, *at* for a woman), are also changed.

The second, more radical strategy is to search for metaphors for God that are perceived to be more explicitly feminine. One of the more popular is *Mekor HaChayim*—God is "the fountain of life" or "the source of life." Implicit in this image is the notion of God birthing the world. More radical metaphors reflect the sense of God as Goddess. Judith Plaskow captures the thrust of these new metaphors. They manifest "a sense of fluidity, movement, and multiplicity, [a] daring interweaving of women's experiences with Jewish, Native American, and Goddess imagery that leaves the reader/hearer with an expanded sense of what is possible in speaking of/to God."[2]

Plaskow acknowledges that God is neither male nor female but insists that symbols of this kind must be taken seriously, though not literally. She defends the radical feminization of God metaphors:

> The Goddess is, of course, God/She, but in a clearer and more powerful way. Not simply a feminine reworking of the masculine deity but an ancient power in her own right, she gathers to her all the qualities and prerogatives of the goddesses of many names. She is Asherah, Ishtar, Isis, Afrekete, Oyo, Ezuli, Mary, and Shekhina. She is lover, creator, warrior, grantor of fertility, lawgiver, maiden, mother, and crone.[3]

Not surprisingly, more traditionalist readers have labeled all of these proposals simple paganism.[4]

The core of the feminist critique is the conviction that the issue is not simply one of language. The language we use both reflects and in turn shapes the way we construct our experience of the world. Plaskow acknowledges that all of these images of God are humanly crafted metaphors, but our metaphors emerge out of specific cultural and political contexts. When these contexts change, the old metaphors must change with them.

> Metaphors for God that might once have been compelling despite—or because of—their political resonance not only have lost their immediacy and power but have become morally suspect and disturbing. Especially those images of God drawn from political and family life have changed in their associations and meanings with changes in and new perspectives on the family and political order. Once images become socially, politically, or morally inadequate, however, they are also religiously inadequate. Instead of pointing to and evoking the reality of God, they block the possibility of religious experience.[5]

Plaskow's conclusion bears on the broad assumptions of the entire study. All our metaphors for God are designed to facilitate our experience of God, to reveal God, to open our eyes. They work like a pair of spectacles. A student once suggested the analogy of *The Wizard of Oz,* where Dorothy has to don a pair of spectacles in order to see the city of Oz. Sometimes, however, after a change in cultural conditions, instead of revealing, the metaphors blind. That can apply across the board. Some have suggested, for example, that the metaphor of God as King or Sovereign that pervades the High Holiday liturgy no longer works for people who don't live under a monarchy.

That's precisely the complaint of Jewish feminists. They reject both metaphors—the king metaphor because of its hierarchical associations, and the paternal metaphor because it excludes their distinctive female experience. The world has changed, and so must our divine images. The entire issue is still very much a work in progress. Prayer books from the more liberal wings of the religious community have incorporated the less radical process of substituting gender-neutral God language. More radically, feminist prayer books have replaced the male metaphors with feminine ones.[6]

Nevertheless, despite the gender issue, there is absolutely no ambiguity about God's protective concern for Israel in the rabbinic homily on Exodus 14:19–20. The biblical passage describes how God shielded Israel from the pursuing Egyptian army, following the Exodus: "The angel of God, who had been going ahead of the Israelite army, now moved and followed behind them; and the pillar of cloud shifted from in front of them and took up a place behind them, and it came between the army of the Egyptians and the army of Israel."

The midrash reads:

> What is this like? It is like a man who was walking on the road and was leading his son in front of him. When robbers came from in front in order to capture the son, the man took his son from in front and placed him behind. When a wolf came from behind, he took his son from behind and placed him in front. When robbers came from in front and wolves from behind, he took his son in his arms. When the son began to suffer from the sun, his father spread his cloak over him. When the son was hungry, he fed him. When he was thirsty, he gave him to drink.[7]

The Teacher

Judaism is the paradigmatic text-centered religion. The substance of God's wishes for Israel and the world are embodied in a book. The immediate implication of that claim is that the paramount Jewish obligation is to study the book. Study becomes the gateway to understanding God's will. No other culture exalts the act of studying, the student, and the teacher as does Judaism. Whom else did parents want their daughter to marry if not the outstanding student in the local yeshiva? The study of Torah is "weighted against all the other commandments," according to the *Mishnah* (*Pe'ah* 1:1), because how are we to understand how to perform all the other commandments if not by studying Torah? Judaism is the only religion in which study is equivalent to worship. My late teacher Rabbi Louis Finkelstein used to say, "When I pray, I speak to God; when I study, God speaks to me." Again, in the words of the liturgy:

> Blessed are You, Lord our God, Sovereign of the universe...who commanded us to study the words of Torah. May the words of Torah...be sweet in our mouths and in the mouths of all Your people so that we, our children, and all the children of the House of Israel may come to love You and to study Your Torah.... Blessed are You, Lord, who teaches Torah to the House of Israel.

Note the tense of the verb: God "teaches," not "has taught," Torah to Israel. God, then, is a teacher not only at Sinai, in antiquity, but today as well, and not only today but also in the world to come. The souls of the righteous who have perished are described as having gone to "the yeshiva on high," where God will be their teacher and will elucidate all the puzzles of the Torah that were never clarified while they lived on earth.[8]

God as spouse, lover, parent, healer, judge, and shepherd are all quite conventional metaphors, but God is also teacher! That is a striking and uniquely Jewish image. It is also significantly free of the tensions that pervade even the positive images of God that we have studied thus far. However, those tensions are very much at the heart of the negative metaphors for God, to which we now turn.

5

God Is Not Nice (Sometimes)

The "Down" Metaphors

But God is not always nice. Our ancestors were as fully aware of that as we are. Sometimes God seems to abuse people—even righteous people, even the Jewish people, whom God is supposed to love in a special way. When they felt that way, they tried desperately to justify God's behavior so as to integrate their disappointment with their image of a loving God. But often the negative feelings slip through the cracks and the tension is exposed for all to see.

Yet even then, their anger at God's behavior was always expressed from within their long-standing relationship with God. They never allowed their sense of being mistreated by God to drive them out of the religious community and its belief structure. Some probably did drop out; but understandably, with at least one striking exception, our texts preserve no record explaining their motivations. On the other hand, there are many texts that do record the feelings of those who, despite their overt anger at God, remained committed and believing Jews. These people wrote psalms to this abandoning God or told stories about God's behavior that channeled their disappointment into a challenge. They never apologized for their anger at God. They understood it to be a totally legitimate dimension of every interpersonal relationship; it did not have to signify that the relationship was dead. Indeed, to abandon the relationship would have deprived them of the very grounds they needed for their challenge.

These negative experiences and the feelings they prompted were embodied in what we can call the "down" images of God that pervade our classical literature. We may wonder what these texts are doing in the Bible, but our ancestors who were responsible for canonizing the Bible, the Talmud, and the liturgy recognized that people sometimes felt this way about God, that they themselves had these feelings, and that these feelings were part of the broad and complex repertoire of encounters between God and human beings.

In the Bible itself and in much of post-biblical literature, the conventional way of integrating the negative experiences of God was to ascribe them to God's punishment for human sinfulness. In a stroke, this image of a judgmental and punishing God accomplished a great deal: it vindicated God's behavior, it canceled out the feelings of abandonment, and it provided a means for restoring the original positive relationship—namely, repentance and return to God. The classical statement of the equation that sin brings about punishment (and virtue brings all manner of blessing) is Deuteronomy 11:13–21, the second of the three paragraphs of the *Shema*, which Jews recite at least twice daily. If we hearken to God's commands and serve God with all our hearts and our souls, then we shall enjoy rainfall, fruitful crops, food, and drink; if we rebel, our land will not yield its fruits and we will be banished from the land.

Our ancestors could vindicate God's behavior because they believed that God's judgments were always fair and honest. Today we recognize that some human judges are corrupt, but that God was a corrupt judge was unthinkable to our ancestors. To this day, when a Jew hears of a death, the immediate liturgical response is *Barukh dayan ha-emet*. The literal translation of the phrase is

"Blessed be the Judge of truth," or "the true Judge," or "the Judge who judges truthfully" or "accurately," or "whose judgment is truthful." A student recently suggested a more colloquial translation: "Blessed be the Judge whose judgment is right on!" That captures the intent of the Hebrew remarkably well.

However we translate the phrase, its underlying metaphor is that God is a fair judge and that our suffering is well deserved. Thus, a potentially negative experience of God becomes a positive one. We may be uncomfortable with the notion that God sits in judgment of people in the first place—we tend to prefer nonjudgmental relationships—but first, there is an inherent judgmental dimension to all interpersonal relationships; and second, the practical implication of viewing God as judge is to teach us that we are accountable for the lives we live. Since God is a fair judge, we can expect a fair judgment, maybe even a compassionate judgment, for God is also compassionate.

Nevertheless, there are texts that describe God's abandonment that are totally devoid of even the slightest implication of guilt. We have studied two such statements, Psalms 13 and 44. The first is a plaintive challenge by some individual who feels deserted by God in a moment of crisis and pleads that God look at him once again, respond to him, and rescue him. The second is an even more painful challenge—this time on behalf of the people of Israel, who have been ravaged by their enemies. In neither of these texts is there even a hint that God's punitive behavior is deserved. In fact, the second psalm asserts the very opposite: it is precisely because of the community's loyalty to God that it is being destroyed. The only possible conclusion is that God must be asleep!

God has overslept? God's alarm clock did not ring on time? This bitter sarcasm, however painful it is to read, is canonized in Hebrew Scripture. It is nothing less than a gift to our own post-Holocaust generation. It frees us to express our own bitterness. It gives us a language for our own challenge.

Job

The image of God in those two psalms is negative enough, but it becomes even more painful in the first two chapters of the Book of Job. Of the Book of Job, it can preeminently be asked, "What is this book doing in the Bible?" Job was a righteous man, we are told. God boasts of Job's piety to the satan—the "adversary," or "prosecuting angel"—who counters that Job is righteous only because God has never tested him. So God gives the satan the right to damage his property and, in chapter 2, to injure his person, as long as he doesn't cause his death. Throughout all this Job remains faithful to God. Job's wife urges him to "Blaspheme God and die!" but Job responds, "Should we accept only good from God and not accept evil?" (2:9–10).

Job's "comforters" arrive and evoke the classical Torah interpretation of suffering: Job must have sinned. But Job retorts that he has not sinned, or that he has not sinned nearly enough to justify this punishment. At the end of the book, God addresses Job in the speeches "out of the whirlwind." These are a paean to God's power and to the complexity of God's creation. Their message is "Job, don't try to understand Me. Don't try to capture Me in your moral categories. I am God; you are a human being." Surprisingly, Job acknowledges the difference:

> I know You can do everything,
> That nothing You propose is impossible for You....
> I had heard You with my ears,
> But now I see You with my eyes;
> Therefore, I recant and relent,
> Being but dust and ashes.
>
> —*Job 42:2, 5–6*

This implies that Job has now achieved a clearer understanding of God's ways and a measure of closure. God then "shows favor to Job" (42:9) and restores Job's fortunes, "twice what he had before" (42:10), and Job dies "old and contented" (42:17)—the same phrase used to describe Abraham's death (Genesis 25:8).

There is another translation of the last verse that puts a very different spin on the conclusion of this book. We can also read the last two verses as "Word of You had reached my ears, but now that my eyes have seen You, I shudder with sorrow for mortal clay." In this translation, Job may have achieved a measure of closure, but he has by no means recanted on his challenge to God. He challenges God to the very end. In effect, he tells God: "If that's the kind of God You are, then I shudder for human beings who have to live under Your sovereignty." The God who praises Job at the very end of the book and restores his fortunes is a God who has lost. Paradoxically, God's loss is also God's victory, for we now know that this is a God who treasures Job's impiety and welcomes Job's challenge.[1]

Three issues never fail to trouble me whenever I return to this impossible book. First, Job is never told why he suffered. The readers, who have that first chapter describing the satan's challenge, do know, but Job never finds out. Abraham, at the end of the story of the binding of Isaac (Genesis 22), is told that it was all a test of his loyalty. Job never gets an explanation. I sometimes fantasize what would have happened if Job and Abraham had met and shared their experiences over a cup of coffee some time down the road. What would they have said to each other? I can't get beyond the look on Job's face when Abraham tells him that he was told, at the end, that God was testing his faith. "At least you know why it happened. I never found out," Job might have said. Yet another part of me is thrilled that he was never told. How would Job have felt at learning that his suffering was designed to win God's bet with the satan?

Second, in 42:7 God explicitly rejects the theology of the comforters that Job's suffering was punishment for sin; in fact, God tells Job that if he will intercede for them, God will forgive them.

This is nothing less than a total repudiation of the Torah's normative explanation for human suffering. What theological *chutzpah* on the part of this biblical author! Yet, those who canonized the Book of Job by including it in the Bible must not have been troubled by this apparently heretical reversal. To put a positive spin on this conclusion, we can learn from this that it is also legitimate for us moderns to reject ancient Jewish doctrines when they no longer seem acceptable to us.

Finally, and most painfully, whereas in Psalms 13 and 44 we are left wondering why God is so neglectful, here in Job we are given a glimpse into God's motivations. It was simply God's vanity in the face of the satan's challenge. God views Job's piety as testimony to God's power. When the satan challenges that assumption, God replies, "So test him, and we'll see who is right." No wonder God does not disclose this exchange to Job at the end of the book.

Probe this image of God for a moment. Indeed, however we interpret the closing passage referred to above, what is it like to live in a world ruled by this kind of God? It would be like living in a world that is ruled by a vain, capricious, but all-powerful sovereign who relates to people in totally unpredictable ways and doesn't even feel the need to account for his behavior. There is no hint of a divine dualism here; the satan is clearly subservient to God. He needs God's permission to test Job. God is clearly the exclusive sovereign of the world, but what kind of God is this? If we recall that Abraham's original decision to leave his native land and its paganism was motivated by a vision of living in a world ruled by a God who espouses justice and righteousness, Job seems to subvert that entire vision. What we do learn from this book, however—particularly if we accept the alternative interpretation of the last verse in Job's concluding address—is that God welcomes our challenge, even our impiety. That is no insignificant lesson!

The fact remains that only one verse from Job made its way into the later liturgy. We recite "The Lord has given, and the Lord has taken away; blessed be the name of the Lord" (1:21) at every Jewish burial. This statement should not be understood as an attempt to justify or vindicate God, a way of making God "nice." It is not a theological statement, not an abstract conceptual claim about the nature of God. Rather, it is a cry from the heart, an affirmation of God's sovereignty and absolute power over our destinies, uttered precisely at the moment when we are most tempted to question that principle. The words are performative; they are a verbal formulation of the act of bowing our heads and accepting God's judgment, whatever it may be. This is precisely what Job did. That's why we continue to recite these words when confronted by death.

Is God Ethical?

On a more abstract level, the cry does raise a genuine theological issue. Boldly stated, is God ethical? The most accurate answer to this would be that it depends on what you mean by ethical. The traditionalist response to this question would be to dismiss it as heretical. What is ethical is defined by God, not the other way around. Whatever God does is, by definition, ethical. Of course God is ethical!

Some of us challenge that opinion. We prefer to bring our own independent code of ethics to bear on God's activity and then to decide whether or not God passes our test. The traditionalist would challenge us: What makes your own ethical code authoritative? Why should God be subservient to some set of human values? One answer might be the passage in Genesis 18:19, part of the story of Abraham's challenge to God over the fate of the inhabitants of Sodom and Gomorrah, where the "way of the Lord" demands "doing what is just and right." To this the traditionalist would simply respond that it is God, not humanity, who determines what is just and right in any particular situation. We, however, might insist that our own conscience is also a gift from God and that we can therefore bring our conscience to bear on God's behavior.

This tension is played out throughout the Bible and the later tradition, as we see in two biblical narratives. Numbers 31:1–18 relates how God commanded Moses, "Avenge the Israelite people on the Midianites." The reference is to an earlier narrative where Moabite women, in a plot hatched by the Midianites, had seduced Israelite men into sexual licentiousness and idol worship (Numbers 25:1–9). Israel is now to take revenge on Midian. We are told that Moses assembled an army; that this army slew every male Midianite, spared the women and children, and brought them and the booty back to Moses; and that Moses became very angry:

> You have spared every female! Yet they are the very ones who, at the bidding of Balaam, induced the Israelites to trespass against the Lord.... Now, therefore, slay every male among the children, and slay also every woman who has known a man carnally; but spare every young woman who has not had carnal relations with a man.
>
> —*Numbers 31:15–18*

Each year, when I reencounter this story during the annual Torah reading cycle, I bridle. I have no choice but to read the text—another example of how the liturgy serves as the cutting edge of theology. I can't simply eliminate it from the Torah, but I can and do grit my teeth each year. The story offends my humanistic values. Is killing masses of women in any way morally justifiable? The Torah justifies the behavior by noting that it was precisely the women who had led Israel into sin. If so, why slaughter the Midianite men? Furthermore, does the punishment fit the crime? Is mass slaughter ever justified?

A similar story is recorded in 1 Samuel 15. Here the prophet Samuel tells Saul, Israel's king, to exact vengeance on Amalek.

Amalek had attacked the Israelites immediately upon their liberation from Egypt (Exodus 17:8–14), leading God to command the Israelites to "blot out the memory of Amalek from under heaven" (Deuteronomy 25:19). Now that promise is to be fulfilled.

Saul gathers his troops, proceeds to defeat Amalek, and puts the people to the sword. However, he spares the Amalekite king, Agag, together with the sheep and cattle and everything that was of value. He proudly returns to Samuel, who is furious at him. Saul has disobeyed God's command to extirpate all of Amalek. Saul defends his behavior by saying that he wanted to save the flocks to sacrifice them before God. Samuel replies:

> Does the Lord delight in burnt offerings and sacrifices
> As much as in obedience to the Lord's command?
> Surely, obedience is better than sacrifice,
> Compliance than the fat of rams.
> — *1 Samuel 15:22–23*

Above all, God demands obedience, especially from Israel's king, who is God's anointed. Saul does not raise the ethical issue here; he doesn't question the morality of slaughtering innocent animals. His argument is that God wants animal sacrifices. To this Samuel replies, quite properly, that God doesn't depend on animal sacrifices for God's own sustenance. Sacrifices are for people, not for God; they are designed to enable humans to worship God, but never at the price of obedience to God's explicit command.

Samuel then slaughters Agag and informs Saul that God has torn the kingship from him and his descendants. Shortly thereafter, Samuel crowns David king of Israel. For many of us, however, the ethical issue is precisely the heart of the matter. The postscript to this story is that in the Book of Esther, Haman, one of Israel's legendary enemies, is identified as "the Agagite" (3:1). Saul's decision to spare Agag thus becomes the ultimate cause of another painful episode in Jewish history. The Bible therefore gives us an ex post facto reason why Saul should have killed him—a pragmatic justification for the command to kill him at the outset.

The traditionalist justifies Samuel's anger at Saul for not having killed Agag by invoking the story in Esther. What about the innocent animals? Why should they have to be slaughtered because of the sins of their owners? Here again, we see the tension between our modern humanistic values and the will of God. God demands obedience, Samuel insists, and by definition, whatever God demands is ethical.

To be fair to the biblical stories, it is possible to argue that they are cultural artifacts, shards of a more primitive era in which slaughtering one's enemies was totally acceptable in a military context. It could also be claimed that absolute evil has to be absolutely destroyed, precisely on moral grounds. In our own day, Holocaust survivors understand that resolution of the issue perfectly well. This may also justify the extermination of Midian and Amalek; in each case, the slaughter is punishment for the nation's treatment of Israel. However, this brings us back to Job, where God explicitly rejects the notion that Job's suffering was God's punishment. We are left with the image of an all-powerful God who decrees the destiny of individuals and nations in ways that are beyond human understanding, sometimes with horrific results.

The Death of Rabbi Akiva

In a similar vein, read the talmudic account of the death of Rabbi Akiva. Akiva was the second-century C.E. rabbinic master whose teachings decisively shaped rabbinic Judaism in the post-biblical period. Akiva also became a leader of the Jewish revolt against Roman rule in 132–135 C.E. He was subsequently arrested by Rome and died the death of a martyr. The talmudic narrative begins with

Moses' ascent to Sinai to receive the Torah. Moses finds God painstakingly inscribing curlicues on the letters of the Torah. When asked why, God responds that there will one day be a great sage, Akiva by name, who will derive countless new laws from each of those curlicues. "Permit me to see him," Moses says. He is then transported in time to Akiva's classroom, where, to his dismay, he cannot follow Akiva's argument. When asked by his students whence he derived his teachings, Akiva answers, "From Moses at Sinai." Moses' feelings are assuaged.

In the last portion of the story, Moses asks God:

"Lord of the universe, You have such a man and You give the Torah through me!" God replied, "Be silent, such is my decree." Then said Moses, "Lord of the universe, You have shown me his Torah, show me his reward." God replied, "Turn yourself around." Moses turned and saw them weighing out his [Akiva's] flesh at the market stalls. "Lord of the universe," Moses cried, "such Torah and such a reward!" God replies, "Be silent, such is my decree."[2]

There is no attempt to justify Akiva's martyrdom; there is absolutely no question of punishment here. God does not even permit Moses to voice the protest. God decrees, and Akiva dies a martyr's death. God's final retort is an expression of sheer power.

Three methodological questions arise, all of which are familiar to us by now. First, what in the author's life experience impelled a story of this kind? Second, why didn't the author simply drop out? Third, what is it like to live under the sovereignty of such a God? How can one continue to worship such a God?

The Talmud does preserve the record of a sage who rebelled at God's injustice and became an apostate. There are a number of accounts of what led Elisha ben Avuyah, a contemporary of Rabbi

Akiva, into apostasy. One of these accounts refers to Deuteronomy 22:6–7, which instructs us that should we chance upon a bird's nest with fledglings and a mother sitting over them, we should let the mother go and take only the young "in order that you may fare well and live a long life." As the story goes, Elisha once saw a man climb a tree, take the mother, and come down unharmed. The next day, he saw another man climb the tree, chase the mother, and take the fledglings, but when he came down a snake bit him and he died. This led Elisha to proclaim, "How did this man fare well, and how did he live a long life?" He then became an apostate, and his rabbinic colleagues no longer referred to him by name. He is called, contemptuously, *Acher*, "The Other One." An interesting postscript to this story says that Elisha apparently did not know of the rabbinic interpretation of the passage in Deuteronomy: that when the Torah refers to the reward of living a long life, it refers to life in the world to come, not necessarily this life. This is another frequently used rabbinic device for vindicating God's apparently unjust behavior.[3] Our tradition seems to have been very much aware of the possibility that an experience of God's apparently abusive behavior could drive someone out of the community of believers.

A popular formulation of the dilemma posed by these texts is to make three claims:

1. **God is righteous, just, and nice.**
2. **God is omnipotent.**
3. **Job (or Akiva) was blameless.**

Then it is asserted that we cannot accept all three claims simultaneously. One of the three must be rejected. Job's consolers reject the third claim, but God weighs in at the end to reprimand them for doing so and confirms Job's blamelessness. So Job remains blameless.

We are left, then, with having to reject one of the first two claims. If a blameless Job suffers terribly, then how can God be either omnipotent or just? The weight of the Jewish tradition, together with God in the last chapters of the book, rejects the apparent contradiction by insisting that our human understanding of righteousness, justice, and niceness is not necessarily God's. God then remains both omnipotent and righteous, and God's treatment of Job and Akiva is vindicated.

There is no questioning the power and persistence of this resolution of the tension. We hear it again and again in eulogies over a particularly tragic, seemingly absurd death. It's our fallback position; we invoke it when we see no other way out of our dilemma. God acts in mysterious ways. We can't hope to comprehend God's motives; we must simply accept God's decree. In fact, the resolution is not really an explanation. We recite "Blessed be the God whose judgment is truthful!" which, like Job's plaintive cry, "The Lord has given and the Lord has taken away; blessed be the name of the Lord," is a verbal bowing of our heads in the face of God's inscrutable power. Then we must go back to our everyday lives and worship this God.

God Is Not Omnipotent

Some modern Jewish thinkers have suggested that, when confronted with the incompatibility of the three claims, we should reject the second one, the claim that God is omnipotent. When Mordecai Kaplan responds to a child's question, "Why did God make polio?" he begins, "God did *not* make polio. God is always helping us humans to make this a better world, but the world cannot at once become the kind of world He would like it to be." Kaplan then lists all the good things that God does: motivate doctors and nurses; stimulate medical, pharmacological, and technological research;

provide the love and the support of families and friends. Then, he continues:

> Do not feel that God does not care for you. He is helping you now in many ways.... Maybe someday you will be restored by His help to perfect health. But if that does not happen, it is not because God does not love you. If He does not grant you all that you pray for, He will find other ways of enabling you to enjoy life.[4]

Kaplan's definition of God is "the power that makes for salvation." The implication of that definition is that God is one specific power in the world, the one that makes for "salvation" or fulfillment in the form of creativity, love, and value. The world includes other powers over which God has no control, such as a power that makes polio, or AIDS, or genetic diseases, or earthquakes and floods. God combats that other power, rages over it, and may in time defeat it, but not yet. Kaplan's notion is of an intrinsically limited God. Kaplan's God is simply not omnipotent.

Kaplan's thesis is expanded in what is arguably one of the most widely read Jewish books of our generation, Harold Kushner's *When Bad Things Happen to Good People*. Kushner's book was his attempt to deal with his grief over the death of his young son from a rare disease. The book is primarily a pastoral guide for the suffering and the bereaved, but it also articulates a theological position, and that position is thoroughly Kaplan's. To the question "If God does not cause the bad things that happen to good people, and if He cannot prevent them, what good is He at all?"

Kushner answers:

> First of all, God has created a world in which many more good things than bad things happen.... God helps by inspiring people to help.... God gives us the strength and perse-

verance to overcome [calamity].... [God] plant[s] in me a little bit of His own divine outrage at injustice and oppression.[5]

In another context:

It may be that God finished His world of creation eons ago, and left the rest to us. Residual chaos, chance and mischance, things happening for no reason, will continue to be with us, the kind of evil that Milton Steinberg has called "the still unremoved scaffolding of the edifice of God's creativity." In that case, we will simply have to learn to live with it, sustained and comforted by the knowledge that the earthquake and the accident, like the murder and the robbery, are not the will of God, but represent that aspect of reality which stands independent of His will, and which angers and saddens God even as it angers and saddens us.[6]

Regarding our three claims, Kaplan and Kushner would agree that Job was blameless and that God is, by definition, just, righteous, and loving. What God is not, however, is omnipotent. We are then left with the following choice: Is God an all-powerful Being, who controls our destiny, decrees our fate in mysterious ways, and demands that we accept those decrees without question? Or is God a limited Being, who may rage or weep over human suffering but is incapable of eliminating it? Which would you choose?

In the Wake of the Holocaust

A post-Holocaust Jew would reformulate the three claims as follows:

1. God is righteous, just, and nice.
2. God is omnipotent.
3. The victims of the Holocaust were blameless.

We cannot accept all three. Which one do we reject?

Some extreme traditionalist circles reject the third claim. They ascribe the Holocaust to God's punishment for the "sins" of the Emancipation, the Enlightenment, Zionism, liberal Jewish movements such as Reform, or, more generally, to the impulse for assimilation on the part of modern Jews. However, that option has been strenuously rejected by the vast majority of Jewish thinkers, who find it simply obscene. In fact, many pious, traditional Jews were also slaughtered. Besides, does this "punishment" fit the crime?

Most of us believe that the victims of the Holocaust were blameless. We are then left with the first two claims: God is righteous or God is omnipotent. Intuitively, we would prefer to maintain both, and the most common strategy for accomplishing this is to insist that the Holocaust was not the work of God but rather of human beings. Once God created us free, God has to stand by even if people behave toward each other in the most terrifying ways. We discussed this option at length in chapter 2. This image of God is not Kaplan's notion of an intrinsically limited God. This God is limited not intrinsically but because of a decision that God has made—namely, to create people with free will. No one would question the value of human freedom, whatever the cost. We call this God a "self-limiting" God, in contrast to Kaplan's "intrinsically limited" God.

This position effectively dismisses the Holocaust as a theological problem; it is, rather, an anthropological, sociological, political, and psychological problem. It is no longer an issue of why God acts in certain ways but of why human beings act in these ways. Its explanation belongs to the social sciences. This resolution may work for the Holocaust, where the perpetrators were human beings acting freely, but it has absolutely no impact in the case of Harold Kushner's son, where the "perpetrator" was nature. Yet, even with the Holocaust, can God be so easily let off the hook? Many would argue not: the suffering was simply too immense, particularly for Israel, God's chosen, beloved people. We are back to choosing between God's omnipotence and God's righteousness.

Holocaust theology is a discipline that remains very much a work in progress. Of the wide range of theological responses that have been proposed, two are worth noting. Each furthers our own inquiry, but in different ways. One of these reappropriates a classical Jewish resolution of the dilemma, but in a modern garb. Recall our earlier discussion of Psalms 13 and 44, two expressions of the experience of God's inexplicable abandonment—the first, of an individual, and the second, of Israel. The Bible refers to this experience as one of God "hiding God's face." That phrase appears in both psalms, in 13:2 and 44:25. A contemporary formulation of that notion is developed by the contemporary theologian Irving Greenberg:

> Faith is living life in the presence of the Redeemer, even when the world is unredeemed. After Auschwitz, faith means there are times when faith is overcome. Buber has spoken of "moment gods": God is known only at the moment when Presence and awareness are fused in vital life. This knowledge is interspersed with moments when only natural, self-contained, routine existence is present.... We now have to speak of "moment faiths," moments when Redeemer and vision of redemption are present, interspersed with times when the flames and smoke of burning children blot out faith—though it flickers again.[7]

There are "moments" when God is God and faith is a living reality, and there are moments when God is not God and faith is impossible. Most important, both are true; neither stage can be sacrificed for the other. The two stages live in tension, as do belief and atheism.

This ends the easy dichotomy of atheist/theist, the confusion of faith with doctrine or demonstration. It makes clear that faith is a life response of the whole person to the Presence in life and history. Like life, this response ebbs and flows. The difference between the skeptic and the believer is frequency of faith, and not certitude of position. The rejection of the unbeliever is literally the denial or attempted suppression of what is within oneself.[8]

What is new and strikingly modern in this position is the acknowledgment of unbelief as a legitimate moment in the life of faith, and of God's mysterious, equally momentary absence as one totally legitimate piece of the God-puzzle. The authors of Psalms 13 and 44 never embraced atheism; they wrote challenges to God. Greenberg takes their protest one step further. Now, in our post-Holocaust age, we are perfectly justified to deny, momentarily, that there is a God in the world.

Greenberg seems to reject the notion of God's righteousness. There is no attempt here to justify or vindicate God's behavior: How could we possibly justify a righteous God's withdrawal when Israel was in such peril? What about God's omnipotence? Greenberg's answer here is not clear. What he has done is to forge an image of God that reflects our fragmented experience. Sometimes we experience God's presence in the world, and at other times we sense God's absence. Sometimes God is perceived as good; sometimes God is perceived as bad.

The Death of God

A much more radical theological response to the Holocaust is that of Richard Rubenstein. Rubenstein, a prolific scholar of religion, adopts a phrase taken from Christian theology and proposes that at Auschwitz, God died.

No man can really say that God is dead. How can we know that? Nevertheless, I am compelled to say that we live in the time of the "death of God." This is more a statement about man and his culture than about God. The death of God is a cultural fact.... When I say that we live in the time of the death of God, I mean that the thread uniting God and man, heaven and earth has been broken. We stand in a cold, silent, unfeeling cosmos, unaided by any purposeful power beyond our own resources. After Auschwitz, what else can a Jew say about God?[9]

Rubenstein takes the step that the psalmists refused to take: he pronounces the entire Jewish belief system to be dead. Note that he cannot claim that God has died. How could anyone possibly know that? Rather, what has died is the classical Jewish metaphorical system. It simply no longer works for us. Rubenstein rejects both God's omnipotence and God's righteousness—the entire package. In effect, Rubenstein stands the traditional punishment theme on its head. Instead of God punishing us for our sins, we punish God.

It is not surprising that Rubenstein's resolution has been rejected by most committed Jews. It is clearly too radical, too much a departure from normative Jewish thinking. The notion that God can die is an intrinsic dimension of Christian thought, but does it work as a Jewish response to tragedy? The notion that we can bring God to the bar of justice for God's treatment of human beings, that God can be found guilty, and that God must repent for God's misdeeds—all an extension of Greenberg's charge that God is a "moment" God—is familiar. Recall the story of the Hasidic master who opened the Yom Kippur service by addressing God:

God, we know that we have sinned and that on this day You commanded us to repent of our sins. But You, God, have also sinned. So I'll strike a bargain with you: If you repent of Your sins, we will repent of ours.

We have claimed again and again that the ultimate cutting edge for theological development is in the liturgy. Liturgical texts that we encounter daily force us to determine where we are and who we are theologically. Scholars may debate the notion of God's culpability, but the discussion remains abstract until it enters the prayer book. That final step has been adopted by David R. Blumenthal in his book *Facing the Abusing God: A Theology of Protest*. This is a wide-ranging, rigorous study of what we have called the "down" metaphors for God, but at the very end Blumenthal suggests that we incorporate our protest to God in our liturgy. We referred earlier to the *Avinu Malkenu* prayer in the traditional High Holiday service, which begins, "Our Father, our King, we have sinned before You." Blumenthal then inserts, "Our Father, our King, You have sinned against us." The traditional prayer continues, "Our Father, our King, we have no King other than You." Blumenthal adds, "Our Father, our King, You have no special people other than us."[10]

How many of us would be comfortable reciting this prayer on Yom Kippur? That reluctance is the most powerful testimony to the power and persistence of the traditional responses to suffering. We are then left with all the tensions outlined above. We are also left with a sense of gratitude to our ancestors for having been honest enough to include these problematic texts in our traditional literature. Their candor liberates us to be as honest as they were in expressing our own discomfort with the way God has treated us.

6

God Can Change

What Changes?

We moderns are not the first to realize that some biblical images of God are not flattering. Sometimes, as in Psalms 13 and 44 and in the Book of Job, the Bible simply preserves the negative image without comment; we have admired the candor with which it does that. At other times, it vindicates God's behavior by viewing human suffering as God's punishment for sin. In still other instances, the ancients implicitly concede their discomfort by replacing an earlier, unflattering metaphor with a later, more flattering one. At times they even advertise what they are doing. They quote a phrase of the text that reflects the negative image, thereby calling our attention to that earlier description, and then add a few words to the older text that give it an entirely different spin.

That God does not change was a central doctrine in medieval Jewish philosophy. The reason is simple enough. For God to change from one state to another implies that the God of the first state lacked something that the God of the second state now possesses. But how can God lack anything? God is perfection, eternal and unchanging, the embodiment of all ideals. Here is Maimonides' formulation of that principle:

So too, it is said "Do they provoke me to anger?" (Jeremiah 7:19); and yet it is said "I am the Lord, I change not..." (Malachi 3:6). If God were sometimes angry and sometimes rejoiced, He would be changing. All these states exist in physical beings that are of obscure and mean condition, dwelling in houses of clay, whose foundation is in the dust. Infinitely blessed and exalted above all this, is God.

—Mishneh Torah, *Basic Principles of the Torah 1:12*[1]

Human beings change; God does not. For Maimonides, the principle of God's changelessness is the immediate implication of his definition of God as perfect; by definition, God cannot change. For we moderns, the principle is a result of the limitations of our mind. Since we know nothing objectively about God, how can we say that God has changed?

What do change, however, are our human images of God, and these can change precisely for the reason that Maimonides cites. Maimonides, we recall, insisted that all our images of God are metaphors, designed for human beings. Thus, if our images of God are subjective expressions of our own experience, and if we humans change, then certainly our images of God can change as well. In other words, what changes are the metaphors, and at times we can watch the change taking place before our very eyes.

There are many striking examples of that process in the traditional texts. We will study two of them. Both deal with the same issue, God's relationship to human sinfulness—not an incidental theme in any religion, and certainly central in Judaism. The first traces the evolution of a set of metaphors through the Bible, rabbinic literature, and the later liturgy. The second traces that evolution within the context of a single medieval liturgical poem. Understandably, both liturgies are recited on the High Holidays, the season of forgiveness. The first example is somewhat complicated because the evolution takes place in a series of five distinct stages, described below.

Sin Is Punished—Immediately

Begin by rereading the stories of Adam and Eve (Genesis 3), Cain and Abel (Genesis 4), and the generation of the flood (Genesis 6–9). In all of these early Genesis narratives, sin is immediately punished; the punishment follows automatically by cause and effect. Nothing intervenes between the sin and the punishment. The one possible exception to this rule is Cain's protest to God in Genesis 3:13–14: "My punishment is too great to bear! Since You have banished me this day from the soil, and I must avoid Your presence and become a restless wanderer on earth, anyone who meets me may kill me!" Cain challenges not the legitimacy of God's punishment but only its severity. That Cain has sinned, and that his sin must be punished, is assumed even by Cain himself. Astonishingly, God does slightly mitigate the punishment by placing a mark on Cain lest someone kill him—but God does not cancel the punishment. Sin must be punished.

In these other Genesis stories, the sinners are punished immediately. Noah makes no attempt to intercede before God on behalf of his generation, nor does he try to persuade them to change their ways. He simply saves himself and his family. The rest of humanity is exterminated in the flood.

The Punishment Must Be Just

Now read Genesis 18:16–33, the remarkable dialogue between God and Abraham over the fate of the sinful cities of Sodom and Gomorrah, which we studied in chapter 3. The core of Abraham's challenge to God is the assumption, shared by both God and Abraham, that God must act justly—not that God has the power to punish the sinful cities, but that the punishment has to be justified. That shared principle is articulated by God at the very outset (Verses 17–18) in the statement that the "way of the Lord" consists in doing "what is just and right." This becomes the basis for Abraham's challenge to God (Verses 23–25). Verse 25 says it all: "Shall not the judge of all the earth deal justly?" Abraham challenges God precisely on the basis of their mutual commitment to justice.

We have now gone beyond the earlier Genesis narratives. Now punishment no longer inevitably follows sin. It can, but only if the punishment is just. Now a new factor enters into the equation: God's commitment to justice—not compassion, not mercy, but simply justice. Here Abraham appears as the paradigmatic intercessor before God on behalf of humanity.

The Punishment May Be Deferred

This text is crucial. The immediate context is Exodus 32–34, the story of the golden calf. Moses is on Mount Sinai, where God is imparting the Torah. Below the mountain, the Israelites have become impatient. Moses seems to have disappeared, so they appeal to Aaron, Moses' brother, to make them a god. Aaron takes their gold jewelry and fashions a calf. The Israelites worship the calf, eat, drink, and dance. God alerts Moses to what's happening below, and Moses returns to the community, observes the orgy, and smashes the calf and the twin tablets of the covenant that he had brought down from his meeting with God.

There follow three separate responses to this event. In the first response (Exodus 32:11–14), Moses uses the "What will the nations say?" argument, what we referred to earlier as a form of blackmail, to persuade God to renounce punishment. In the second response, Moses summons the Levites, and they slay three thousand Israelites (Exodus 32:25–29). In the third response, Moses returns to intercede with God once again on behalf of Israel. God replies that those who have sinned must be "erased" from God's record, and God sends a plague upon the people (Exodus 32:30–35).

The Bible then devotes two more chapters to this story. The first, Exodus 33, is an extended exchange between God and Moses, of which, for our purposes here, the most significant is Moses' plea: "Now, if I [Moses] have truly gained Your favor, pray let me know Your ways, that I may know You and continue in your favor" (33:13). Note the term *ways*. As we saw in our discussion of the Sodom and Gomorrah episode, that is precisely the term God uses in identifying Abraham: one who keeps "the *way* of the Lord by doing what is just and right" (Genesis 18:19). Moses seems to be dissatisfied with that description, because if the criterion is God's justice, then his people are doomed.

God's response to Moses' plea is the burden of Exodus 34. Moses crafts two new tablets and ascends the mountain. God then comes down "in a cloud" (34:5) and reveals a new version of God's ways. The text that follows, God's reply to Moses, is one of the more striking passages in the Bible and is the core of our discussion here:

> The Lord passed before him [Moses] and proclaimed: "The Lord! The Lord! a God compassionate and gracious, slow to anger, abounding in kindness and faithfulness, extending kindness to the thousandth generation, tolerating iniquity, transgression, and sin; yet He does not remit all punishment, but visits the iniquity of parents upon children and children's children, upon the third and the fourth generation."
>
> —*Exodus 34:6–7*[2]

This passage, commonly called, "[God's] Thirteen Attributes," reverberates throughout later biblical and post-biblical texts. What does it tell us about God's ways?

The first point to note is that here, it is God who speaks. In Genesis 18, we are given God's private deliberations, but here we have God's own words. God tells Moses what kind of God this God is, what are this God's ways. The second point is that God's self-description is what might be called a "mixed bag." The first part of the passage is completely positive and introduces a new criterion for God's relationship with sinners. In the Abraham story, God is just. Now God is "compassionate and gracious, slow to anger, abounding in kindness and faithfulness." This is a radically new image. As the passage continues, however, we find that God's compassion is qualified. God may be compassionate, but God can (only) tolerate sin, not ignore it. God "does not remit all punishment." In fact, God even "visits the iniquity of parents upon children and children's children."

However compassionate God may be, sin must nevertheless be punished. God's compassion therefore lies in God's readiness to "tolerate" human sin. God does not punish immediately. God will bear, live with, and accept human sinfulness for a while, but eventually it must be punished. The punishment may be deferred, but it must come in time. A "mixed bag" God, indeed!

A confirmation of this understanding of Exodus 34:6–7 can be found in another incident, recorded in Numbers 13–14. Here the sin is the report of the ten spies who maligned the Promised Land. Again, God is furious at Israel's faithlessness, and again Moses intercedes on Israel's behalf. In this intercessory speech, Moses quotes God's own words from Exodus 34 almost verbatim (Numbers 14:18). Here, to Moses' plea for pardon, God replies:

> I pardon, as you have asked. Nevertheless...none of the men who have seen My Presence and the signs that I have performed in Egypt and in the wilderness, and who have tried Me these many times and have disobeyed Me, shall see the land that I promised on oath to their fathers; none of those who spurn Me shall see it.
>
> —*Numbers 14:22–23*

This response captures quite accurately the thrust of Exodus 34:6–7. God is compassionate, to a point. God may tolerate sin for a while, but God does not remit all punishment. Sin must be punished, but not immediately; the punishment may be deferred. The generation who was influenced by the sinful spies will not die now, but they will never make it into the Promised Land.

In both of these narratives, this qualified compassion is an immense improvement over the Abraham episode. Now it is no longer justice alone that governs God's dealing with human sin, but also compassion—a limited compassion, but compassion nevertheless. Now Moses plays the role of intercessor, as Abraham did earlier; now, however, Moses' claim is not that God must be just, but rather that God must be compassionate.

Repentance Enters the Picture

The passage from Exodus 34:6–7 is referred to numerous times in prophetic literature, but with one significant change. One clear instance of this further development is in the Book of Jonah, one of the shortest but most fascinating books in the entire Bible. It is also, not coincidentally, the prophetic reading for the afternoon service on Yom Kippur.

The story of Jonah is familiar to us, and we referred to it in chapter 2. The paradox in this book is that the only successful biblical prophet feels that he has failed. He won. Nineveh repented and was spared, yet Jonah is furious at God, and he protests:

> O Lord! Isn't this just what I said when I was still in my own country? That is why I fled beforehand to Tarshish. For I know that You are a compassionate and gracious God, slow to anger, abounding in kindness, renouncing punishment.
>
> —*Jonah 4:2*

Note that here Jonah is talking to God. Moreover, he quotes God back to God. He uses God's own words from Exodus 34:6–7. The author of the Book of Jonah is clearly familiar with what we have called the "mixed bag" Exodus passage, but he accepts only part of it—the first part, the image of the compassionate God. When he gets to the last part of the passage, in which God states that although sin may be tolerated it must eventually be punished, he replaces it with the very opposite claim, "renouncing punishment." God is now all compassion—period. When I read this passage, I fantasize that Jonah accompanies this speech with a sly wink, as if to say, "We both know that this is not precisely what You said back in Exodus, but we also know that the earlier passage is no longer operative. We both understand that in our day, if people repent, You will cancel punishment completely." It's like the advertisement for a Yiddish theater's performance of *Hamlet*: what we are invited to see is *Hamlet* "translated and improved."

This new reading of God's will is possible because repentance is now part of the relationship between God and human beings—specifically, what we may call "preemptive repentance," repentance that enters into the picture between the sin and the punishment and hence preempts punishment. This is new; it is a major innovation of the prophetic tradition. Until now, repentance has only followed punishment (Deuteronomy 30:1–5). Now repentance has the power to cancel punishment. Now God is all compassion. That's the message of the last verses in Jonah 4, in which God accuses Jonah of lacking the kind of compassion that God manifests to people and even to animals. Finally, since this is read on Yom Kippur and we are all repenting, we have a guarantee that we too will be pardoned. That's why we read this book on that day.

Why this change in God's image? Why must God grant us the power to repent? The answer, I believe, is in Psalm 103:3–14. The passage as a whole effusively proclaims God's readiness to pardon, and it begins with another clear reference to the same first portion of the Exodus 34 passage that Jonah quotes back to God: "The Lord is compassionate and gracious, slow to anger, abounding in steadfast love" (Psalm 103:8). As in Jonah, the quotation ends here. For the last portion of the Exodus 34 passage, the psalmist substitutes a series of images that are diametrically opposed to Exodus 34:

> He [God] will not contend forever,
> or nurse His anger for all time.
> He has not dealt with us according to our sins,
> nor has He requited us according to our iniquities.
> For as the heavens are high above the earth,
> so great is his steadfast love toward those who fear Him.
> As east is far from west,
> so far has He removed our sins from us.
> —*Psalm 103:9–12*

Then comes the theological underpinning for the power of repentance: "For He knows how we are formed; He is mindful that we are dust" (Psalm 103:14). God grants us the power of repentance because God knows how we were created: from the dust (Genesis 2:7). The unwritten implication of this statement is that in some way God is responsible for human sin. God made us that way! That's why God must give us a way out of our predicament.

Jonah 4 and Psalm 103 mark a total subversion of the earlier images of God. What has changed? Obviously not God—or, if so, we can't know that. What has changed is our collective perception of God, and with that change comes a corresponding change in the metaphor.

Finally, what happens to the very last part of the Exodus 34:6–7 passage, the part that claims that God will visit the sins of the parents onto the third and fourth generations? It too is simply and quickly abrogated in three biblical passages: Deuteronomy 4:16, Jeremiah 31:29–30, and Ezekiel 18:2–4. The last of these is particularly interesting, because here it is God who abrogates what God said back in Exodus:

> What do you mean by quoting this proverb..., "Parents eat
> sour grapes and their children's teeth are blunted"? As I
> live—declares the Lord God—this proverb shall no longer
> be current among you in Israel. Consider, all lives are Mine;
> the life of the parent and the life of the child are both Mine.
> The person who sins, only he shall die.

This is intrabiblical revisionism with a vengeance, accomplished with minimum effort. God simply says that what God said then is no longer operative. God basically says, "I've changed my mind on that point!"

The Yom Kippur Liturgy

The talmudic discussion of Exodus 34:6–7 seals Jonah's interpretation of Exodus in a formal covenant between God and Israel:

> "And the Lord passed by before him [Moses] and pro-
> claimed..."(Exodus 34:6). Rabbi Jochanan said: "Were it
> not written in the [biblical] text, it would be impossible for
> us to say such a thing: this verse teaches us that the
> Blessed Holy One donned a prayer shawl like the emissary
> of a congregation [who leads the congregation in prayer],
> and showed Moses this order of prayer [Exodus 34:6–7].
> God said to Moses: 'Whenever Israel sins, let them carry
> out this service before Me, and I will immediately forgive
> them....'" Rabbi Judah said: "A covenant has been made
> with the thirteen attributes that Israel will not be turned
> away empty-handed...as it says, 'Behold I make a
> covenant...'" (Exodus 34:10).[3]

This talmudic passage is stunning in its imagery of a God who wears a prayer shawl and points to a biblical text. Jonah's theological redefinition of God is now concretized in God's promise:

Whenever Israel sins, the people should remind God of this passage—not the original version, but Jonah's revised version—and God will immediately pardon.

Which is precisely what we do again and again throughout the Yom Kippur liturgy. The *vidui*, the confessional portion of the Yom Kippur liturgy that is repeated throughout the day, quotes a slightly expanded version of the Exodus text that still follows Jonah's dropping of the "not nice" part of the text. The recitation of this passage is preceded by a liturgical introduction that dates from the early Middle Ages:

> Almighty King, who sits on the throne of mercy, governs with kindness, pardons the iniquities of His people. He removes [their sins] one by one; increasing pardon to sinners, and forgiveness to transgressors; acting charitably with all mortals, not requiting them according to their sinfulness. O God, You have taught us to recite the Thirteen Attributes; remember this day in our favor the covenant of the Thirteen Attributes, as You have made known to the meek one [Moses] of old, as it is written: "And the Lord descended in a cloud...And the Lord passed before him [Moses] and proclaimed. 'The Lord! The Lord!' A God compassionate and gracious, slow to anger, abounding in kindness and faithfulness, extending kindness to the thousandth generation, forgiving iniquity, transgression, and sin, and acquits" (Exodus 34:5–7).

On Yom Kippur, then, we do what God instructed us to do and what Jonah did: we too quote God back to God, again in its amended form, and we have God's promise of forgiveness. This time we quote somewhat more of the Exodus passage, but again we subvert the sense of the original concluding words by proclaiming that God simply "acquits."

We have come a long way from the God of the early Genesis narratives—from a God who punishes immediately to one who insists on justice, to one who exhibits a qualified compassion but eventually must punish, to one who is all and only compassionate, and, finally, to a God who promises to forgive. Note how this revision is accomplished: not by erasing the earlier unflattering image—an impossible strategy, for the Exodus passage was already regarded as sacred—but precisely by quoting part of it again and again, in its amended form.

Unetaneh Tokef

Our second instance of a radical transformation of a divine image is in a single liturgical poem, dating from the early Middle Ages, which we also recite on the High Holidays, entitled *Unetaneh Tokef* ("Let us proclaim the sanctity of this day" are the first words of the poem). Once again, the theme is God's dealings with human sinners, but in contrast to the previous example, where the transformation takes place gradually through the Bible and post-biblical literature, here it takes place within the poem itself.

For many Jews, this prayer marks the high point of the High Holiday season. It captures starkly the sense that this is the season when all of creation comes before God in judgment. The theme of divine judgment and our human accountability before God for the lives we lead is the central theme of Yom Kippur. However, the rabbinic tradition extends the theme back to Rosh Hashanah, ten days earlier, calling the entire ten-day period "The Days of Repentance." We therefore recite this poem on the three festival days. The setting is the celestial court:

On this day Your throne of compassion is established and
You sit on it firmly. It is true that You are judge, prosecutor,
and witness, and that you inscribe and seal and record and

count. You remember all that is forgotten. You open the book of memories, and it is read aloud. The signature of every human being is recorded there.

In one stroke, that first sentence summarizes the complex interpretive history of Exodus 34:6–7. It repeats the opening sentence of the Yom Kippur liturgical passage cited above, that in this season God is seated on the throne of compassion. The criterion for judgement is no longer justice but rather compassion.

Look at the flood of judicial images for God: in this courtroom, God is judge, prosecutor, witness, bailiff, and court stenographer. Even more, God remembers all that is forgotten. To use a contemporary analogy, God is the ultimate database, the ensemble of all memories. The poem then assumes an apocalyptic tone:

The great shofar is sounded. A still small voice is heard. Angels tremble; they are seized with fear and terror, as they proclaim, "Behold the Day of Judgment on which the heavenly host are judged!" For before You, even they are not freed from judgment. All who enter the world pass before You as soldiers on review. As a shepherd musters his flock, and causes them to pass beneath his staff, so do You review and count and record the destiny of all living things. You determine the fate of every creature and You record their verdict.

When I read these words, my mind shifts to images of Dante's *Inferno*, or to the *Dies Irae* (literally, "Days of Wrath") portion of the Christian Requiem Mass as scored by Mozart, Verdi, or Berlioz: trumpets blare, tympani bang, the strings become increasingly agitated, and the piece is played fortissimo. This is the Final Judgment, the ultimate day of reckoning for all of creation, even for the angels. The range of verdicts is spelled out:

On Rosh Hashanah it is inscribed, and on Yom Kippur it is sealed: How many shall pass away, and how many shall be born. Who shall live and who shall die. Who will attain the measure of his days and who will not. Who by fire and who by water.

The list of possibilities—twenty-one in all—concludes with "who shall be brought low and who shall be exalted."

It is the phrase "Who shall live and who shall die" that is singularly responsible for the terror that has gripped generations of worshiping Jews at this moment. Each year, at this point in the service, I recall my own childhood experience, sitting in a synagogue surrounded by elderly Jews, their heads wrapped in prayer shawls, weeping silently as the cantor chanted this passage. I remember wondering which of those men would still be here next year and which ones would be gone.

Abruptly the mood changes. The poet has remembered that God is sitting on the throne of compassion. All is not lost; there is hope. He formulates that hope in a liturgical outburst, a protest, addressed by the congregation to the cantor: "But repentance, prayer, and deeds of righteousness avert the severe decree."

The poet has us remind the cantor of what he wrote at the outset. God is now sitting on the throne of compassion, not of justice. Therefore our fate is not predetermined. We have been granted a reprieve, an escape hatch, a way of avoiding our verdict, simply by doing the familiar things that Jews are expected to do daily throughout their lives: repent, pray, and be righteous. It's not the final judgment, after all, because every day is a day of judgment, and every day we are given ways to redeem ourselves before God. This is probably the most significant claim of the poem as a whole. It is nothing less than a validation of the everyday life of the Jew in the here and now.

The poem then concludes with a theological justification for God's compassion:

You are slow to anger and ready to forgive. You do not desire the death of the wicked but that we return from our evil way and live. Even until our dying day, You wait for us, perhaps we will repent, and You will immediately receive us. Our origin is dust and we return to the dust. We earn our bread at the peril of our life. We are like a fragile potsherd, as the grass that withers, as the flower that fades, as a fleeting shadow, as a passing cloud, as the wind that blows, as the fleeting dust, and as a dream that vanishes. But You are ever our living God and sovereign![9]

The echo of Psalm 103:14, quoted above, is unmistakable here. God must forgive because God above all knows what it means to be a human being and to live a human life. God not only knows our fragility and our vulnerability, God is also responsible for the way we are because God created us that way. God must then provide us with a way of escaping our verdict.

Note also the transformation of the courtroom metaphors for God. God is no longer only the judge, prosecutor, witness, bailiff, and stenographer. Now God also becomes the defense attorney, arguing on our behalf before the heavenly court—in fact, before God who is the ultimate judge. The God who is the ensemble of all memories must also remember the righteousness of our ancestors, whose merit accrues to us. This entire transformation takes place within the forty or so lines of the poem.

Changing Metaphors

We began this chapter by noting that we are not the first generation of Jews to be uncomfortable with how God appears in our classical texts. What we have traced here is the way that our ancestors handled these texts. We have quoted portions of the text and then shown how a new spin on that text subverts its original meaning.

In the first example, the process is drawn out and reflects historical development through centuries. In the second, the entire process is clearly within the mind of the author from the outset. That's probably because the medieval author had the entire earlier progression before him when he began to write.

What has changed, then, is not God but our human images of God. It is certainly tempting to suggest that these changes are always for the better, that they represent growth or maturation—first within human beings and then by projection—on God's part. We surely feel better about the new images than we did about the earlier ones, but this claim implies that our own value system is superior to that of the original texts and their authors. It may or may not be.

What is much more important is that the changes are impelled by a deeply felt human need—the need central to the High Holiday mood to wipe our individual slates clean, to begin the new year without the burdens of our past failures, to know that God is infinitely understanding and forgiving of erring humanity. To put it simply, we could not live with the God of the early Genesis narratives, or even the God of Exodus 34:6–7, the God who does not rise to the defense of humanity before the heavenly court. The metaphors change because we demand that they change.

Note also the central role of the liturgy. Liturgy represents the cutting edge of theological development. Jews encounter the prayer book daily, far more frequently than they encounter the Bible or the Talmud. More than any other text, it is the prayer book that shapes the Jewish sensibility. That's why, to this day, our own place in the range of the possible Jewish religious identities that abound about us becomes clearest when we confront the words of a specific prayer in a specific version of the prayer book, and we determine that we can or cannot recite this particular prayer and that we therefore belong in this community or in a different community with a different prayer book. To be accepted, every significant change in Jewish thinking must eventually find its liturgical expression.

Finally, the fact that our ancestors felt free to transform or even subvert some of Judaism's classic images of God legitimizes our doing the same. For again, we are changing not God but rather our own evolving images of how God appears to us today, in our own historical and cultural context. If the ancients could say that, to them, God could not be experienced as purely punitive, then we can say, for example, that God should not be portrayed exclusively in male terms. Some of us will agree, and others will not. Some will change the liturgy, and others will not. That tension is a source of vitality.

7

God Creates

Creation, Revelation, and Redemption: The Triad

The notion that three themes—creation, revelation, and redemption—capture three distinctive modes in which God relates to the world is both very new and very old. It provides the explicit structure for the twentieth-century German philosopher Franz Rosenzweig's *The Star of Redemption,* one of the most influential contemporary readings of Judaism. It also structures the traditional liturgies for the daily morning and evening worship services, canonized centuries ago. The heart of those liturgies is the recitation of the three paragraphs of the *Shema,* but that is preceded by two units, one dealing with God's creation of the world and the other with God's revelation of Torah. It is followed by a third unit, which praises God for having redeemed Israel from Egypt and for the promised final redemption to come.

The traditional names for these three units capture the three themes: (1) *Yotzer* ("Creation"), (2) Torah (for what God revealed was Torah), and (3) *Geulah* ("Redemption"). The liturgists who composed these texts were not systematic theologians. They were not consciously using these three models in their abstract form, as Rosenzweig does, but when they deliberated on what belief every worshiping Jew should recite daily, they determined that God should be praised for these three moments in which God turned to the world in particularly striking acts of relationship. What integrates the three moments, what makes them three-in-one instead of simply three discrete units, is the theme of God's relationship to the world. To use Abraham Joshua Heschel's language, they represent three dimensions of "the divine pathos." God's pathos, God's ongoing concern for the world, serves as the "ground tone" for these three more particular manifestations.

To put this in a more striking way, the common theme that unites all three is that human beings complement and extend God's work. To use the traditional formulation, we are "partners with God" in creation, revelation, and redemption. In each case, God demands a human contribution in order to fulfill the relationship. This is a statement both about human responsibility and about God's intrinsic nature or, more precisely, about how the ancients perceived God's nature. We then have to ask: What kind of God would grant a substantive role to human beings in completing God's work?

Note a subtle change in the focus of our inquiry. Thus far we have focused on the ways in which our ancestors tried to capture the nature of God, what God *is*. Now we turn to the equally varied ways in which they captured what God *does*. The distinction is by no means clear. A person's behavior usually reflects his or her nature; a "just" God will act justly, and from this behavior we infer something about God's nature. The change in emphasis from God's nature to God's behavior appeals to the sensibilities of many thinkers—Maimonides is the primary example—who are reluctant to say anything at all about God's nature. We may know nothing about God's nature, but we experience God's activity in the world daily. Our new question provides a different point of entry into our broader discussion.

God Creates Something

Posted prominently on the door of my office is a cartoon called "Frank and Ernest" by Bob Thaves. The cartoon portrays swirling patterns of light or energy. To the right, we find a large, oldish, shaggy-haired, smiling God, and to God's left, a much smaller, incredulous-looking creature, confronting this God. The caption reads: "You made it all out of QUARKS? ...Get outta here!"

I love this cartoon. It captures perfectly well how this seemingly simple notion of God as creator of the world is actually quite perplexing. For traditional believers of whatever stripe, that God created the world is an unquestioned principle of faith. For the secularist, the claim has been decisively dismissed by science and reason. The debate between creationists and scientists of all stripes began in antiquity and continues with unabated fervor to this day. Our cartoon captures and questions one somewhat whimsical resolution of that tension.

That God created the world, that without God there would be no world, is a pillar of Jewish thought. It is the theme of the opening chapters of the Bible. It appears everywhere in rabbinic homilies and in the very opening words of Maimonides' *Mishneh Torah*:

> The basic principle of all basic principles and the pillar of all sciences is to realize that there is a First Being who brought every existing thing into being. All existing things, whether celestial, terrestrial, or belonging to an intermediate class exist only through His true existence. If it could be supposed that He did not exist, it would follow that nothing else could possibly exist. If, however, it were supposed that all other beings were non-existent, He alone would still exist. Their non-existence would not involve His non-existence. For all beings are in need of Him, but He...is not in need of them nor of any one of them.
>
> —Mishneh Torah, *Basic Principles of the Torah 1:1–3*[1]

It also appears, in slightly different words, as the very first of Maimonides' Thirteen Principles of Faith:

> [God] is the cause of all existence. In Him all else subsists
> and from Him derives. It is inconceivable that He not exist,
> for should He not exist, the existence of all else would be
> extinguished, and nothing could persist. If we imagine the
> absence of any other existent thing, however God's exis-
> tence would not thereby be extinguished or diminished.[2]

In both of these formulations, Maimonides assumes that there is a tight congruence between the doctrine of creation and the existence of God. The first assumes the second; creation assumes a creating God. In fact, medieval philosophers devote much energy to proving the doctrine of creation on rational grounds, precisely because once they have proved creation, they have ipso facto proved the existence of a creating God. Proofs of creation become proofs of the existence of God.

Once we move beyond this apparently straightforward claim, however, questions abound. What does the claim mean? How (and why) did (or does) God create the world? What did (or does) God create—the world as we know it, or quarks? Despite the conventional belief that the first chapter of Genesis is Judaism's classical statement on this topic, the Bible and the post-biblical tradition preserve at least four separate answers to these questions.

Creation as Cosmic Ordering

The majestic narrative that appears in the opening chapter of the Bible portrays a God who creates the world by speaking it into existence. God's creative work accounts for everything: light, the earth below, and the heavens above—from the sun, moon, and stars to birds, animals, and fish, and as a climax, the human being. God creates, in this account, by imposing order on a state of primordial anarchy. "When God began to create heaven and earth"—this is probably the most accurate translation of those first seven Hebrew words of the Bible—God had to deal with a preexistent set of conditions, outlined in the parenthetical clause that follows immediately: "the earth being unformed and void, with darkness over the surface of the deep and a wind from God sweeping over the water." Then "God said, 'Let there be light'; and there was light." God speaks, and there is a world. One of the liturgical names for God is the One "who spoke, and [behold!] there was a world."

In this Genesis account, God does not create the world "out of nothing." Here, when God begins to create, God has to deal with an "earth" that is "unformed and void" (despite the apparently contradictory notion that God was about to create the earth) as well as with darkness, the deep, and a sweeping wind. God's creative work is portrayed as bringing order out of a preexisting anarchy, cosmos out of chaos. By *chaos,* we mean what the verse describes as *tohu va-vohu,* frequently translated as "unformed and void," a condition in which boundaries are blurred, distinctions obscured, and confusion rampant. In contrast, throughout this chapter God is portrayed as creating distinctions, separating elements from one another: heaven from earth, light from darkness, waters above the heaven from waters below, and birds, fish, and mammals. Finally, at the end, one day, the Sabbath, is separated from the remaining six days. Every piece of creation has its legitimate place. Distinctions impose form on the "formless." Where there was primordial chaos, there now reigns cosmos.

The literary character of this chapter also reflects this ordering work. Every portion of the created world has its distinctive day. Each day's account begins and concludes with the same words: "God said, 'Let there be'" at the outset, and "God saw that it was good. And there was evening and there was morning, a [number] day" at the end. The days are explicitly numbered. The literary form of the text underlines its substance. Both point to creation as ordering.

There are two further characteristics of the Genesis 1 account: Here, God's creative work is unopposed. God speaks, and the world comes into being as a manifestation of God's transcendent power. Here, too, the creation of the human being comes at the very end of the process. The story provides the broad context into which the human being has his and her (because in this account, God creates the first human as male and female) own place in the ordered world. Only if the world is fundamentally ordered does everything have its proper place.

We might ask: why did medieval philosophers abandon this reading of Genesis 1 in favor of the doctrine of creation "out of nothing"? The notion that something else coexisted with God before creation implied a theological dualism that was probably anathema to these thinkers. In this Genesis account there was God *and* there was all of this other preexisting stuff. Where did this preexistent stuff come from? Was the chaos another god? Then there would be two gods, and that doctrine was simply unthinkable to the medieval commentators. Furthermore, they were being challenged by the influential Aristotelian notion that an original creation in time was simply wrong: the world, or at least undifferentiated matter, existed eternally. That notion seemed to contradict Genesis 1, so Genesis 1:1 had to be clarified and revised.

A useful analogy might be our experience of building a house out of blocks of wood. In the Genesis account, the blocks are piled on the floor in an indiscriminate, chaotic heap, and then we select blocks and order them into a house. For the medieval commentators, first we make the blocks and then we build the house. The biblical account is not interested in proving the existence of God, however; that was simply assumed. Nor was whoever wrote Genesis 1 challenged by Aristotelian science. Genesis 1 was written as it was because that's how someone's experience suggested it happened.[3]

The Centrality of the Human Being

Modern biblical criticism claims that Genesis 2 and 3 preserve a second, separate creation story. The evidence for this conclusion is both substantive and literary. On the literary front, scholars point to differences in vocabulary, in style, and in names for God in the two documents. The substantive differences are also striking. The scope of the first account is cosmic; the second, narrowly anthropocentric. In the first, God creates everything else and then, on the last day, human beings; in the second, the creation of the "everything else" *follows* the creation of the first man (2:9 for trees, and 2:19 for beasts and birds). The parenthetical clause in 2:5 explicitly claims that the human being, here only a male, was created before everything else. The rest of the account deals with the creation of the garden, the other creatures, and the woman, and finally with the adventures of these first humans that led to their expulsion from Eden.

It is understandable why traditional biblical commentators see these two accounts as one single story, with the first part setting the cosmic stage for the creation of human beings and the second part describing in more detail how the first humans were created. The second part is viewed as building on and extending the last verses of the first part. For religious scholars concerned with preserving the integrity and inner coherence of the text as a whole, this solution seems eminently reasonable; for modern biblical critics the contradictions are too sharp to ignore.

These contradictions are anticipated in the opening words of the two accounts. In the first, God creates "heaven and earth" (Genesis 1:1); in the second, "earth and heaven" (Genesis 2:4). The change is subtle but significant. In the earlier account, the scope of God's creation is the broadest possible natural canvas, beginning with heaven and then proceeding to earth and its inhabitants. In the second, that ultimate canvas is dismissed as irrelevant. God's singular concern is with what happens on earth and, even more narrowly, with the creation of the first human being, which took place *before* anything else was created (Genesis 2:4–7). This "everything else" was then created for and on behalf of the human being.

Furthermore, in the first account we are never told how the first humans were created, just that God created them. In the second, God created the first man by breathing the breath of life into a clod of earth (Genesis 2:7), and the first woman subsequently from the man's rib or side. In the first, the original human creature was a hermaphrodite (Genesis 1:27); in the second, God created only the male at first. Finally, the second account follows the lives of these two human creatures—their eating of the fruit of the tree of knowledge of good and bad, the suffering imposed on them because of this act of rebellion, and their banishment from the garden. Essentially, this account explains why things are the way they are for human beings in the post-Eden world in which we live to this day: why men earn their bread by the sweat of their brow, why women experience pain in childbirth, and why we die. None of this is described in Genesis 1.

The shift in focus of the two accounts is a shift in the nature of God's ultimate concern. Is God concerned primarily with the world as a whole or with human beings? Were humans created for the sake of the world, or the world for the sake of humanity? It is also, then, a shift in God's values. In the first, God is concerned with nature as a whole and with human beings as part of that canvas. In the second, God cares preeminently about human beings, how they were created, how they behaved, and their subsequent destiny in and out of Eden.

The exalted status of the human being, so distinctive to this second creation narrative, emerges most strikingly in the notion that humans are "partners with God in creation." That rabbinic formulation is an extension of the notion that "The Lord took the man and placed him in the garden of Eden, to till it and tend it" (Genesis 2:15). The sense of the passage is that God's created world needed more work, tending and tilling the earth, and that this task was assigned to the first human. The partnership formula appears in the following commentary on Genesis 2:1, "And heaven and earth were finished":

Rabbi Hamnuna said: "He who prays on the eve of the Sabbath and recites 'And heaven and earth were finished,' Scripture treats him as though he had become a partner with the Holy One, blessed be He, in the Creation, for it is written, 'And they [heaven and earth] were finished.' Do not read 'and they were finished,' but rather, 'and they finished.'"[4]

The point is subtle and requires a familiarity with the Hebrew text. By a midrashic sleight of hand, Rabbi Hamnuna reads the passive verb "they were finished" as an active verb, "they finished." The "they" is obviously Adam and Eve. They finished the work of God's creation, and this made them God's partners in creation. When we recite the passage on Friday evening, we share in this partnership.

Our own experience extends and confirms this notion. Every use we make of the world requires a substantive human contribution. God did not create bread; we create bread from what God has previously provided. God did not create medicine; we create medicine out of the plants and other substances that God provided. Human sharing in creation is also not limited to the material world. God may have created justice, but the application of that mandate in concrete human exchanges is a human responsibility: "Every judge who judges with complete fairness, even for a single hour, Scripture gives him credit as though he had become a partner with the Holy Blessed One in the creation."[5]

In an even more unusual application of this notion, the Rabbis note that God could have created the first male already circumcised but did not do so. We are responsible for completing God's work here, as well. The text then expands: "Observe that everything that was created during the six days of creation needs finishing: mustard needs sweetening, vetches [a plant] need sweetening, wheat needs grinding, and even man needs finishing."[6]

This is as much a statement about God as about human beings. God did not create a perfect world, even a perfectly just world. God requires the help of people here in creation and, as we shall see, also in revelation and redemption. This exalted role is assigned to human beings.

Both of these versions of creation are to be found, unreconciled, in the Bible, but pluralistic understandings of creation are even more numerous than these.

A Primordial Combat

Whatever the differences in these two accounts of creations, they agree on one significant point: God's creation was unopposed. Apart from the rebellion of the first human beings in the second account—not an insignificant exception—there is nary a hint of any challenge to God's power from any other force within or beyond the created world. God speaks or wills, and everything falls into place.

Genesis 1 teaches that God formed the cosmos out of primordial chaos. A closer reading of the text suggests that God did not simply banish or abolish the chaotic element in the world, the *tohu va-vohu*, the darkness, and the deep—God could surely have done that—but rather set boundaries so that it would be controlled. God separates light from darkness, the sea from the earth, and the waters above from the waters below the earth (Genesis 1:4, 7). That the setting of boundaries may be challenged is only implicit in Genesis 1. It becomes explicit in other creation stories in the Bible. Here are three texts that suggest that God's creative work was not as effortless as Genesis 1 portrays it—that, in fact, God's creation of the world demanded a battle with forces that resisted God's work and had to be controlled.

Psalm 104 is a majestic description of God's power over nature, but it also reflects another implicit creation narrative. It is recited, appropriately, at the conclusion of the morning service on every Rosh Chodesh, the celebration of the new month in the Jewish calendar, and again during the Sabbath afternoon service during the winter months:

> [God] established the earth on its foundations,
> so that it shall never totter.
> You made the deep cover it as a garment;
> the waters stood above the mountains.
> They fled at Your blast,
> rushed away at the sound of Your thunder,
> —mountains rising, valleys sinking—
> to the place You established for them.
> You set bounds they must not pass
> so that they never again cover the earth.
>
> —*Psalm 104:6–9*

What we have here is a different spin on Genesis 1. If the Genesis 1 account tells of God imposing order on primitive anarchy, this account relates in more detail just how God did it. It also suggests some resistance on the part of nature: waters rush, mountains rise, and valleys sink, none of which is in Genesis 1. At the end, God instructs the waters that they must not cross the divinely imposed boundaries, implying that they still have the power to do just that.

Even more explicit is Job 38:8–11, part of God's response to Job's demand that God justify Job's apparently undeserved suffering. Again, it is a paean to God's power and reflects a creation narrative:

> Who closed the sea behind doors
> When it gushed forth out of the womb,
> When I clothed it in clouds,
> Swaddled it in dense clouds,
> When I made breakers My limit for it,

And set up its bar and doors,

And said, "You may come so far and no further;

Here your surging waves will stop?"

Here again the effortless creation of Genesis 1 is replaced by the notion of a primordial battle between God and the sea. God wins the battle, but the sea does not yield passively. God bounded it about, set up its "bars and doors," but it remains a threat to God's mastery. Otherwise, why the need for bars and doors? Were it not for God's ongoing presence, it might transgress its assigned boundaries. In fact, that's precisely what the waters do in Noah's day in the story of the flood: "All the fountains of the great deep burst apart, and the floodgates of the sky broke open" (Genesis 7:11). They can do all this because God has released them from their imposed boundaries, but God could do this because their original power had not been totally vanquished. In contrast, following the flood, God promises that the boundaries of nature that God established will never again be violated: "So long as the earth endures, seedtime and harvest, cold and heat, summer and winter, day and night shall not cease" (Genesis 8:22).

Even more explicit is this passage from Psalm 74:13–17:

It was You who drove back the sea with Your might,

who smashed the heads of the monsters in the waters;

it was You who crushed the head of Leviathan,

who left him as food for the denizens of the desert;

it was You who released springs and torrents,

who made mighty rivers run dry;

the day is Yours, the night also;

it was You who set in place the orb of the sun;

You fixed all the boundaries of the earth;

summer and winter—You made them.

The verbs in this passage—"drove back," "smashed," and "crushed"—imply a full-fledged combat between God and the primordial forces of nature, which seem to have strenuously resisted God's power; that's why they had to be "crushed" and "smashed."

This version of creation is much more than an arcane mythic detail. If the order of creation implies that the forces of nature have not been totally subdued, then we can understand why, from time to time, they erupt to engulf God's established boundaries. The theological implications of that shift are startling. The most obvious implication is that it denies God's ultimate sovereign power. What we seem to have here is a biblical proof-text for the notion of a limited God. Even more striking, this notion of a primordial combat between God and the forces of nature helps us to understand why it is that although in nature God's control of chaos appears to be secure, in history that control is far from evident. Just look at Israel's historic suffering at the hands of its enemies! We studied that discrepancy in chapter 2.

It is also explicit in Psalm 74, which in verses 13–17 deals with God's suppression of natural chaos. That passage is a setup for the main point of the psalm, which is a challenge to God for failing to control the anarchical forces in history. That's how the psalm begins: "Why, O God, do You reject us, do You fume in anger at the flock that You tend?" It continues with a description of Israel's defeat at the hands of its enemies:

> They made Your sanctuary go up in flames;
> they brought low in dishonor the dwelling place of Your
>   presence.
> They resolved, "Let us destroy them altogether!"
> They burned all God's tabernacles in the land.
>
> —Psalm 74:7–8

This provides the context for verses 13–17, in which the psalmist recalls how God's power crushed the forces of nature. Then the original theme returns: "Do not deliver Your dove to the wild beast; do not ignore forever the band of Your lowly ones, Look to the covenant!" (Psalm 74:19–20).

God is supposed to be the ultimate master of all things, nature and history together, but there is a yawning gap between nature and history. The anarchic forces of history are still active, seemingly immune to God's control. The major challenge to God's power is still human beings, whom God created free even to flout God's will, in history to this day as in Eden in the beginning. God is supposed to have made a covenant not only with nature (after the flood, in Genesis 9:9) but also with Israel at Sinai. Therefore the psalm makes the appeal "Look to the covenant!" It means both covenants.

We have revisited the discrepancy between God's power in nature and in history in this context because the modern reader does not necessarily share the psalmist's conviction that God has indeed mastered natural anarchy. How should we deal with the devastation wreaked upon innocent people by earthquakes, floods, and tornados? We experience God's limitations in both realms, which is why this third account of creation speaks so clearly to us. Again, how we understand creation determines how we picture God.[7]

Creation Continues Daily: The Liturgy

When the rabbinic authors of the daily liturgy wanted to codify a theology of creation in words that worshiping Jews would articulate every single day, they chose neither Genesis 1, which would seem to be the preeminent text because of its placement at the very beginning of Torah, nor the other accounts studied thus far, but still another biblical account, Isaiah 45:7:

I form light and create darkness,
I make order [*shalom*] and create bad [*ra*]—
I the Lord do all these things.[8]

We studied this text in chapter 1. In its original context, it was a rejection of Zoroastrian theological dualism. There is only one God, this prophet insists, not a god of light and a god of darkness, not a good god and a bad god. This God is responsible for "all things." But when this passage was placed at the opening of the first daily blessing, it was reworded this way: "Blessed are You, Lord our God, Sovereign of the universe, Who forms light and creates darkness, who makes *shalom* and creates all things."

Two new themes emerge immediately. First, God now creates darkness; in Genesis 1, darkness preexisted creation. God may have separated it from light, but it was there all along, before the creation of light. Second, what happened to the notion that God creates evil, too? That is simply dropped and replaced with the concluding words of the Isaiah text: now God creates "all things," which may include evil as well, but only implicitly. The liturgists felt no discomfort at having God create darkness, but they did not want to have God explicitly identified with the creation of evil.

This text rejects, or at least ignores, the thrust of the other creation accounts we have examined. Creation is not order out of anarchy; now God creates the anarchy (and the darkness) as well. Creation is not anthropocentric; the author is not interested in the order of creation. Finally, this is no limited God. This God creates all things!

As this liturgy expands on the Isaiah passage, another surprise is in store for us: "[God]...illuminates the earth and those who dwell upon it with compassion, and in God's goodness, renews daily, perpetually, the work of creation." Creation is no longer an act that occurred once upon a time, eons ago. It occurs today, daily, perpetually. The doctrine of creation is no longer simply a statement about how things came into being at the outset, but rather about how the world continues to be from moment to moment. It is now a statement about the world's continuing dependency on God's perpetual presence and power. Note also that these words are to be recited at dawn, precisely at the threshold moment when we are most conscious of the daily cycle of nature.

We should not for a moment minimize the theological implications that God created evil or chaos. We have seen that when we try to understand why innocent human beings suffer, we have two options: that the suffering takes place within God's purview, or that it escapes God's power. This prophet clearly opts for the first, which leaves us with the disturbing conclusion that an apparently good God is directly responsible for the suffering. However, the second option is equally disturbing: God is simply not omnipotent.

Why Four Creation Accounts?

We need different accounts of creation because to speak of how the world originated takes us outside time and space into realms that neither the human mind nor human language can describe in literal terms. I once asked a noted astronomer if the "big bang" was loud. He smiled and responded, "In fact, there was no air, so there was no sound," but then he added, "The big bang itself is beyond the boundaries of scientific inquiry. Scientists can tell you what happened a nanosecond after the big bang, but the big bang itself belongs to the realm of poetry, of myth, or," he added with a wink after asking me what I taught, "theology."

We are all obsessed with a need to understand how everything began, just as we are obsessed with a need to understand how everything will end. That intuitive need to make sense of our world is what impels both science and religion. If we pursue the chain of inquiry back to the very, very earliest moments in time, as far back as we can go, we eventually confront a wall of mystery. There always remains at least one further step back in the chain of time that our minds cannot penetrate. To characterize that last, furthest step, we have to depart from ordinary language, and then we slip into poetry or myth. Then we talk of Genesis 1, or of quarks. At that moment we are functioning imaginatively, not scientifically. We have no data against which to measure our hypotheses. No one has ever directly observed a quark; we can only observe the tracks that quarks leave behind, as we infer a big bang from the traces of the primordial event that we do observe. The scientific assumption is that if the world works as it seems to work, there must have been a big bang, and so there must be something like quarks. The Bible does the same thing, and so we have Genesis 1.

All four answers are true in that sense. Each captures part of the truth; each is a partial view; they complement one another, and none alone conveys the whole truth. It is true that our world maintains an uneasy balance between order and anarchy. It is true that it manifests one grand, overarching, coherent pattern or system, something like the scientists' "grand unified theory." It is true that among creation, the human being has been granted exceptional standing and value. After all, we are apparently the only creatures who think about how the world was created in the first place! It is also true that this incredibly complex world somehow maintains itself, day after day, moment after moment, perpetually.

There is one major difference between the scientific and the biblical understandings of creation. The purpose of the biblical answers is not primarily to provide an accurate account of how things came into being in the first place, but rather to provide imaginative visions of what the world and human life mean. They are all concerned with issues of ultimate meaning; they all try to locate the meaning of a human life within the broadest possible canvas. In one way or another, they are all attempts to isolate the distinctive character of the human experience. One message tells us that we humans beings are creatures of inestimable value; that's what the Bible wants to convey by noting that we were created in "the image of God." Another teaches us that we have the responsibility to "tend" the world. A third tells us that human life is lived on a precipice, on the edge of chaos. A fourth says that the world and hence our lives are not self-dependent. These different messages are all manifestly true. That's why the very presence of the four messages is a gift to us. Our ancestors were speculating about what life is all about, and they included all these possibilities to encourage us to do the same.

What unites all four biblical messages is God. How could it be otherwise? For our ancestors, God was not the conclusion of an argument but rather its point of departure. They began with the conviction that there was a God in the world and that the world was all God's work. They didn't reason *to* God from their experience—that was the route of medieval rationalism—but rather *from* God as a way of understanding their experience.

Understood this way, the conflict between creationism and evolutionism is not about conclusions but about assumptions. On this issue, the assumptions are all equally poetic or mythic. God may have created the world out of quarks, but a quark is also an imaginative construct of the human mind. Besides, who created the quark?

8

God Reveals

The Principle of Revelation

Creation and redemption represent the broad parameters of God's engagement with the world: creation marks its beginning, redemption its conclusion. In between, the period in which we now find ourselves, can be referred to as the period of "history."

In the Bible, history is not cyclical but rather vectoral. It moves from a beginning toward an ending, from creation to redemption, in which redemption is understood as the emergence of a world or an eon in which all of the promises of God's original creation are fulfilled. The term *redemptive history*, frequently applied to the Jewish understanding of the historical process, is the story of how human civilization may, progressively and with God's help, realize the vision of an ideal age. Throughout this intermediate age of history, we carry with us a dynamic impulse toward fulfillment—our own fulfillment as individual human beings, of the Jewish people, and of the world as a whole.

A God who cares enough to create a world in the first place, and who hopes that this created world will eventually achieve its ideal state, will also care enough to provide humanity with the resources to bring that longed-for ideal into being. That resource is what Jews call *Torah*. Torah (literally, "Instruction") provides the structures through which we are to shape our individual and communal lives to further the task of redemption.

Torah is the fruit of the middle moment of our triad, revelation; revelation occurs within, and is a product of, the age of history. Because revelation takes place after creation, it reflects the reality of the world as it is, but it also impels the dynamic that leads to the world as it might yet be. Torah is the impulse behind redemptive history. To put this another way, revelation is the bond that lends integrity to the triad as a whole. Given the way we are here in this created world, and given our vision of the world that might yet be, Torah brings us from here to there.

That's why Jews have understood Torah to be an expression of God's love for Israel, as God's gift to Israel. The daily evening liturgy reads: "With eternal love have You loved the House of Israel, Torah and commandments, decrees and statutes have you taught us." The daily morning liturgy expands and extends the implications of that gift. It is then our responsibility to "understand and to grasp, to listen, learn, teach, guard, perform all of teachings of Your Torah with love." If Torah is an expression of God's love for Israel, then Israel's engagement with Torah is the expression of its own reciprocal love for God.

That Torah is an expression of God's love for Israel is the source of the often troublesome doctrine of Israel as God's "chosen" people. The connection is explicit in the first of the blessings that Jews recite upon being called to the liturgical reading of the Torah: "Blessed are You, Lord our God, Sovereign of the universe, who has chosen us from among all peoples by giving us His Torah. Praised are You, Lord, giver of the Torah." Another translation of this text reads, "who has chosen us from among the peoples *and* given us His Torah," but the first translation captures more accurately the notion that it is through the giving of Torah that God expresses God's distinctive love for Israel. It is inevitably a statement of exclusivity, but first it is Israel's own self-understanding of its relation with God (not God's explicit choice); second, despite the notion that it is God's gift, it also represents a unique burden.

The tension between Torah as gift and Torah as burden is a recurring theme in the literature of the Jewish tradition.

A God who creates and redeems must be a God who also reveals. Revelation is the central element of the complex metaphorical system through which Jews view God—what we have called, using Abraham Joshua Heschel's term, God's pathos, God's concern for the world. This is a God who cares enough to provide us with a sense of what a fulfilled world will be like as well as to embed within us the impulse and the resources to achieve that goal.

But Does God Choose?

However we understand the blessing over the Torah, the notion that God has chosen one people "from among all peoples" is troublesome to many of our contemporaries. To choose implies to select, and when we select something we seem to be expressing a preference for that something over another. That easily slips into the notion that whatever we have chosen is superior to what we have not chosen. Recent history has offered ample proof of the depravity to which theories of national or racial superiority can lead. That's why Mordecai Kaplan, among other notable twentieth-century Jewish thinkers, has simply eliminated or reformulated all liturgical references to the doctrine of Israel as the chosen people. Kaplan's version of the Torah blessing reads: "Blessed be Thou, O Lord our God, King of the universe, who has brought us nigh to Thy service and hast given us Thy Torah."[1]

However, to be chosen does not have to imply superiority. Offer me a bowl of fruit and I may decide to choose the peach. That choice certainly implies that I prefer the peach to the apples, pears, and plums, but it does not imply that peaches are in some way superior to apples or that I don't also like apples. It does not rule out that on some other occasion I might have chosen the pear, nor does it mean that I will think ill of someone else who chooses the plum. Similarly, the fact that we choose a spouse suggests that we prefer this particular man or woman, but it does not imply that all other men or women are inherently inferior to the one that we have chosen.

The notion that God has "chosen" Israel has come to signify that God prefers Israel to other peoples. For some people, this has led to the notion that Israel is better than other peoples, that these other peoples occupy a lower rank in God's esteem than Israel does. It is beyond dispute that many people, Jews and non-Jews alike, have understood the doctrine in these ways.

First and foremost, as I noted above, the doctrine of Israel as God's chosen people is Israel's self-perception, not God's own perception of Israel. We have made this point again and again. No human being knows objectively what God wants, feels, or does. God transcends human understanding. One interpretation of revelation that follows in this chapter is explicit in claiming that at least to many modern Jews, Torah as a whole is Israel's very human understanding of its distinctive history, its relationship to God, and God's claims on its behalf—not at all God's explicit will or word.

Israel perceived itself to be chosen by God because that's the way it chose to make sense of its distinctive history, beginning with Abraham and reaching its climax with the redemption from Egyptian bondage. Those events, woven into the pattern that we have called redemptive history, then became concretized in the Sinai covenant, the seal for Israel's unique relationship with God. Again, this notion of redemptive history is nothing more or less than Israel's way of understanding itself and human history as a whole. Israel wrote this redemptive history, not God.

In addition, Israel's "daughter religions" inherited the notion of redemptive history, which led them to believe that God's choice had passed to another, different community. The first Christians understood that God's revelation in and through Jesus of Nazareth superseded the Sinai covenant with "the old Israel." (In this post-Holocaust age, however, many Christians have come to question the accuracy of this reading of Christian Scripture and to abandon it.) Islam claimed that God's revelation to Mohammed in the Arabian desert in the seventh century C.E. constituted the seal of prophecy, God's final revelation. The Mormons hold a similar view regarding God's revelation to Joseph Smith in upstate New York in the 1820s. In all these cases, the new community became God's chosen, leading—ironically in many instances—to violent persecution of the original chosen people. Again, in all these instances, what these communities claimed reflected only their own self-perception, not God's choices.

The conventional translation of the Hebrew word *bachar*, used in the Torah blessing above, is indeed "chose." However, the issue is more complicated. Consider this blessing that Jews recite before reading the selection from prophetic literature that follows the Torah reading on the Sabbath and festivals. The text reads: "Blessed are You, Lord, who chooses [in Hebrew, *bocher*] the Torah, Moses, God's servant, and Israel, God's people." We can understand why God may "choose" Moses (from among other people) and Israel (from among other nations). In what sense, however, does God "choose" the Torah? Did God consult a whole series of sacred books and then "choose" this one? Obviously not.

The word, then, does not necessarily mean "select" or "choose." It could also mean "single out," or "distinguish" as a synonym for "separate." Something that is "distinguished" or separated can easily become "distinguished" in the sense of "special." This is clearly what has happened in our case, but it doesn't have to acquire that second meaning. The bottom line is that the claim that God has chosen Israel can mean nothing more than that God loves Israel, but God may also love many other peoples, as a parent loves all of his or her children. In fact, Judaism has never claimed that God does not love the other nations. The prophet Amos puts it this way:

To Me, O Israelites, you are
Just like the Ethiopians, declares the Lord.
True, I brought Israel up
From the land of Egypt,
But also the Philistines from Caphtor
And the Arameans from Kir.

—*Amos 9:7*

To equate God's redemption of Israel from Egyptian bondage with God's redemption of other nations—indeed, a nation such as the Philistines, one of ancient Israel's enemies—is a striking acknowledgment that God loves all peoples equally.

The Issue of Revelation

In principle, then, intrinsic to God's concern for people is that God is a revealing God. But what, in fact, did God reveal, and how did God reveal it? These issues have bedeviled Jewish thinkers throughout history, never more so than in our own day.

These questions are far more than an attempt to recapture, with some precision, events that occurred millennia ago. First, they raise fundamental questions concerning the nature of God. Various answers to these questions suggest various metaphors for imaging God. Second, they raise the issue of the truth of competing religions. Did God reveal only to Israel at Sinai? Or did God also reveal through the person and career of Jesus of Nazareth and/or in a book dictated to Mohammed? Are all of these revelations equally expressions of God's will, differing only for the individual community to which the revelation is directed? Are all these religions equally "true"? Why do we accept one of these revelations and dismiss the others? If they are all equally true, why be Jewish, Christian, Muslim, or Mormon? A detailed inquiry into all of these questions is beyond the scope of this study, but what cannot be avoided is a third issue that arises from these questions, the issue of the authority of this body of teachings. For contemporary Jews, these questions raise the issue of the authority of the Torah in Jewish life today.

For Jews, what precisely was the "content," the substance of God's revelation to our ancestors? Torah can be defined in many ways. It can be understood as (1) the first five books of the Bible (the *chumash,* or Pentateuch, both referring to "five"); (2) the entirety of Hebrew Scripture, from Genesis to 2 Chronicles; (3) all of Scripture *plus* the body of rabbinic interpretation that emerged in the talmudic era (from the first to the seventh centuries C.E.); or, even more broadly, (4) the ongoing interpretation of that material to our very own day. However we define it, Torah is a complex body of doctrines, history, narratives, prayers, and legal codes. It constitutes the entire body of Judaism's distinctive religious message. What authority does this body of teaching have for us? Are we to accept the entire body of tradition as absolutely binding on all Jews for eternity? How free are we to depart from it, and how do we decide? The different answers to these questions account for the denominational structures that characterize the Jewish community today, from right-wing Orthodoxy to left-wing Reform and everything in between.

The Traditionalist Option

The classic biblical account of revelation is in Exodus 19–24. Exodus 20 begins with the ten commandments, followed, in the rest of Exodus 20 through the end of Exodus 23, by the first comprehensive biblical code of law, and in Exodus 24 by the ritual solemnization of the Sinai covenant. Exodus 20:1 introduces all this material with the claim that God "spoke all these words" to the Israelite community. Exodus 19 is a narrative prelude that describes the setting for this revelation, its date (in the third month after the Exodus), its site (the wilderness of Sinai), and the manifestations of God that accompanied the revealing of the message itself.

This complex narrative is wrapped in obscurity. God is described as descending on the mountain and Moses as ascending the mountain (and also descending to the people), all accompanied by thunder, lightning, a cloud, fire, and the blast of the shofar. The metaphor of the cloud on the mountain is singularly appropriate. The impression conveyed by the narrative as a whole is one of mystery. Whatever is taking place on the mountaintop is veiled, beyond literal description. The chapter can be read as a poem, an evocation of some mysterious event, not a historical account.

Traditionalists take this passage as the proof-text for the authority of Torah as a whole. Proponents of the traditionalist understanding of revelation insist that this text is to be understood literally. The "contents" of the Torah were the explicit words that God conveyed first to Moses, and later to Israel, on that specific day at that spot on earth. What the text recounts is pure history, the founding event in the history of Israel. As a result, everything in Torah is eternally binding on all Jews throughout history; all of it consists of God's explicit words. Should there be a conflict between Scripture and the changing cultures of different ages, culture must bow before the ultimate authority of God's will and word.

The significant accomplishment of this understanding of Sinai is to absolutize the authority of Torah. It leads implicitly to another series of claims: Torah alone is God's authentic revelation; the other pretenders (e.g., Jesus of Nazareth) are simply false. Judaism, then, is the only "true" religion. Second, Torah represents one internally coherent and consistent document. Third, the contents of Torah, including the very words in which it is conveyed, were determined by God. God alone created Judaism. Fourth, no human being or community can override the Torah. We are then left with two options: either accept the divine authority of Torah in our lives, or reject the package as a whole, which is the ultimate heresy because it effectively denies God's power.[2]

This is an admittedly oversimplified characterization of the traditionalist option, and we shall see that thinkers throughout the ages have questioned specific pieces of the position. The Talmud is replete with instances where Moses says that God commanded something that does not explicitly appear in the Torah itself. Take one significant example of major importance to contemporary Jewish feminists. In preparing for the Sinai revelation, God commands Moses:

> Go to the people and warn them to stay pure today and tomorrow. Let them wash their clothes. Let them be ready for the third day; for on the third day the Lord will come down, in the sight of all the people, on Mount Sinai.
>   —*Exodus 19:10–11*

Three verses later, we have Moses' version of the command: "Moses came down from the mountain to the people and warned the people to stay pure, and they washed their clothes. And he said to the people, 'Be ready for the third day: do not go near a woman'" (Exodus 19:14–15).

The phrase "go near a woman" is obviously a circumlocution for sexual intercourse. In biblical religion, a seminal emission is a source of ritual impurity. Because the community is to receive the Torah in a state of ritual purity, the men should avoid sexual activity for three days prior to the revelation. God says nary a word about that kind of preparation, however. Apparently, Moses introduces it on his own authority.

The issue is not at all trivial. Feminists remind us that this text—one of the most central in the Torah as a whole, the text that captures God's primary revelation to Israel—is being addressed to a male audience. Moses could have said the same thing in a more inclusive way. He could have said, "Don't have sexual relations for the next three days," but he doesn't. Instead, he says, "Don't go near a woman," thereby excluding women from his audience. Again, this is Moses' contribution, not God's. However exalted Moses' role, he remains a human being, one who in this instance extends and transforms God's own words, a remarkable anticipation of what rabbinic authorities were to pursue later in Jewish history.

In its general outline, the traditionalist position has become dogma for many modern Jewish thinkers, the very hallmark of Jewish religious authenticity.[3]

In terms of our broader inquiry, consider the image of God reflected in Exodus 19–24. This God chooses to be manifest in thunder and lightening, as God was earlier manifest in plagues and burning bushes and later in the sea that split. This God speaks to people. These are all demonstrations of God's power over nature and history and of God's love for Israel.

Contrast this God with the image of God in the Joseph story (Genesis 37–51). The God of Joseph never speaks a word to anyone. None of the events here is miraculous. The entire narrative can be read as an account of what normal people do in the course of leading their normal lives—the good and the bad, generosity and deception, parental manipulation and sibling rivalry. Occasionally we are reminded that it is God who really runs the show, but God does so in a remarkably restrained way. This is the "hidden hand" of God. The God of Sinai is hardly hidden.

Finally, near the end of Moses' career, in his final address to the Israelite community, Moses has this to say about God's covenant with Israel: "I make this covenant, with its sanctions, not with you alone, but both with those who are standing here with us this day before the Lord our God and with those who are not with us here this day" (Deuteronomy 29:13–14). In other words, every Jew throughout the generations stood at Sinai. The issue of the authority of Torah is not simply the accuracy of some event that occurred centuries ago, but of the impact of Torah in our lives to this day. It applies to us as well, as it has applied and will continue to apply to every heir of that tradition. It's not only their issue, it's ours as well.

The Liberal Option

Liberal thinkers, myself included, challenge every detail of this traditionalist version of revelation on three grounds. First, on theological grounds, they claim that God does not literally "speak." Humans speak; God may "speak," but only metaphorically. If the claim that God spoke to Moses is not a literal claim, then the "words" of Torah did not originate with God. If they are not God's words, the only other possibility is that they are human words. Rarely in the entire Torah is God characterized in such starkly anthropomorphic terms. Apart from "speaking," this God "descends" onto a specific spot on earth on a specific day. This God functions in space and time. Is this characterization of God literally true? Is it not again metaphorical? To accept it as literally true seems to diminish God. Space and time are human constructs, human ways of structuring our experience of the world. God is beyond both.

Second, liberal theologians take seriously the findings of modern biblical criticism. The Pentateuch is not one coherent book, these scholars claim, but rather a composite of at least four distinctive units, composed and canonized at different times over the centuries and edited into its present form in the time of Ezra (c. 550 B.C.E., approximately seven centuries after Moses' death. This explains the many overlappings, contradictions, gaps, and duplications in the text as we have it. It also explains the multiple borrowings from ancient Near Eastern literature throughout the book, such as the flood story, the parallels in biblical legislation to the Code of Hammurabi, and the very notion of covenant (in Hebrew, *brit*), the linchpin of God's relationship with Israel, which, Bible scholars believe, derives from Hittite suzerainty treaties.

Third, the anthropological implications of the traditionalist position are troubling. What does it say about the status and the role of humanity? Here, God alone is active; the human community is totally passive. Any substantive human contribution to the contents of Torah is dismissed as a dilution of God's authority. For modern liberal Jewish thinkers, this probably represents the core of the issue. Deny from the outset a substantive human contribution to Torah, and you also rule out the right of future generations to revisit the original revelation in terms of its ability to evoke modern religious impulse, to abandon laws that seem to be immoral today (such as those affecting the status of women in Jewish ritual and liturgical practice), and to change still others. The traditionalist position diminishes the human factor; the liberal position accords the community a shared role in shaping Torah. We become God's partners in revelation. God accords us that power in explicit recognition of our standing in God's eyes.

The net impact of these claims is that the authority for what is in Torah is as much human as it is divine. How much is human and how much is divine, and what is the nature of each contribution? On this modern thinkers disagree. What is agreed upon, however, is that people were partners with God in revelation from the very beginning, and therefore divine authority over Torah is substantially diluted. Modern quarrels with Torah are not necessarily with God but rather with prior human understandings of God's will. People can disagree on how to understand God's will, and these understandings can change and continue to change throughout history. The authority of Torah is no longer absolute and eternal; it has now become relativized. This change is hardly trivial. Religion, it is commonly believed, should represent a source of absolute values in this age of rampant moral confusion. Now Torah seems to have become one additional source of ambiguity.

A thorough discussion of the specific formulations of the liberal position is beyond the scope of this inquiry, but here are three brief versions of the position, as adopted by three influential twentieth-century theologians: Abraham Joshua Heschel, Franz Rosenzweig, and Mordecai Kaplan. In each case, we will capture the position through a brief quotation from the author's writings and then add an equally brief explication of the position.

Abraham Joshua Heschel: "As a report about revelation, the Bible itself is a midrash."[4]

A midrash is an interpretation, usually of a biblical narrative, verse, or word. It goes beyond the explicit sense of the original in order to disclose a more elusive or hidden meaning in the text. Heschel's startling claim is that Exodus 19–24 is itself a midrash, an interpretation of the Sinai event that is beyond explicit, literal expression. God revealed Torah, but what Israel has is our ancestors' interpretation of that event, not an accurate, literally true, historical account. If the entire account is a midrash, then the substance of Torah, what the text refers to as God's "words," is part of the midrash, part of the human interpretation. Torah may have originated as God's words, but what has reached us has passed through the screen of human understanding and human language. What we have is a human attempt to render an event that surpasses those words.

Franz Rosenzweig: "Thus revelation is certainly not Law-giving. It is only this: Revelation. The primary content of revelation is revelation itself."[5]

The difference between Rosenzweig's position and Heschel's is that for Heschel, God revealed a substantive Torah, of which we have the human version; for Rosenzweig, the substance of revelation is God's presence. What God revealed was God's self in an intimate relationship with Israel; the Torah itself was not explicitly revealed but represents Israel's later attempt to capture the sense of what God's self-revelation implied in terms of the life experience of the community. It is a human response to the revelation, not its substance. In what sense, then, can we speak of Torah as revealed?

> Mordecai Kaplan: "I can understand why our ancestors believed the Torah (and its authoritative interpretations) to have been 'divine revelation.' For me, however, those concepts and values explicitly conveyed or implied in it which I can accept as valid represent discovery, partial and tentative glimpses into the true nature of human life."[6]

This statement is not Kaplan's own, but rather that of his most prominent disciple, Rabbi Ira Eisenstein. However, Kaplan would surely agree. Kaplan was a religious naturalist: Religion (including Judaism) is a thoroughly natural, intuitive creation of human communities. The result is that, for Kaplan, what we call "revelation" is really "human discovery" of the values and ideals that this community determined were indispensable for living in the presence of God. Note the difference between reveal and discover. The first attributes the initiative to God; the second, to human beings. This human discovery remains God's revelation because it is God, operating thoroughly within and through the human community, who prompted these discoveries. As we have noted, Kaplan's God is not a transcendent being but rather a power or impulse operating within and through the natural order.[7]

These three versions of the liberal option differ in the respective roles assigned to God and human beings. On this issue, Heschel is closer to the traditionalist position and Kaplan is the furthest removed, but they agree on one central claim: in each case, the human factor plays a decisive role in determining what God wills. In contrast, the traditionalist position insists that what we have is precisely what God wills.

One more striking statement of this position is in a comment of a nineteenth-century Hasidic rabbi, Mendel of Rymanov, as reported by Gershom Scholem, the late, undisputed scholar of Jewish mysticism. (We say "reported" here because Scholem does not document the statement.) Rabbi Mendel's view is that God's revelation consisted solely of the first letter of the first word of the ten commandments, the *aleph* of the Hebrew word *anokhi* ("I" in the phrase "I am the Lord Your God"). Scholem continues:

> In Hebrew the consonant *aleph* may be said to denote the source of all articulate sound.... To hear the *aleph* is to hear next to nothing; it is the preparation for all audible language, but in itself conveys no determinate, specific meaning.... Thus...Rabbi Mendel transformed the revelation on Mount Sinai into a mystical revelation, pregnant with infinite meaning, but without specific meaning. In order to become a foundation of religious authority, it had to be translated into human language, and that is what Moses did.[8]

In teaching this text, I frequently use a modern analogy. It is as if at Sinai, God gave Moses a blank computer disk and then let Moses fill it with content. What was revelatory about Sinai was God handing Moses the disk. What was human was what Moses put on the disk. There is no more striking portrayal of the substantive human contribution to Torah than this.

Heteronomy versus Autonomy

The tension between the traditionalist and liberal options on revelation stems from a basic disagreement on both the nature of humanity and the nature of God. It is a difference between two models for human behavior: one portrays humanity as bowing to an authority that is "other than," or beyond the world of humanity (the heteronomous model, from the Greek: *heter* = other; *nomos* = law); the second finds the source of authority within the individual (the autonomous model, also from the Greek, *auto* = self). In practice, we function with both models. We bow to the laws of the state, but those same laws guarantee us basic freedoms through which we express our personal values. How do these two models apply in regard to the dictates and practices of religion? The traditionalist option accentuates the heteronomous model: God spoke, we obey. The liberal model accentuates the autonomous model, or at least redresses the balance between the two. Whatever God commands and however we understand that process, the ultimate authority for determining our obligations lies within the human community, which in our day includes ourselves, for we too were standing at Sinai.

This anthropological distinction reflects a theological distinction. In one model, God is all-powerful, transcendent, and absolute. In the second, God is more vulnerable, dependent, and generous. God shares God's power with humanity and accords human beings at least an equal role in shaping the contents of Torah. These two polarities in Judaism's understanding of God's nature emerge in two frequently quoted rabbinic homilies, advanced by thinkers who seek to promote one of the two images over the other. The first begins with a legal discussion on a relatively arcane detail of the laws of ritual purity and impurity. It focuses on a certain type of oven and on whether or not an oven constructed that way is susceptible to becoming ritually impure. The vast majority of the court decided that it was; one sage alone, the late first-century C.E. Rabbi Eliezer ben Hyrkanos, disagreed. Rather than bowing to the will of the majority, Rabbi Eliezer continued to argue in favor of his position and invoked a series of miraculous, divine actions supporting his view: a carob tree was uprooted, a stream flowed backward, the walls of the schoolhouse tilted, but all to no avail. Finally, he called upon a heavenly voice to support his view, whereupon a heavenly voice called out, "Why do you dispute with Rabbi Eliezer, seeing that in all matters the *halakhah* (Jewish law) agrees with him?" Whereupon,

> Rabbi Joshua, the head of the court, arose and exclaimed:
> "It [Torah] is not in heaven"[quoting Deuteronomy 30:12].
> What did he mean by this? Said Rabbi Jeremiah: "...The
> Torah has already been given at Sinai; we pay no atten-
> tion to a heavenly voice, because You have long written in
> the Torah at Mount Sinai, 'Incline after the majority'
> [Exodus 23:2]."[9]

This is a powerful statement of the case for human autonomy
and for the legitimacy of independent human legal reasoning. Note
also that it is God who, in the very same Torah, legitimatizes this
autonomous human role. Whatever God "really" willed is irrelevant. God now wills whatever the majority of the human court
determines.

The conclusion of the story confirms our autonomous model.
We are told that another rabbi, Rabbi Nathan, met Elijah, who,
according to Scripture, never really died but ascended to heaven
alive in a fiery chariot (2 Kings 2:11–12). He is portrayed as
appearing again and again to individual rabbis. Rabbi Nathan
asked Elijah: "What did the Holy Blessed One do in that hour?"
"He [God] laughed and replied, saying, 'My children have defeated me. My children have defeated Me.'"[10]

It is abundantly clear why this story is constantly advanced in
support of the autonomous position. It is a powerful affirmation of
the place of the human factor in determining God's will and therefore of the status of human beings in God's creation. It is also a
statement about the nature of God. This is a God who surrenders
God's own power to humanity and not only accepts the human verdict but even laughs.

The contrary, heteronomous posture emerges in the following
brief comment on Exodus 19:17: "Moses led the people out of the
camp toward God, and they took their places at the foot of the
mountain" (or, more literally, "under the mountain"). Commenting

on the phrase "at the foot of the mountain," Rabbi Abdimi ben Hama ben Hasa said: "This teaches that the Holy Blessed One overturned the mountain upon them like a barrel, and said to them, 'If you accept the Torah, it is well [for you]. If not, here shall be your graves.'"[11]

There is not much autonomy in this version of Sinai! Apparently Israel was not overly eager to receive the Torah; God had to force the people to do so on pain of death. It also suggests a very different image of God. This God compels people to do God's will. The human role is passive. God demands total submission.

Both of these texts are included in classical Jewish literature, even though they reflect a fundamental disagreement on the part of the Rabbis regarding the nature of God, the status of human beings, and the authority of Torah. So do the plurality of images that the different views on revelation imply.

We Are Partners with God in Revelation

The Rabbis were very much aware of the fact that their expansion of Jewish law went far beyond anything explicitly written in the Torah. The elaborate system of dietary laws concerning the mixing of meat and milk, for example, rests on one single biblical injunction, repeated three times in the Torah: "You shall not boil a kid in its mother's milk" (Exodus 23:19; 34:26, and Deuteronomy 14:21).

God also tells the angels that the very determination of the day on which the festival of Rosh Hashanah, which opens the season of judgment, is to be observed is Israel's:

If the [human] court declares, "Today is Rosh Hashanah," God says to the angels: "Set up the [heavenly] court, let the defense attorneys arise, let the prosecuting attorneys arise, because My children have declared that today is Rosh Hashanah." If the [human] court...decides to postpone it to the next day, God says..."Remove the [heavenly] court, let the prosecuting attorneys leave, because My children decided to postpone it to tomorrow."[12]

The contemporary American-Israeli traditionalist thinker David Hartman portrays the heteronomy-autonomy tension this way:

> On the one hand, there is an unconditional acceptance of revelation.... For the Talmud, no autonomous human authority can set aside the divine revelation embodied in the written Torah. On the other hand, it is clear to anyone familiar with the Talmud that rabbinic teachers exhibit enormous interpretive freedom and mastery over the revealed text. God...in the end must submit to the procedural rules of human academies of learning.[13]

Contemporary traditionalist thinkers accept this notion of a human partnership with God in elaborating the further (i.e., rabbinic) substance of Torah, although they would insist that even here it is God who is guiding the deliberations of the human authorities and that these later innovations were also revealed to Moses, who transmitted them orally to his successors, the rabbis of the Talmud, and contemporary rabbinic authorities. However, these thinkers also maintain that this view in no way impinges on the Sinai revelation itself, which was all God's work. Liberal theologians, on the other hand, extend the notion of a substantive human contribution to Torah to include the Sinai revelation itself. The human factor was present from the outset.

The tension between heteronomy and autonomy is then resolved in many different ways, reflecting the explicit or implicit theologies of different thinkers. The range of possible resolutions enriches our own struggle with this issue.

9

God Redeems

To Redeem Is to Save

One day some months ago, as I was working on this book, I was confounded by the fact that my word processor had decided to ignore all my commands. As I was banging my head in frustration, a student knocked on my office door. I immediately realized that like all of my students, he really knew word processing. As he walked in, I exclaimed, "I know that my redeemer lives!" I was quoting Job (19:25), admittedly in a slightly more trivial setting than Job's, but at that moment I totally identified with Job's situation. I was in deep trouble, and this student was going to rescue me. He did, in about thirty seconds.

To *redeem* means to rescue or to save. The claim that God redeems, has redeemed, and will again redeem Israel and all of humanity means that God has, and will, save or rescue—but save or rescue from what?

In Jewish sources, the earliest answer to that question was the Jewish people from slavery in Egypt; this was the founding event in Jewish history. The original manifestation of God's rescuing was on behalf of the Jewish people; its focus was national. However, since every event in Jewish history was understood to have a religious dimension as well, and since Jews believed that it was precisely God who had redeemed the Jewish people from oppression, that redemption was understood to be a religious claim as well as a national one. There simply was no distinction between the national or political dimension of Jewish history and its religious dimension. Eventually, because the God of Israel was the God of all humanity, God's redemptive power soon acquired a universal dimension. God was, at least potentially, the redeemer of all humanity—indeed, of the world as a whole.

The Exodus from Egypt served as the prologue for God's everlasting covenant with Israel, later to be sealed at Mount Sinai. The very opening words of that covenantal statement in Exodus 20 identify the God who now enters into that covenant as "the Lord Your God who brought you out of the land of Egypt, the house of bondage" (Exodus 20:2). There follows an implied "Therefore," and the rest of Torah flows from that initial identification. The Exodus and Sinai were actually one single transformatory event that created both the Jewish people and Judaism as we know it to this day.

Jews are commanded to remember the day of their departure from the land of Egypt every day of their lives (Deuteronomy 16:3), which is why the theme appears in the third paragraph of the *Shema* liturgy (Numbers 15:37–41), which Jews recite at least twice daily, morning and evening. The concluding words of the Redemption benediction, which follows the recitation of the *Shema* as the Creation and Revelation benedictions precede it, praises God, "Who redeemed Israel."

From History to Eschatology

In the post-biblical tradition, God's national, political, and religious act of rescuing Israel from bondage becomes the guarantor for God's repeated rescuing of Israel from all its future travails. Not unexpectedly, that guarantee appears explicitly in this text from the Passover *haggadah*, the liturgy that is used for the Passover *seder*, the home celebration of the Exodus. Its source is the tenth chapter of *Mishnah Pesachim,* which outlines the rituals and liturgies to be followed on Passover eve.

The primary purpose of this celebration is to tell the story of the Exodus. When our children or our guests ask why we observe Passover, we are to explain to them, "It is because of what the Lord did for me when I went free from Egypt" (Exodus 13:8). The *Mishnah* is not at all explicit on the precise details of how we are to tell the story, but it does make one stipulation: we are to "begin with the disgrace and end with the glory" (10:4). More colloquially, we are to begin with the bad news and end with the good news. The Passover *haggadah* that we use today, dating at the earliest from the ninth century C.E., suggests various versions of the bad news: Egyptian bondage, the idolatry of Abraham's ancestors, and Jacob's persecution at the hands of his uncle, Laban. It is unanimous about the good news: the redemption from Egypt.

The *Mishnah* (10:6) also stipulates that we conclude the telling of the story with this benediction—dubbed, appropriately, the *Geulah,* or Redemption benediction: "Blessed are You God, Lord of the universe, who redeemed us and redeemed our ancestors from Egypt, and has enabled us to reach this night whereon we eat unleavened bread and bitter herbs."

Two points about this statement are worth noting. First, the redemption from Israel was not simply an event in the past, not just history; it is also contemporaneous, an event in the present. Not only were our ancestors redeemed, but so were we, so were all generations of Jews. The Exodus did not happen *then;* it happens *today,* every day, to us as well. A similar claim is made by all cultures in regard to the great transformatory events in their histories. These events inhabit a perpetual present. For example, on Easter Sunday Christians do not say, "Christ arose!" but rather "Christ is risen!" This claim is not disingenuous. The great events in the life of a community enjoy a perpetual, ongoing resonance. They remain eternally present.

Second, the *Mishnah* identifies the author of the text as Rabbi Tarfon, a mid-second-century C.E. rabbi. At that time, the Jewish People were again suffering through a period of oppression, this time at the hands of the Roman empire. Jerusalem and the Second Temple had been destroyed (in 70 C.E.), and the Jews had begun to scatter into exile. The *Mishnah*, then, is not content with Rabbi Tarfon's statement, and so it suggests an addition in the name of his contemporary, Rabbi Akiva (10:6):

> Therefore, O Lord our God and God of our ancestors, bring us in peace to the other forthcoming feasts and festivals, while we rejoice in the rebuilding of Your city [Jerusalem] and in Your worship; and there, may we [again] eat the sacrifices and the Passover offerings.... We will [then] chant a new song to You for our redemption and for our deliverance. Blessed are You who has redeemed Israel.

Today we recite both texts consecutively. The historical memory of God's initial deliverance becomes the basis for a plea for God's further deliverance from oppression, originally of Akiva's day and now of our own day. Indeed, the earlier deliverance serves as a paradigm for—or, more precisely, assures—the later ones. Note the use of the word "Therefore," which introduces Rabbi Akiva's prayer; it connects the past redemption to the forthcoming one, for we are painfully aware that in historical time, oppression, in one form or another, will always be with us. The final step in the evolution of the doctrine of divine redemption is the expectation of some ultimate act of deliverance that will destroy all manner of oppression, this time forever.

God's redemptive power is the centerpiece of Jewish eschatology (from the Greek: *eschaton* = last things; *logos* = discourse), the umbrella term for the body of teaching that describes the events that will occur at the end of days, at the culmination of history as we know it. Jewish eschatology is a singularly complex and imaginative body of teachings because it purports to discuss events that no human eyes have ever witnessed. This doctrine also evolved throughout Jewish history. In its fully developed form, dating from the talmudic period, it describes events that will take place in three dimensions: a universal dimension (events that will affect the entire cosmos), a national dimension (affecting the Jewish People), and an individual dimension (affecting each individual). In one way or another, each of these scenarios describes God as the initiator of the drama. All eschatologies stem from one common impulse: the sense that things as they are now are deeply flawed. The redemptive scenarios then proceed to describe how at the end of time God will transform the flawed into the perfect. All speak of a God who saves, rescues, and delivers people or, ultimately, the cosmos as a whole, from an imperfect state.

God Redeems the World

In the universal dimension, the flawed state of affairs is a world where injustice, warfare, oppression, and social evils of all kind govern human relations. At the end of days, God will abolish all of these and create a new world order in which peace, justice, and compassion will pervade all human relationships. Idolatry will be abolished, and all the nations of the world will acknowledge the God of Israel as their God.

This is the most ancient statement of Jewish eschatology, and its power persists to this day. It is the impulse that inspires every movement that challenges us, our governments, and our social structures to improve the lot of the oppressed in our midst. It is implicit in one of the central themes of all prophetic literature, the biting prophetic critique of social evil. Its earliest statement is in fact in prophetic literature—for example, in this memorable vision of the sixth-century B.C.E. prophet whose writings are included in the Book of Isaiah, recited appropriately as the prophetic reading for the fast day of Yom Kippur. The prophet describes the "fasting" that God really desires above all. God speaks:

> No, this is the fast I desire:
> To unlock the fetters of wickedness...
> To let the oppressed go free;
> To break every yoke.
> It is to share your bread with the hungry,
> And to take the wretched poor into your home;
> When you see the naked, to clothe him
> And not to ignore your kin.
>
> *—Isaiah 58:6–7*

In the vision of the opening chapter of the Book of Isaiah, the very first chapter in the collection of prophetic writings, God again speaks:

> Wash yourselves clean:
> Put your evil doings
> Away from My sight.
> Cease to do evil:
> Learn to do good.
> Devote yourself to justice;
> Aid the wronged.
> Uphold the rights of the orphan;
> Defend the cause of the widow.
>
> *—Isaiah 1:16–17*

These are the flaws that pervade our social structure and that demand redemption. Therefore, in the chapter that follows immediately—the juxtaposition is not at all coincidental—there follows the noble prophetic vision of the ideal age to come. A society that embodies the prophet's moral vision will lead the world into an age in which the greatest of social evils, warfare, will disappear.

> In the days to come,
> The Mount of the Lord's House
> Shall stand firm above the mountains....
> And the many peoples shall go and say: "Come,
> Let us go up to the Mount of the Lord
> To the House of the God of Jacob;
> That He may instruct us in His ways,
> And that we may walk in His paths."
> For instruction shall come forth from Zion,
> The word of the Lord from Jerusalem.
> Thus He will judge among the nations
> And arbitrate for the many peoples,
> And they shall beat their swords into ploughshares
> And their spears into pruning hooks:
> Nation shall not take up
> Sword against nation;
> They shall never again know war.
>
> —*Isaiah 2:2–4*

Reflecting on this passage, my teacher, the late Professor Heschel, once said: "No other thinker in all of antiquity ever dreamed of an age when there would be no more war." That vision continues to exercise its power to this very day.

God Redeems Israel

The national dimension of Jewish eschatology extends the theme of God's redemption of Israel from Egypt: God will once again rescue Israel from the oppression of foreign nations, and Israel will return to its own land, freed from the yoke of the exile and as the master of its own destiny. Jerusalem and the Temple will be rebuilt, and the sacrificial cult will be restored. Israel will also teach the nations to worship the God of Israel.

One of the earliest statements of this theme appears in prophetic literature, this time in the Book of Jeremiah. Jeremiah is commonly understood to be a prophet of doom, but his work includes this striking prophecy of consolation that will follow God's imminent destruction of Jerusalem:

> For thus said the Lord...:
> I will bring them [Israel] from the northland,
> Gather them from the end of the earth—
> The blind and the lame among them,
> Those with child and those in labor—
> In a vast throng they shall return here....
> I will turn their mourning to joy,
> I will comfort them and cheer them in their grief....
> Truly, Ephraim is a dear son to Me,
> A child who is dandled!
> Whenever I have turned against him,
> My thoughts will dwell on him still.
> That is why My heart yearns for him;
> I will receive him back in love.
>
> *—Jeremiah 31:7–20*

The subsequent evolution of this national dimension of Jewish eschatology is considerably more complicated than the universal one. The Temple and Jerusalem were destroyed in 586 B.C.E., just a few short years after Jeremiah's prophecy, and Israel was exiled to Babylonia, but Jeremiah's prophecy of redemption was soon to be fulfilled. Israel did return from that exile, but the Temple and Jerusalem were destroyed again, centuries later, by Rome. Once again Israel experienced exile, and that exilic experience lasted until our own day with the reestablishment of an independent Jewish state in 1948. Jews who read modern Jewish history in religious terms view this event as the beginning of a renewed redemptive process. In that spirit, the prayer for the State of Israel, recited in many synagogues in our own day, asks that God bless the State of Israel, "the first flowering of our redemption." But contemporary secular Jews, either American or Israeli, along with the more extreme religious Jews who do not recognize the modern state as fulfilling God's will, do not recite this prayer.

God Redeems from Death

Finally, on the individual dimension, God will rescue human beings from the ultimate flaw that pervades human existence: death. Human bodies will be resurrected from their graves and reunited with their souls. Thus reconstituted, as we once were on earth, all of humanity will come before God in judgment. Death itself will die at the hands of God, whose sovereignty and power will now be ultimate.

This final aspect of Jewish eschatology was the latest to enter into Jewish thought. In most of the Bible, death was understood to be final. Only in the middle of the second century B.C.E. do we find a biblical text that suggests that God will raise the dead from the graves: "Many of those that sleep in the dust of the earth will awake, some to eternal life, others to reproaches, to everlasting abhorrence" (Daniel 12:2). The doctrine of bodily resurrection became canonized in Jewish liturgy in the second benediction of the *amidah*, which praises God as one "who resurrects the dead" or "gives life to the dead." In the modern age, many Jews have found this doctrine to be repugnant. Reform prayer books, for example, replace these words with the more neutral phrase "who gives life to all things" or "source of life." In place of the doctrine of bodily resurrection, many modern Jews have embraced an equally ancient Jewish doctrine that originated in Greek philosophy, the doctrine of the immortality of the soul. At death, our souls leave our bodies and join with God; this constitutes human immortality.[1]

As for the ultimate death of death, that theme emerges in the concluding stanza of the Passover hymn *Chad Gadya* ("One Single Goat"), with which we conclude the Passover seder. In this stanza, the Holy Blessed One is portrayed as slaughtering the Angel of Death. God's power will then be unchallenged, even by death.

This entire eschatological drama is to take place under the aegis of either a singularly endowed human king or, in other traditions, a divine or semidivine being who came to be called the Messiah (in Hebrew, *mashiach,* or "anointed one," because in antiquity, and even in our own day, sovereigns are crowned by anointing them with oil). It is God who, in God's own time, will send the Messiah. Until then, we simply await his coming.

We have now moved well beyond the original, narrow national sense of redemption. All eschatologies are inherently mythical statements—complex, imaginative metaphors that take us well beyond our everyday human experience, beyond what we can ever hope to see with our eyes. As with all great myths, their goal is to help us infuse our lives with the kind of meaning that we could never hope to achieve through reason alone. At this point, the theme of redemption becomes profoundly religious in the deepest sense of that term; it addresses the most persistent issue posed by human existence, the sense that our lives and the world we inhabit are, in some profound sense, flawed. All eschatologies are visions of an age of cosmos against the backdrop of the chaos that pervades human life as we live it in the here and now. They impose order over anarchy, meaning over senselessness. If God is really God, then this God must have redemptive power.

The World Is Not Yet Redeemed

That God is a redeeming God is testimony to God's power, but that redemptive power is strangely ambiguous, for if God's redemptive power will be manifest only at the end of days, then the inescapable implication is that in the here and now God's power is not fully manifest. The concluding verse from the prophet Zechariah (14:9), with which we conclude every formal Jewish service of worship and which we studied at length in chapter 1, has a significant implication here. The context is a vivid description of "the day of the Lord," a common prophetic characterization for the age that will mark the culmination of history as we know it. The vision is apocalyptic: the familiar structures of nature will be overturned; there will be neither sunlight nor moonlight, just one continuous day; God will wage war against the evil nations and smite them with a plague. All who survive will make a pilgrimage to Jerusalem to worship the God of Israel. And then "the Lord will be king over all the earth; on that day there shall be one Lord with one name," or as other translations would have it, on that day "the Lord alone shall be worshiped and shall be invoked by His true name."

All of this will happen "on that day," but that day has not yet come to pass. In the time in which the prophecy was uttered—Zechariah lived in the sixth century B.C.E.—most of the Israelites were still living in Persia, and although Jerusalem and the Temple were beginning to be rebuilt, the dead had still not been resurrected, nor was God "alone" being worshiped by all the nations of the earth. Nor had any of the other events long prophesied as characterizing the ideal age to come yet taken place. Nor have any of those events taken place in our own day, when we continue to recite this verse daily.

We confront here the same ambiguity that we have seen throughout this study. In theory, God's power is absolute; in practice, it is far from that. At the end of days, God's power will be manifest; today, in historical time, it remains muted. God may be a redeeming God, but the full flowering of that redemption lies in the indefinite future.

The ambiguity is reflected in the various forms that the Hebrew word for redeemer, *goel,* appears in the liturgy. Return to the closing words of the two redemption benedictions that we studied above, the one that follows the recitation of the *Shema* and the one that concludes the Passover narrative. In both, the word appears in the past tense: *ga'al,* translated as "has redeemed," and referring to God's redemption of Israel from Egyptian slavery. There is also a redemption benediction in the daily *amidah,* and there it appears in the present tense, *goel,* translated as "Redeemer of Israel" or "Who redeems Israel." In this context, the meaning seems to be that even though God may not be in the process of redeeming Israel in the here and now, God still has the power to redeem Israel. In a similar vein, the second benediction of the *amidah* speaks of God, "Who brings a redeemer to [Israel's] children's children." Again the verb is in the present tense.

Also note the references to a God who "resurrects" or "gives life to the dead," one of the central events in the classical Jewish eschatological drama. Again the verb is in the present tense, even though that resurrection has clearly not yet taken place. Why didn't the author of this benediction use the future tense of the term? Again the implication seems to be that God has the power to resurrect the dead, even though God has not as yet done so. Why not?

We pointed to that very same ambiguity in our earlier discussions of God as creator and revealer. As in those two other dimensions of God's relationship with humanity, God does not work alone. God depends on humanity for the full manifestation of God's power. In historical time, God and humanity are partners in redemption, as in creation and revelation.

Partners in Redemption

The most striking expression of that theme can be seen in the teachings of the sixteenth-century mystic Rabbi Isaac Luria. Luria, who lived and taught in the city of Safed in Palestine in the wake of the expulsion of the Jews from Spain at the end of the fifteenth century, wove ancient rabbinic and mystical traditions into a highly original myth of redemption for a generation of Jews that had once again tasted the bitter reality of exile and national trauma. These Jews were confronted, in the starkest way possible, with the fact that the world that they inhabited was profoundly flawed. Where indeed was God's redemptive power?

Luria's answer, far too complex to be traced in detail here, centers on the notion that from the very outset, God's entire creation was flawed. God created the world by emanation out of God's own being, so to speak, from an original "God-stuff." This emanation was designed to be contained in "vessels" that God had created so that the created world would emerge ordered or structured. However, those vessels were not strong enough to fulfill their assigned role. They shattered in a primordial catastrophic event, and the sparks of God's creative impulse came to be scattered throughout the cosmos. This scattering of the divine sparks accounts for the presence of all evil in the world, both natural evil and historical evil. In effect, the world was born flawed; it emerged broken from God's very hand.

The implication of that creation myth is that God is responsible for the evil in the world, but Luria's theory is even more radical. Since creation occurred as an emanation out of God's own being, the created world, with all its flaws, is at the same time an inherent part of God. Therefore, the flaws in the world are at the same time flaws within God. The world is broken, and so is God.

Luria posited that there were two faces to God: God in God's intrinsic essence, which he dubbed *Ein Sof* (literally, "Infinity" or "Without End"), the transcendent or hidden God; and *Shekhinah* (literally, "Presence"), God as immanent, manifest or present in creation. In that primordial catastrophe, these two faces of God were split asunder. Luria called that dislocation in God's being "the Exile of the *Shekhinah*." If Israel is in exile, then so is God.

Repairing the World

To this creation myth Luria now added a myth of redemption. The world needs to be mended or repaired, and so does God. The responsibility for mending the world is assigned to Israel, and the means of accomplishing this mending are the mitzvot, God's commands to Israel. Every mitzvah performed by a Jew, accompanied by the proper inner focus, is redemptive, an act of repairing the world. Since the world and God together form one cosmic system, as we repair the world we also repair the split within God. To use another metaphor, the entire cosmos is one giant pool. Drop a pebble in one corner of the pool, and the ripples affect the entire pool. The material world in which we live is but the outermost edge of this cosmic pool. Performing one simple command affects the entire system, up to and including God.

The Hebrew term for what we call "inner focus" is *kavanah*. Lurianic mystics composed brief liturgical statements, also called *kavanot* (plural for *kavanah*), to be recited before the performance of the commandments to ensure that we will indeed perform these commands with the proper intent—namely, to repair the split within God; reciting the words of these brief prayers serves to focus our thoughts. Before donning the *tallit* (the shawl Jews wear during prayer), for example, Jews were to say: "For the sake of the unification of the Holy Blessed One and His *Shekhinah*, in trembling and in love, to unify the name *Yod Heh* with *Vav Heh* in perfect unity, in the name of all Israel."

This is an incredible statement. First, the name "Holy Blessed One" (in the original Aramaic, *Kudshah Brikh Hu,* or in Hebrew, *Kadosh Barukh Hu*) is one of the traditional names for God. In kabbalistic thought it becomes a synonym for what we called *Ein Sof,* "Infinity," God in God's essence, the transcendent or hidden God. *Shekhinah* is God's presence in and through creation. They are now split apart, but we are about to perform a commandment that will repair or mend that split and unify God.

As the text continues, that responsibility is given even greater emphasis. The four Hebrew letters *Yod, Heh, Vav, Heh* form the Tetragrammaton, the unpronounceable, four-letter name of God, usually rendered in English as YHWH or YHVH (as in "Yahweh" or "Jehovah"). The split in God's nature is reflected in the split between the first two and the last two letters of God's holy name. By performing the command of donning the *tallit*, now with the proper inner focus or intent, we are helping to reunify God's name and, symbolically, the two faces of God.[2]

The conclusion is inescapable. Not only are Jews partners with God in redeeming the world, they are also partners with God in redeeming God. God too needs redemption. There is no more powerful statement of God's dependence on humanity.

Now place this myth of redemption in its historical context. In a very direct way, Jews had just experienced, once again, the full reality of a deeply flawed world. In this context, Luria provides them first with a measure of consolation: you are in exile, but so is God. Second, he provides them with the resources to mend the world and God. These resources are immediately at hand: they are the familiar, day-to-day responsibilities of every Jew, the divine commandments, such as donning the *tallit*. Testimony to the effectiveness of the myth is the fact that within a few generations, it led to one of the most traumatic events in Jewish history, the messianic movement centered on Shabbatai Zevi.

Shabbatai Zevi (1626–1676) was a Turkish Jew who proclaimed himself to be the Messiah, inflamed the Jewish people with his vision that the long-awaited end of days had finally arrived and that redemption was finally at hand, then converted to Islam and plunged the Jewish world into a renewed despair that took generations to overcome. The story of this failed Messiah is long and complex.[3] What is important to us here is its implicit testimony to the effectiveness of Luria's redemptive myth: Jews were fully prepared to believe that their work of repairing the world had accomplished its goal. That Shabbatai Zevi turned out to be a false or failed messiah is another story. The Achilles heel in all myths of redemption is the risk that they may be falsified by history. Myths of this kind are effective as long as they remain visions or dreams, always slightly out of reach. When they become so concrete that they lie within our immediate grasp, they inevitably disappoint. Redemption is always around the corner. The main purpose of the vision is less to forecast events that lie ahead than to make the here and now bearable. The redemptive myth must remain a dream deferred.

Luria's Hebrew term for "repairing" or "mending" the world was *tikkun*. That term has achieved renewed popularity in our own day in the phrase *tikkun olam*—literally, "repairing the world." It is used to characterize social and political activities undertaken by Jewish groups that have the general purpose of making the world a better place. The term itself is ancient. It appears originally in the *Mishnah,* where it is used to justify a series of legal enactments that were promulgated for the public welfare—literally, "in order to repair the world." To give one example, *Mishnah Gittin* 4:3 teaches, "Hillel ordained the *prozbol* in order to repair the world." According to Deuteronomy 15:1–3, in every seventh, or sabbatical, year, all debts are to be remitted. However, the Bible also warns us lest, as the sabbatical year approaches, we avoid lending money to the poor (Deuteronomy 15:9–11). To avoid that eventuality, Hillel, the first-century C.E. rabbinic master, enacted a procedure whereby on the eve of the seventh year the creditor may make a declaration before the court that would insulate his loans from the law of remission. That declaration was called *prozbol* (from the Greek for "before the court"). The purpose of the declaration, then, was broadly redemptive; it was designed to guarantee the availability of loans for the poor.

The phrase occurs in another rabbinic passage, that same closing paragraph of the daily Jewish worship service that concludes with Zechariah's prophecy that we noted above. The paragraph begins with these words:

> We hope in You, Lord our God, soon to see Your splendor, when You will sweep away idolatry so that false gods will be utterly destroyed, when You will repair the world under Your kingship, so that all of humankind will invoke Your name.

That text, together with its opening paragraph, also dates from the rabbinic period; it was composed as an introduction to the recitation of the passages proclaiming God's sovereignty, part of the High Holiday *musaf* ("additional")—an additional service in the daily morning worship on Sabbaths and festivals. Here, it is God who will in time "repair" the world. In the case of Hillel's *prozbol,* we act to perfect the world. Luria's use of the term takes us far beyond these earlier references. Now repairing the world also effects a repair within God's very being.

The Power That Makes for Salvation

For Mordecai Kaplan, redemption defines God. Kaplan was far from enamored of Jewish mysticism. He was far too hard-headed and rational a thinker. However, note two aspects of his thought. First, Kaplan's characteristic definition of God is that God is the power that makes for salvation. Second, recall that Kaplan was a naturalist theologian. God is not a being located in some supernatural realm. Kaplan placed God, this salvational impulse, precisely in the world, in people, in nature, and in history.

Here is one of Kaplan's many definitions of salvation:

Man, once his physiological needs are satisfied, begins to experience the need to overcome such traits as self-indulgence, arrogance, envy, exploitation and hatred, or to bring under control the aggressive forces of his nature. That constitutes man's true destiny. Therein lies his salvation.[4]

Kaplan characterizes the next step in his argument as "no blind leap into the dark":

The next step is to conclude that the cosmos is so consti-tuted as to enable man to fulfill this highest human need of his nature.... *The fact that the cosmos possesses the resources and man the abilities—which are themselves part of those resources— to enable him to fulfill his destiny as a human being, or to achieve salvation, is the Godhood of the cosmos.*

The entire world—literally, all there is—is pervaded with an elemental power, force, or impulse that Kaplan likens to a magnet-ic force and that drives all things to achieve perfection. That power is itself God; it is not caused by God, not created by God; it *is* God. This God is most immediately experienced within us—within our hearts, our minds, and our behavior—precisely at those moments when we strive to banish "those aggressive forces" of our nature. True, that very same power exists outside us, where it serves to complement human efforts, but without our efforts there is no sal-vation. The world may furnish us with the resources to conquer dis-ease, but without scientists to work with these resources, cures will never result. The resemblance to Luria's mystical myth is uncanny.

The parallels between Luria and Kaplan are even deeper, for in the present time, in history, Kaplan's God's redemptive power is not yet fully manifest. Kaplan's God is not all-powerful. The world may well be infused with this power that makes for salvation, but other powers are also at work in the world: counter-salvational impulses, the powers of chaos and anarchy. We may have found a cure for polio, but what about AIDS? Kaplan's God needs redemption, too. Again, it is humanity that can help to achieve God's own redemption.

We are left with the inescapable conclusion that the image of God portrayed in Jewish sources is very different from the popular conventional image. We were all trained to believe that God, at least, has it all together. This is not so, say our sources. In theory it may be true, but in practice it is not. The God that we experience is a God who needs humanity to achieve God's own purposes. This is a God who is frustrated, who dreams dreams for humanity and the world, who is rebuffed but returns again and again, with infinite yearning, pleading for our help to achieve God's purposes and our own as well. That may well be God's most striking tribute to us.

Epilogue

Upon reviewing the final draft of this book, I am left with feelings of both astonishment and liberation: astonishment at the sheer audacity of a community that concedes that the God whom it worships daily remains beyond human understanding, but yet writes voluminously about this God's wishes, thoughts, feelings, and behavior; astonishment at the candor with which the members of this community record how they experience God—the joy and the pain, the nurturing and the punitive, the bright side and the dark side—and at the richness of the images that these feelings generate; astonishment at the plurality and fluidity of these images, how they blatantly contradict one another, how they evolve as the texts parade before our very eyes and as we traverse the liturgical day, week, month, and year and the cycles of our lives.

I also feel liberation, however, because if our ancestors reveled in the freedom to speak of God in all these ways, then so can we. Their awareness of God's transcendence might well have left them mute, paralyzed by the fear that to speak of God was somehow to betray God. Instead, they acknowledged the inherent limitations of their humanness and proceeded to ignore it. They drew their images from their most familiar relationships: parent, judge, spouse, lover, military general, shepherd, teacher. Indeed, the more familiar, the better, for to them God was close at hand, intimately related, and, above all, concerned. Out of these images they composed stories, psalms, laws, liturgies, midrashim, mystical and philosophical texts, and sermons—the entire body of what we call Torah.

We can do the same. Of course, I hope that this book will be read, taught, and studied. However, it will fulfill its ultimate purpose if it impels you, its reader, to reach into yourself, come in touch with your own religious experiences, create your own images—the less conventional the better—and put them on paper, and share them with your family and friends.

For some years now I have asked my students to do just that, and their statements are collected in a rapidly expanding file in my office. Don't be intimidated. Most people confess that the first sentence is the most difficult to write, but then the rest flows naturally. I never fail to be amazed at what emerges. There are profound theological depths in the hearts and minds of the people I meet in the course of my teaching.

Writing is important. We all have significant experiences, but they tend to fade under the pressure of our daily tasks. Writing forces us to externalize them. Now we can look at them, consider them, and share them. Out of the sharing comes community, the sense that others think and feel as we do, or don't feel as we do but still care as we do, and then we can talk.

The talking is the most amazing phenomenon of all. There is an unrequited thirst for religious sharing among people today. People think about these issues but never talk about them. We talk about politics, sports, the stock market, the condition of our lawns and our cars. We rarely talk about the ultimate issues: our dread of death, our sense of loneliness and isolation, our failed relationships, the fragmented quality of our daily lives, and the desperate need to find a measure of meaning, to counter the absurdity that seems to pervade all we do. If we don't talk about these questions, however, then we are truly alone.

So read, write, share, and talk.

Notes

Introduction

1. Abraham Joshua Heschel, *Who Is Man?* (Stanford, Calif.: Stanford University Press, 1965).
2. The translation is from Isadore Twersky, *A Maimonides Reader* (West Orange, N.J.: Behrman House, 1972), 44–45.
3. Adapted from Philip Birnbaum, trans., *High Holiday Prayer Book* (New York: Hebrew Publishing Company, 1951), 127–128.

Chapter 1: God Is *Echad*

1. Twersky, 410.
2. Ibid., 46.
3. The 1985 Jewish Publication Society (JPS) translation of this last passage reads: "I make weal and create woe—I the Lord do all these things." I appreciate the alliterative value of that translation (although the alliteration is not present in the original Hebrew), but "weal" and "woe" are unfamiliar terms to modern ears, and the translation fails to capture the order/chaos dualism that is the very point of the prophet's message. The Hebrew for "weal" is *shalom,* which is conventionally translated as "peace" but which literally means "harmony" or "cosmos." The Hebrew for "woe" is *ra,* which, in Genesis 2:9, JPS translates as "bad" ("the tree of knowledge of good and bad"). Thus, the tension is between "good" and "bad" or between "cosmos" and "chaos."
4. For an elaboration of the implications of this polytheistic view of the world, see E. A. Speiser, "Introduction," *The Anchor Bible Genesis* (New York: Doubleday, 1964), xliii—lii.
5. *Mekhilta d'Rebbi Ishmael, Massekhta d'Bachodesh,* chapter 5.
6. For this notion of God's loneliness, I am indebted to Sherry H. Blumberg, in *"Ehad*: God's Unity," collected in *Ehad: The Many Meanings of God Is One,* edited by Eugene B. Borowitz, *Sh'ma* (1988): 9–12.

Chapter 2: God Is Power

1. Twersky, 43–44.
2. See chapter 1, note 3.
3. For this entire discussion, I am indebted to Jon D. Levenson, *Creation and the Persistence of Evil: The Jewish Drama of Divine Omnipotence* (San Francisco: Harper & Row, 1988), particularly Part 2.

Chapter 3: God Is Person

1. Abraham Joshua Heschel, *God in Search of Man* (Philadelphia: Jewish Publication Society, 1956).
2. Heschel's most rigorous elaboration of what he means by "divine pathos" is in *The Prophets*, chaps. 12–18 (Philadelphia: Jewish Publication Society, 1962).
3. *Pesikta d'Rav Kahana* 12:6.
4. Judah Halevi, "Lord, Where Shall I Find You?" in T. Carmi, ed. and trans., *The Penguin Book of Hebrew Verse* (Harmondsworth, Middlesex, England: Penguin Books, 1981), 338.
5. *Midrash Lamentations Rabbah* 1:3. I am indebted to my colleague Dr. Henry Glazer for drawing my attention to this text.
6. Rabbi Jules Harlow, ed. and trans., *Siddur Sim Shalom: A Prayerbook for Shabbat, Festivals, and Weekdays* (New York: Rabbinical Assembly and United Synagogue of America), 252–253.
7. Heschel, *The Prophets*, 283.
8. Ibid., 257.
9. *Midrash Lamentations Rabbah* 24.
10. Here and following, Mordecai M. Kaplan, *Questions Jews Ask: Reconstructionist Answers* (New York: Reconstructionist Press, 1956), 83–84.

Chapter 4: God Is Nice (Sometimes)

1. Joseph H. Hertz, ed., *Authorized Daily Prayer Book,* rev. ed. (New York: Bloch, 1948). The list appears on the very last (unnumbered) page of the book.
2. Judith Plaskow, *Standing Again at Sinai: Judaism from a Feminist Perspective* (San Francisco: Harper & Row, 1990), 141–142.
3. Ibid., 146.
4. For a sustained critique of Plaskow's position, see Cynthia Ozick, "Notes toward Finding the Right Question," in Susannah Heschel, ed., *On Being a Jewish Feminist: A Reader* (New York: Schocken Books, 1983). For Plaskow's response, see pp. 149ff in her book.
5. Plaskow, 135–136.
6. The literature on Jewish feminism is large and growing daily. Apart from Plaskow, this author also recommends Rachel Adler, *Engendering Judaism: An Inclusive Theology and Ethics* (Philadelphia: Jewish Publication Society, 1998), particularly chapter 3, on the images of God in the liturgy. The most radical revision of the liturgy from a feminist perspective is Marcia Falk, *The Book of Blessings: New Jewish Prayers for Daily Life, the Sabbath and the New Moon Festival* (San Francisco: HarperSanFrancisco, 1998).
7. *Mekhilta BaHodesh*, chapter 2.
8. *Midrash Tanchuma, Vayyiggash*, chapter 12.

Chapter 5: God Is Not Nice (Sometimes)

1. For this more radical interpretation of the closing passage in Job, see Jack Miles, *God: A Biography* (New York: Alfred A. Knopf, 1995), 323–328.

I am grateful to my friend and student Barbara Birnbaum for drawing my attention to this interpretation.

2. Babylonian Talmud, *Menachot* 29b.
3. Palestinian Talmud, *Chagigah* 2:1.
4. Kaplan, 119–120.
5. Harold Kushner, *When Bad Things Happen to Good People* (New York: Schocken Books, 1981), 183–184.
6. Ibid., 55.
7. Irving Greenberg, "Cloud of Smoke, Pillar of Fire: Judaism, Christianity, and Modernity after the Holocaust," Eva Fleischner, ed., in *Auschwitz: Beginning of a New Era?* (New York: KTAV, Cathedral Church of St. John the Divine, and Anti-Defamation League, 1974), 27.
8. Ibid.
9. Richard Rubenstein, in *The Condition of Jewish Belief,* compiled by the Editors of *Commentary* Magazine (New York: Macmillan, 1966), 199.
10. David R. Blumenthal, *Facing the Abusing God: A Theology of Protest* (Louisville, Ky.: Westminster/John Knox Press, 1993), 290–291.

Chapter 6: God Can Change

1. Twersky, 45.
2. I depart here from the JPS translation, which reads "*forgiving* iniquity, transgression, and sin." If God forgives iniquity, then why does God "not remit all punishment"? Accordingly, I translate "*tolerating* iniquity." In what follows in the text I attempt to justify this translation.
3. Babylonian Talmud, *Rosh Hashanah* 17b.

Chapter 7: God Creates

1. Twersky, 43–44.
2. Ibid., 417.
3. For one notable medieval Jewish philosopher's argument in favor of creation out of nothing, see the selection from Saadya Gaon's *Book of Doctrines and Beliefs,* in *Three Jewish Philosophers*, Alexander Altmann, ed. (New York: Atheneum, 1982), 49ff.
4. Babylonian Talmud, *Shabbat* 119b.
5. Babylonian Talmud, *Shabbat* 10a.
6. *Midrash Genesis Rabbah* 11:6.
7. On this version of creation, see Levenson, chapter 2, note 3.
8. On my translation of this verse, see chapter 1, note 3.

Chapter 8: God Reveals

1. Mordecai Kaplan, *Sabbath Prayer Book* (New York: Jewish Reconstructionist Foundation, 1945), 160–161. Kaplan's translation reads "Thy" Torah, but the Hebrew is "His" Torah.
2. For an exceptionally clear statement of this traditionalist position, see Norman Lamm, in *The Condition of Jewish Belief,* compiled by the Editors of *Commentary* Magazine, 124–126.
3. On the feminist understanding of the Sinai revelation, see Plaskow, 25ff.

4. Abraham Joshua Heschel, *God in Search of Man,* 185.
5. Franz Rosenzweig, *On Jewish Learning,* Nahum N. Glatzer, ed. (New York: Schocken Books, 1955), 118.
6. Ira Eisenstein, in *The Condition of Jewish Belief,* compiled by the Editors of *Commentary* Magazine, 16.
7. For Kaplan's own version of this position, see Emanuel S. Goldsmith and Mel Scult, eds., *Dynamic Judaism: The Essential Writings of Mordecai Kaplan* (New York: Schocken Books and Reconstructionist Press, 1985), 89ff.
8. Gershom Scholem, *On the Kabbalah and its Symbolism* (New York: Schocken Books, 1965), 30.
9. Babylonian Talmud, *Baba Metzia* 59b.
10. Ibid.
11. Babylonian Talmud, *Shabbat* 88a.
12. Palestinian Talmud, *Rosh Hashanah* 1:3.
13. David Hartman, *A Living Covenant: The Innovative Spirit in Traditional Judaism* (Woodstock, Vt.: Jewish Lights, 1997; orig. publ. New York: Free Press, 1985), 37–38.

Chapter 9: God Redeems

1. For a thorough overview of Jewish teachings on life after death, see Neil Gillman, *The Death of Death: Resurrection and Immortality in Jewish Thought* (Woodstock, Vt.: Jewish Lights, 1997).
2. That formula is omnipresent in prayer books that follow the Lurianic rite, but it is far less frequent in other prayer books. The instance noted in the text can be found in Rabbi Nosson Sherman, *The Complete ArtScroll Siddur* (New York: Mesorah Publications, 1984), 4.
3. For an exhaustive study of the Sabbatean movement, see Gershom S. Scholem, *Sabbatai Zevi: The Mystical Messiah* (Princeton, N.J.: Princeton University Press, 1973).
4. Here and following, Kaplan, 83–85.

Glossary

Sometimes two pronunciations of words are common. This glossary reflects the way that many Jews actually use these words, not just the technically correct version. When two pronunciations are listed, the first is the way the word is sounded in proper Hebrew, and the second is the way it is sometimes heard in common speech, often under the influence of Yiddish, the folk language of the Jews of northern and eastern Europe. "Kh" is used to represent a guttural sound, similar to the German "ch" (as in "sprach").

Acher (ah-KHER): Also known as Elisha ben Abuya. In the first half of the second century C.E., he was one of the great sages of his day, though he later abandoned Judaism. Because of his apostasy, he is referred to as *Acher*, "The Other One," throughout Rabbinic literature.

Adonai (ah-doh-NYE): God's name as it is pronounced in reading sacred texts such as the prayer book and the Bible. From the Hebrew word *adon* (ah-DOHN), literally meaning "master" or "Lord." See **tetragrammaton**.

Adon Olam (ah-DOHN oh-LAHM): An early morning prayer of unknown authorship, but dating to medieval times, and possibly originally intended as a nighttime prayer, because it praises God for watching over our souls when we sleep. Nowadays, it is used also as a concluding song at many religious services.

amidah (ah-mee-DAH or, commonly, ah-MEE-dah): One of the three commonly used titles for the second of the three central units in the worship service, the first being the **Shema** and Its Blessings and the third being the reading of the **Torah**. It is composed of a series of blessings, many of which are petitionary (except for the Sabbath and holidays, when the petitions are removed out of deference to the holiness of the day). Also called **tefillah** and **shemoneh esrei**. *Amidah* means "standing," and refers to the fact that the prayer is said standing up.

Babylonian Talmud: See **Talmud**.

bachar or *bocher* (bah-KHAR, boh-KHER): From the Hebrew root *b-kh-r*, conventionally translated as "choose," but more precisely meaning "consecrated" or "set-aside." In the Bible, it has a particular theological meaning relating to the people of Israel. This aspect of closeness is the essence of the covenant, which signifies the fundamental relationship between God and Israel.

Bar Kokhba (bahr KHOHKH-bah): The leader of a messianic movement in the second century C.E.

Barukh Atah Adonai (bah-ROOKH ah-TAH ah-doh-NYE): The opening three words of every traditional benediction, usually translated as "Blessed are you, O Lord."

berakhah (b'-rah-KHAH); pl. *berakhot* (b'-rah-KHOHT): The Hebrew word for "benediction."

B'reishit Rabbah (b'-ray-sheet rah-BAH): One of the most commonly referenced midrashic texts compiled in the fifth century C.E., in the Land of Israel, its core is a verse-by-verse treatment of the Book of Genesis.

Chad Gadya (khahd gahd-YAH): Initial phrase and name of a popular Aramaic song chanted at the conclusion of the Passover *seder*. The song seems to have originated in the sixteenth century. Composed of ten stanzas, the verse runs as follows: A father bought a kid for two *zuzim*; a cat came and ate the kid; a dog then bit the cat; the dog was beaten by a stick; the stick was burned by fire; water quenched the fire; an ox drank the water; a *shohet* (slaughterer) slaughtered the ox; the *shohet* was killed by the Angel of Death who was then killed by God.

Chagigah (khah-GEE-gah): The last tractate of the order *Mo'ed* (lit. "seasons," or "festivals"), in the **Mishnah**, Tosefta, and **Talmud**, it deals with the laws of sacrifices which were offered during the festivals, as well as with subjects related to festival observance such as the duty of pilgrimage. *Chagigah* means "festival offering."

chayim (khah-YEEM): Life. Grammatically always expressed in plural form.

chazan (khah-ZAHN or, commonly, KHUH-z'n): A specially trained leader of prayer services, also known as a cantor.

Chelek (kheh-LEHK): The name of the tenth chapter of the **Mishnah** and **Talmud** tractate *Sanhedrin*.

Chumash (khoo-MAHSH or, commonly, KHUH-m'sh): The first part of the Bible, which is read in the synagogue on Mondays, Thursdays, the Sabbath and holidays. Also called the "Five Books of Moses," or the **Torah**, it contains the books *B'reishit* (In the Beginning), *Shemot* (Names), *Vayikra* (And [God] Called), *Bamidbar* (In the Desert), and *Devarim* (Words or Commandments). These names are the first key words mentioned in each book, but they allude to the content of each one. The English names for the five books of the **Torah**—Genesis, Exodus, Leviticus, Numbers, and Deuteronomy—are based on the titles in the Latin Bible, which were drawn from the Greek translations of the Hebrew names.

echad (eh-KHAHD): One. Can express numerical meaning (i.e. "one, not two"), as well as uniqueness (i.e. "the only one").

eid (EYD): A witness.

Ein Sof (EYN SOHF): Infinity. One of many names for God in Rabbinic and mystical literature. Literally translates as "(the One) without end."

Eliezer ben Hyrkanos (eh-lee-EH-zer ben HER-kah-nus): A rabbi who lived during the end of first century or beginning of the second century C.E., he founded an academy in Lydda, where one of his most outstanding students was R. Akiva.

geulah (g'-oo-LAH): Redemption.

haftarah (hahf-tah-RAH or, commonly, hahf-TOH-rah); pl. *haftarot* (hahf-tah-ROHT): The section of Scripture taken from the prophets and read publicly as part of **Shabbat** and holiday worship services. From a word meaning "to conclude," since it is the "concluding reading," that is, it follows a reading from the **Torah**.

Ha-kadosh barukh Hu (hah-kah-DOHSH bah-ROOKH hoo): A name for God, literally, "the Holy Blessed Be He."

halakhah (hah-lah-KHAH or, commonly, hah-LAH-khah): The Hebrew word for "Jewish law." Used as an anglicized adjective, *halakhic* (hah-LAH-khic), meaning "legal." From the Hebrew word meaning "to walk" or "to go," so denoting the way on which a person should walk through life.

Hasidic (khah-SIH-dihk): Of the doctrine generally traced to an eighteenth-century Polish Jewish mystic and spiritual leader known as the Ba'al Shem Tov (called also the *BeSHT,* an acronym composed of the initials of his name). Followers are called *Hasidim* (khah-see-DEEM or khah-SIH-dim); sing., *Hasid* (khah-SEED or, commonly, KHAH-sihd) from the Hebrew word *chesed* (KHEH-sed), meaning "loving-kindness" or "piety."

High Holy Days, or **High Holidays**: Rosh Hashanah (the New Year) and Yom Kippur (the Day of Atonement), ten days later. The period between these two days is known as the Ten Days of Repentance.

Jerusalem Talmud: See **Talmud**.

Kabbalah (kah-bah-LAH or, commonly, kah-BAH-lah): A general term for Jewish mysticism, but used properly for a specific mystical doctrine that was recorded in the *Zohar* in the thirteenth century, and then was further elaborated, especially in the Land of Israel (in Safed), in the sixteenth century. From a Hebrew word meaning "to receive," or "to welcome," and secondarily, "tradition," implying the receiving of tradition.

kavanah (kah-vah-NAH): From a word meaning "to direct," and therefore denoting the state of directing one's words and thoughts sincerely to God, as opposed to the rote recitation of prayer.

koach (KOH-akh): Strength.

ma'ariv (mah-ah-REEV or, commonly, MAH-ah-reev): From the Hebrew word *erev* (EH-rev), meaning "evening"; one of two titles used for the evening worship service (also called *Arvit*).

machzor (mahkh-ZOHR or, commonly, MAHKH-z'r): The prayer book containing holiday prayers. From the Hebrew word meaning "cycle" and referring to the festivals that recur according to an annual cycle of time.

Mekhilta (meh-KHEEL-tah): An exegetic **midrash**, proceeding verse by verse through the Book of Exodus, offering a variety of interpretations of each verse. It was compiled sometime during the amoraic period (third to fifth centuries) in Palestine.

Mekor HaChayim (meh-KOHR hah-KHAH-yeem): Source of Life. A reference to God, Talmudic in origin, and brought back into the liturgical vocabulary through the Reconstructionist movement in an effort to find diverse and non-gender-specific ways of mentioning the Deity.

Menachot (meh-nah-KHOHT): The second tractate in the order *Kedoshim* (lit. "holy things," or "Temple practices"), in the **Mishnah**, Tosefta, and **Talmud**. The meal offering is called *minchah* (meen-KHAH or, commonly, MIN-khah); pl. *menachot* (meh-nah-KHOHT). The text deals with requirements and details of preparation of meal offerings.

midrash (meed-RAHSH or, commonly, MID-rahsh); pl. *midrashim*: From the Hebrew word *darash*, "to seek, search, or demand [meaning from the biblical text]"; also, therefore, a literary genre focused upon the explication of the Bible. By extension, a body of rabbinic literature that offers classical interpretations of the Bible.

Midrash Rabbah: A work made up of ten different midrashic compilations, one of each of the five books of the ***chumash*** and the "Five Scrolls": the Song of Songs, Ruth, Lamentations, Ecclesiastes, and Esther. These ten independent works were compiled at very different times, most probably between the fifth and thirteenth centuries C.E., and in different locales, and they exhibit a variety of midrashic styles. Unlike the **Mishnah**, they are not a code organized by topic; instead, their material follows the organization of the different biblical books. The most well-known anthology of classic midrashic texts.

Mishnah (meesh-NAH or, commonly, MISH-nah): The first written summary of Jewish law, compiled in the Land of Israel about the year 200 C.E., and therefore our first overall written evidence of the state of Jewish prayer in the early centuries.

Mishneh Torah (meesh-NEH toh-RAH or, commonly, MISH-nah TOH-rah): The title of Maimonides' Code of Jewish Law.

mitzvah (meetz-VAH or, commonly, MITZ-vah); pl. *mitzvot* (meetz-VOHT): A Hebrew word used commonly to mean "good deed," but in the more technical sense, denoting any commandment from God, and therefore, by extension, what God wants us to do. Reciting the *Shema* morning and evening, for instance, is a *mitzvah*.

Oral Torah: In Hebrew, *Torah she-Ba'al Peh* (TOH-rah sheh-bah-ahl-PEH). The commentaries, interpretations, legal writings, and legends that students and teachers have woven around the **Written Torah**, or *Torah she-Bikhtav* (TOH-rah sheh-BIKH-tahv), that were thought to have been transmitted out loud rather than in writing.

Palestinian Talmud: See **Talmud**.

Pe'ah (PEH-ah): The second tractate in the order *Zeraim* (lit. "seeds," or "agriculture"), in the **Mishnah**, Tosefta, and Palestinian **Talmud**. *Pe'ah* refers to the corners of the fields which one must not harvest, but should leave for the poor.

Pentateuch: The Greek word for "five-volumed book," referring to the Hebrew Bible because the five parts of the **Torah** were transcribed on separate scrolls. The Hebrew equivalent is *Chamisha Chumshei Torah* (KHAH-mee-shah khoom-shay TOH-rah).

Pesachim (peh-sah-KHEEM): The third tractate of the order *Mo'ed* (lit. "seasons," or "festivals"), in the **Mishnah**, Tosefta, and **Talmud**. The word *pesach* (PEH-sahkh) refers literally to the paschal sacrifice, but is applied more broadly to the festival in general. The tractate deals with the paschal sacrifice, the laws of the festival, the issues of leavened and unleavened bread, and the order and liturgy of the *seder*.

peshat (peh-SHAHT): The simple, straightforward meaning of a verse.

Pesikta de'Rav Kahana (peh-SEEK-tah d'rahv kah-HAH-nah): A homiletic **midrash** compiled of sermons that was put together in the late fifth to early sixth century in the Land of Israel, offering readings for the holidays and special Sabbaths.

pesukei de-zimra (p'soo-KAY d'-zeem-RAH or, commonly, p'SOO-kay d'ZIM-rah): Literally, "verses of song," and therefore the title of a lengthy set of opening morning prayers that contain psalms and songs, and serve as spiritual preparation prior to the official call to prayer.

piyyut (pee-YOOT); pl. *piyyutim* (pee-yoo-TEEM): Literally, "a poem," but used technically to mean liturgical poems composed in classical and medieval times, and inserted into the standard prayers on special occasions.

Sanhedrin (san-HEHD-rin): The **Mishnah** and **Talmud** tractate dealing mainly with legal procedures and the court system.

Second Isaiah: Also known as "Deutero-Isaiah." Modern scholarship notes a differentiation between chapters 1–39 and 40–55 of the Book of Isaiah, calling them First and Second Isaiah, respectively. There are historical, linguistic, and conceptual differences which separate the two.

Shabbat (shah-BAHT): The Hebrew word for "Sabbath," from a word meaning "to rest."

Shabbatai Zevi (shah-bah-TYE z'VEE) (1626–1676): The central figure of Sabbateanism, the largest and most momentous messianic movement in Jewish history. The movement continued for some time even after his conversion to Islam and his death.

shacharit (shah-khah-REET or, commonly, SHAH-khah-reet): The morning worship service; from the Hebrew word *shachar* (SHAH-khar), meaning "morning."

Shekhinah (sh'-khee-NAH or, commonly, sh'-KHEE-nah): God's Divine Presence, considered to be the feminine aspect of the Divine.

Shema (sh'-MAH): The central prayer in the first of the three central units in the worship service, the second being the *amidah* and the third being the reading of the **Torah**. The *Shema* comprises three citations from the Bible. The larger liturgical unit in which it is embedded (called the *Shema* and Its Blessings) contains also a formal call to prayer *(Bar'khu)* and a series of blessings on the theological themes that, together with the *Shema*, constitute a liturgical creed of faith. *Shema*, meaning "to hear," is the first word of the first line of the first biblical citation, "Hear O Israel, **Adonai** is our God, Adonai is One,"which is the paradigmatic statement of Jewish faith, the Jews' absolute commitment to the presence of a single and unique God in time and space.

shemoneh esrei (sh'-MOH-neh ES-ray): A Hebrew word meaning "eighteen," and therefore a name given to the second of the two main units in the worship service that once had eighteen benedictions in it (it now has nineteen); known also as the *amidah*.

tallit (tah-LEET); pl. *tallitot* (tah-lee-TOHT): A prayer shawl.

Talmud (tahl-MOOD or, commonly, TAHL-m'd): The name given to each of two great compendia of Jewish law and lore compiled from the first to the sixth centuries C.E., and ever since, the literary core of the rabbinic heritage. The *Talmud Yerushalmi* (y'-roo-SHAHL-mee), the "Jerusalem Talmud," is the earlier one, a product of the Land of Israel generally dated about 400 C.E. The better-known *Talmud Bavli* (BAHV-lee), or "Babylonian Talmud," took shape in Babylonia (present-day Iraq), and is traditionally dated about 550 C.E. When people say "the" Talmud without specifying which one they mean, they are referring to the Babylonian version. *Talmud* means "teaching."

TaNaKh: An acronym which is derived from the initial letters of the three divisions of the Hebrew Bible: **Torah** (the Five Books of Moses), *Nevi'im* (Prophets), and *Ketuvim* (Writings).

tannaitic: Of, or pertaining to, the Rabbis who lived during the first two centuries C.E. (70 C.E.–200 C.E.), before the compilation of the **Mishnah**. Known as *tannaim* (tah-nah-EEM or, commonly, tah-NAH-yim); sing. *tanna* (TAH-nah), they transformed Judaism from a religion based on land and a sacrificial system to one based on learning and prayer.

Tefillah (t'fee-LAH or, commonly, t'FEE-lah): A Hebrew word meaning "prayer," but used technically to mean a specific prayer, namely, the second of the three central units in the worship service. It is known also as the *amidah* or the *shemoneh esrei*. Also the title of the sixteenth blessing of the *amidah*, a petition for God to accept our prayer.

tefillin (t'-FIH-lin or, sometimes, t'fee-LEEN): Black leather boxes which Jewish adults attach to their head and forearm with black leather straps during weekday morning prayers, in fulfillment of the biblical command to "bind them as a sign upon your arm and...frontlets between your eyes." The boxes contain pieces of parchment with the biblical quotes that command this written on them.

Temple, First and Second: In ancient times, a central building for the worship of God in Israel. The first Temple was built by Solomon, and its construction is described in the first Book of Kings. In 586 B.C.E., King Nebuchadnezzar and the Babylonians conquered Judah and destroyed the Temple, sending the Jews into exile in Babylonia. In 538 B.C.E., the Persians conquered the Babylonians, and a small remnant of the Jews returned to Palestine. Urged on by Zechariah and Haggai, they rebuilt the Temple and reinstated the sacrificial cult. The Temple was destroyed again by the Romans in 70 C.E. The building was razed, but the retaining wall of the Temple mount remains to this day as the "Western Wall."

Tetragrammaton: The technical term for the personal name of the God of Israel that is written in the Hebrew Bible with the four consonants YHWH, and pronounced *Adonai* (ah-doh-NYE). Some early Greek writers of the Christian Church state that the name YHWH was pronounced "Yahweh." Like many other Hebrew names in the Bible, the name

Yahweh is no doubt a shortened form of what was originally a longer name. It has been suggested that the original, full form of the name was something like *Yahweh-Asher-Yihweh*, "He brings into existence whatever exists."

Thirteen Principles of Faith: Maimonides' formulation of the beliefs incumbent upon every Jew.

tikkun olam (tee-KOON oh-LAHM): Literally, "repairing the world"; a focus of Jewish prayer is to make us active agents of God in the world. Commonly used today to characterize Jewish forms of social action.

Torah (TOH-rah): Literally, "teaching" or "direction." Normally, the first part of the Bible, also called the "Five Books of Moses," or the *chumash* (khoo-MAHSH or, commonly, KHUH-m'sh), which is read in the synagogue on Monday, Thursday, the Sabbath and holidays. Used also, by extension, to mean all Jewish sacred literature (the **Written Torah**, or *Torah she-Bikhtav*) and, all the commentaries and interpretations of the Written Torah (known as **Oral Torah**, or *Torah she-Ba'al Peh*).

Unetaneh Tokef (oo-neh-TAH-neh TOH-kehf or, commonly, oo-neh-SAH-neh TOH-kehf): Literally, "Let us declare the power [of the holiness of the day]," a *piyyut* recited on Rosh Hashanah and the Day of Atonement. Written by Kalonymus ben Meshullam Kalonymus of Mayence (eleventh century), the prayer became part of the traditional Ashkenazi, Polish, and Italian liturgies.

Vayikra Rabbah (vah-YEEK-rah rah-BAH): A **midrash** made up of a series of sermons on the triennial cycle portions of the Book of Leviticus *(Vayikra)*, compiled in the late fifth to early sixth century in the Land of Israel.

Yizkor (YIS-kohr): Literally, "He shall remember," it is the title and opening word of the memorial prayer said for departed close relatives on the last day of Passover, Shavuot (the second day in the Diaspora), Shemini Atzeret, and the Day of Atonement.

Yotzer (YOH-TSAYR or, commonly, YOH-tsayr): A form of *piyyut* inserted in the benedictions that precede and follow the **Shema** of the morning prayers. The name is taken from the opening line of the first benediction before the *Shema*: *Yotzer or u-vore hoshekh* etc.…"Who creates light and forms darkness."

Zechariah: One of the twelve minor prophetic books of the Bible dated from the sixth century B.C.E., though there is disagreement as to dating. Zechariah was one of the three prophets to accompany the Exiles who returned from Babylon to Jerusalem in 538 B.C.E. He prophesied together with Haggai and Malachi, in the second year of the reign of King Darius of Persia.

Zohar (ZOH-hahr): A shorthand title for *Sefer Hazohar* (SAY-fer hah-ZOH-hahr), literally, "The Book of Splendor," which is the primary compendium of mystical thought in Judaism; written mostly by Moses de Leon in Spain near the end of the thirteenth century, and ever since, the chief source for the study of **Kabbalah**.

Suggestions for Further Reading

Bialik, Hayim Nahman and Ravnitzky, Yehoshua Hana. *The Book of Legends, Sefer Ha-Aggadah: Legends from the Talmud and Midrash.* Trans. William G. Braude. New York: Schocken Books, 1992.

Blumenthal, David R. *Facing the Abusing God: A Theology of Protest.* Louisville, Ky.: Westminster/John Knox Press, 1993.

Buber, Martin, *I and Thou*: A New Translation with a Prologue "I and You" and Notes by Walter Kaufmann. New York: Charles Scribner's Sons, 1970.

Dorff, Elliot N. *Knowing God: Jewish Journeys to the Unknowable.* Northvale, N.J.: Jason Aronson, 1992.

Green, Rabbi Arthur. *Seek My Face, Speak My Name.* Northvale, N.J.: Jason Aronson, 1992.

Herberg, Will. *Judaism and Modern Man: An Interpretation of Jewish Religion.* Woodstock, Vt.: Jewish Lights Publishing, 1997.

Heschel, Abraham Joshua. *God in Search of Man: A Philosophy of Judaism.* Philadelphia: The Jewish Publication Society of America, 1956.

———. *The Prophets.* Philadelphia: The Jewish Publication Society of America, 1962.

Hoffman, Rabbi Lawrence A., Ed. *My People's Prayer Book: Traditional Prayers, Modern Commentaries*, vols. 1–4. Woodstock, Vt.: Jewish Lights Publishing, 1997–2000.

Kaplan, Mordecai M. *The Meaning of God in Modern Jewish Religion.* New York: The Jewish Reconstructionist Foundation, Inc., 1947.

Levenson, Jon D. *Creation and the Persistence of Evil: The Jewish Drama of Divine Omnipotence.* San Francisco: Harper & Row, 1988.

McFague, Sallie. *Metaphorical Theology: Models of God in Religious Language.* Philadelphia: Fortress Press, 1982.

A Maimonides Reader. Edited, with introductions and notes, by Isadore Twersky. West Orange, N.J.: Behrman House, 1972.

Miles, Jack. *God: A Biography.* New York: Alfred A. Knopf, 1995.

Neusner, Jacob. *The Foundations of the Theology of Judaism*, vol 1. Northvale, N.J.: Jason Aronson, 1991.

Plaskow, Judith. *Standing Again at Sinai: Judaism from a Feminist Perspective.* San Francisco: Harper & Row, 1990.

Siegel, Seymour and Gertel, Elliot. *God in the Teachings of Conservative Judaism.* New York: The Rabbinical Assembly, 1985.

Index

A

Abdimi ben Hama ben Hasa,
Rabbi, 162
Acher, the Other One, 100
Akiva, Rabbi, 17, 168
Akiva martyrdom, 98–101
Anthropomorphism, 7
Authorized Daily Prayer Book, 75
Azikri, Eleazar, 63

B

Babylonian exile, 3–4
Blumenthal, David R., 108
Buber, Martin, 21, 56–57

C

Cain, 111
Chaos, 36, 131, 136, 139
Circumcision, 135
Compassionate and forgiving image
of God, 113–115, 120–123, 170
Creation: cosmic ordering,
130–132; dualistic view,
131–132; four differing
accounts?, 142–144; human
role in and contribution to,
132–136; humans as partners
with God, 128; liturgical doctrine, 140–142; Maimonides'
view, 129–130; from nothing,
ex nihilo, 36–37, 131–132; primordial combat with chaos,
136–140; scientific *vs.* biblical
understanding, 143–144;
Shema, 127; *tohu va-vohu,* 131

D

Death: *Chad Gadya,* 49; dead, resurrection of, 48–50; redemption from, 173–174, 176

Divine-Human relationship. *See
also* Emotions of God. accessi-
bility of God, 58–59; Buber
vision of, 56–57; a caring for
humanity God, 54–56; child
image, 62; God in search of
humanity, 55–56; Heschel theology, 55–56, 64–65, 68;
humanity in search of God,
57–59; Husband and Wife
image, 59–62; I-Thou, 56–57;
Judah, punishment of, 60–61;
Kaplan theology, 64, 67–68,
70; Lover image, 62–63; a loving *vs.* punitive God, 71–72;
Parent image, 63; personhood
of God, 51–52, 66–68;
prophetic vision of, 59–62;
speaking to God, 5–6, 10; vulnerability of God, 56–57
Doctrine of negative attributes, 5–6
Dualistic conception of the world,
26, 27–28, 131–132, 141

E

Ego theory
Ein Sof, 5, 177, 178
Eisenstein, Rabbi Ira, 158
Eliezer ben Hyrcanos, Rabbi,
160–161
Elisha ben Abuyah apostasy,
99–100
Emotions of God. *See also* Judge
image of God. 63–69; anger,
63–65; can God be moved?,
68–69; God as process, alternative interpretation, 66–68; sorrow, 65

End of Days. *See* Eschatology, Jewish

Enlightenment, Jewish, 10

Eschatology, Jewish, 29, 168–174; *Alenu,* 29

Ethical and moral behavior of God, 53; Agag, sparing of, 97–98; Akiva martyrdom, 98–101; Amalekites, massacre of, 96–98; Elisha ben Abuyah apostasy, 99–100; and the Holocaust, 103–108; Job, 92–95, 98, 100–101, 103, 137–138; Midianites, massacre of, 96; Rubenstein theology, 106–108; Sodom and Gomorrah, 52–54, 95, 111

Evil, 35–37

Expressing *vs.* feeling love towards God, 19–20

F

Facing the Abusing God: A Theology of Protest (Blumenthal), 108

Faith and the Holocaust experience, 105–106

Feminist images of God, 11–12, 83–86, 153–154; *Mekor HaChayim,* 12, 84

Finkelstein, Louis, 87

First Temple, destruction of, 3, 65–66

G

God's existence, proving, 15, 16

God's will, knowing, 10–11

Greenberg, Irving, 105–106

H

Halakhah, Jewish law, 10

Halevi, Judah, 57–58

Hamnuna, Rabbi, 135

Hartman, David, 162

Healer image of God, 80–81

Heschel, Abraham Joshua, 1–2, 55, 56, 68, 147, 157, 158, 171

Hillel, Rabbi, 180

History: and the Bible, 145; God's power in, 42–45; redemptive history, 145, 148

Hosea, 60

Human images of God, evolution of, 110–111; changing metaphors, 123–125; compassion and sin, 113–115; justice and punishment, 111–112; punishment for sin, 111; repentance and punishment, 115–118; Yom Kippur liturgy, 118–120

I

Idolatry, sin of, 4–5

Images of God. *See also* Judge image of God; Liturgical images of God; Mysticism; Negative experience of God; Omnipotent image of God; Positive experience of God; Prophetic images of God; Theological metaphors. agnosticism, 10–11; biblical, 2–4; dualistic, 26, 27–28; father, 82–83; feminist, 11–12, 83–86; healer, 80–81; idolatry, 4–5; I-Thou, 21–22; judge, 90–91; masculine, 82–84, 85–86; ordered *vs.* anarchic, 26–27; parent, 81–83; redeemer, 79–80; rock, 79–80; teacher, 86–87

Immutability of God, 109–110

Isaac Luria, Rabbi, 176–181

Isaiah, 3, 35, 64, 140–141, 169–171

Israel: chosenness status issue, 147–150; and God interdependence, 20–22; God's abandonment of, 45–48; God's loyalty to, 20–22

J

Jeremiah, 59, 61, 62, 63, 65–66, 80–81, 172

Jeremiah, Rabbi, 161

Jerusalem, 61

Job's suffering, 92–95, 98, 100–101, 103, 137–138

Jonah, 115–118

Joshua, Rabbi, 161

Judah the Pious, Rabbi, 8
Judge image of God, 53, 90–91;
  Dante's *Inferno,* 121; Rosh
  Hashanah, 162–163; *Unetaneh*
  Tokef, 120–123; Yom Kippur,
  118–120

K

Kaplan, Rabbi Mordecai, 64, 67–68,
  70, 101–102, 103, 147, 181–183
Knowledge and God's nature, 25
Kushner, Rabbi Harold, 102–103,
  104

L

Law of remission of debts, 180
Liturgical images of God, 124–125.
  See also Shema. Adon Olam,
  72–73, 78, 79; *Alenu,* 29; *ami-*
  dah, 37, 79–80, 176;
  Authorized Daily Prayer Book,
  75; *Avinu Malkenu,* 62, 82–83,
  108; *Chad Gadya,* 49, 174;
  doctrine, 140–142; *Geulah*
  benediction, 167–168; *gevurah*
  prayer, 37; *goel, ga'al,*
  175–176; Job's suffering,
  92–95, 98, 100–101, 103,
  137–138; Priestly Benediction,
  58–59; Redemption, 166, 167,
  176, 181; teacher, 87;
  Unetaneh Tokef, 120–123;
  vidui, 119; *Yedid Nefesh,* 63;
  Yom Kippur, 118–120, 119–20
Loneliness and frustration of God,
  30–31
Loving God, 19–20
Loving *vs.* punitive God, 71–72

M

Maimonides: *Commentary on the*
  Mishnah, 23; corporeality of
  God, 8; creation, 129–130;
  doctrine of negative attributes,
  5–6; immutability of God,
  109–110; knowing God, 9;
  Mishneh Torah, 23–24;
  omnipotence of God, 34–35;
  Oneness of God, 22–25;
  Shema, interpretation of,

22–25; Thirteen Principles of
  Faith, 23, 129–130
Masculine images of God, 11–12
Materialism and idolatry, 5
Mekor HaChayim, 12, 84
Mendel of Rymanov, Rabbi,
  158–159
Messiah, Shabbatai Zevi, 179–180
Metaphors, theological. *See*
  Theological metaphors
Mezuzah, 20
Mishnah, 167–168
Mishneh Torah (Maimonides), 7, 129
Monotheistic *vs.* polytheistic views
  of God, 33–34
Moshe ben Maimon, Rabbi. *See*
  Maimonides.
Mysticism: creation, 177; *Ein Sof,*
  5, 177, 178; evil, 177; humans
  as partners in redemption,
  176–181; *kavanah,* 178; know-
  ing God, 5; lover image of
  God, 62–63; *Shekhinah,* 12,
  83, 177; Song of Glory, 8–9;
  Tetragrammaton, 178, 179;
  tikkun olam, 178, 180

N

Nathan, Rabbi, 161
Negative experience of God. *See also*
  Judge image of God; Positive
  experience of God: Akiva martyrdom, 98–101; Amalekites,
  massacre of, 96–98; an abandoning God, 91; Blumenthal
  protest theology, 108; death of
  God theology, 106–108; down
  metaphors, 89–90; Elisha ben
  Abuyah apostasy, 99–100; faith
  and the Holocaust, 105–106;
  Greenberg theology, 105–106;
  the Holocaust, 103–108; Job's
  suffering, 92–95, 98, 100–101,
  103, 137–138; Midianites,
  massacre of, 96; Rubenstein
  theology, 106–108; a sleeping
  God, 91
Noah, 111

O

Omnipotent image of God: ambivalence of, 61–62; biblical, 34, 38; a caring God, 54–56; death, power over, 48–50; and evil, 35–37, 50; face of God, 57–59; frustration and loneliness of God, 30–31; a God asleep, 47–48; and history, 50; and the Holocaust, 45–48; and human free will, 42–44; and Israel's abandonment, 45–48; Kaplan's view, 101–102, 103; Kushner's view, 102–103, 104; limitations of, 37–40, 50; Maimonides' view, 34–35; monotheistic *vs.* polytheistic views, 33–34; Moses' vision, 38–39; over the forces of nature, 37, 136–140; and repentance, 40–42; self-limitation, 39–40; vulnerability of God, 56–57

P

Paganism, 28

Passover seder, 166–167

Pathos of God, 55, 147

Pentateuch, biblical criticism of, 155

Performative language, 22

Personhood of God. *See* Divine-Human relationship

Plaskow, Judith, 84, 85

Poetic images of God. *See* Liturgical images of God

Positive experience of God. *See also* Negative experience of God. compassionate and forgiving image of God, 120–123; father, 81–83; feminist images, 83–86; healer, 80–81; loving *vs.* punitive God; parent, 81–83; protector of all, 72–79, 86; rock, 79–80; teacher, 86–87

Priestly Benediction, 58–59

Prophetic images of God, 3–4, 35

Prozbol, 180

Punishment and sin. *See also* Sin. biblical, 111–118; in Book of Genesis, 111; compassion and, 113–115; golden calf, 112; Israel's abandonment, 45–48; Judah, Kingdom of, 60–61; Moses' plea for forbearance, 39; and repentance, 40–42, 115–118; Sodom and Gomorrah, 52–54, 95, 111; Temple, destruction of, 3, 65–66; *Unetaneh Tokef,* 120–123

R

Rahab, 43

Redeemer image of God, 79–80

Redemption, 127; an unredeemed world, 174–176; *Chad Gadya,* 174; Christianity, 167; from Death, 173–174, 176; Exodus story, 165–166; *Geulah* benediction, 167–168; *goel, ga'al* in liturgy, 175–176; Heschel views, 171; humans as partners in, 176–181; of Israel from oppression, 171–172; Jerusalem and the Temple, 171–172; Kaplan theology, 181–183; Messiah, 174; and mitzvot, 178; mystical position, 176–181; Passover *haggadah,* 166–167; Rabbi Akiva prayer for, 168; Shabbatai Zevi, 179–180; and *tikkun olam,* 178, 180; the World to Come, 169–171; Zechariah vision of, 175, 181

Religious education, task of, 16

Repentance. *See also* Punishment and sin. Jonah's experience, 40–42, 115–118; power of, 40–42; prophets' intercession role, 40; *teshuvah,* 40

Resurrection of the dead, 48–50

Revelation, 127; chosenness status issue, 147–150; Christianity, 149; Eliezer ben Hyrcanos position on, 160–161; feminist

views, 153–154; Heschel theology, 157, 158; heteronomy *vs.* autonomy, 159–162; and history, 145; human partnership with, 162–163; Islam, 149; Kaplan theology, 158; Liberal position on, 155–159; Mendel of Rymanov position, 158–159; Mormonism, 149; Rosenzweig theology, 157, 158; Scholem view, 159; Sinai, 159, 161–162; Torah role, 145–147; traditional position on, 150–155; *vs.* discovery, 158
Rock image of God, 79–80
Rosenzweig, Franz, 127, 157, 158
Rosh Chodesh, 137
Rosh Hashanah, 162–163
Rubenstein, Richard, 106–108

S

Scholem, Gershon, 159
Shabbatai Zevi, 179–180
Shekhinah, 12, 83
Shema: God's loyalty to Israel, 20–22; loving God obligation, 19–20; Maimonides' interpretation, 22–25; mutual interdependency, 20–22; oneness of God, 22–25; ordered world view within, 25–28; origins of, 17–18; readings and meanings for, 18–19; and redemption, 166; sin and punishment, 90; uniqueness, 20
Sin: of the golden calf, 38; idolatry, 4–5; sinfulness, human, 3
Sleep and death images, 74, 77
Sleeping image of God, 91
Spain, Jewish expulsion from, 177
Speiser, E. A., 33
Star of Redemption (Rosenzweig), 127
Steinberg, Milton, 103

Suffering. *See* Evil; Job's suffering

T

Tarfon, Rabbi, 168
Tefillin, 19, 20
Temple, destruction of, 3, 65–66
Teshuvah, 40
Tetragrammaton, 178, 179
Theologians visions of God: death of God theology, Rubenstein's, 106–108; Heschel's theology, 68; Holocaust theology, 103–108; Kaplan's theology, 67–68, 70; medieval Jewish philosophy, 109; process theologians, 67; protest theology, Blumenthal's, 108
Theological metaphors, 6–7, 52; agnosticism and, 10–11; description of, 6–7; and ego theory, 14–15; magnetic force analogy, 67–68; Maimonides', 7; seeing the invisible, 13–16; tension of, 11
Thirteen Principles of Faith, 23, 129–130
Tikkun olam, 178, 180
Torah: biblical criticism of, 155; role in revelation, 145–147; study and worship equivalence, 87; as word of God, 11

U

Unknowability of God, 3–4

W

When Bad Things Happen to Good People (Kushner), 102

Y

Yahweh, 178
Yedid Nefesh, 63
Yizkor Memorial Service, 1
Yom Kippur, 170

Z

Zechariah, 175, 181
Zoroastrianism, 27, 141

About JEWISH LIGHTS Publishing

People of all faiths and backgrounds yearn for books that attract, engage, educate and spiritually inspire.

Our principal goal is to stimulate thought and help all people learn about who the Jewish People are, where they come from, and what the future can be made to hold. While people of our diverse Jewish heritage are the primary audience, our books speak to people in the Christian world as well and will broaden their understanding of Judaism and the roots of their own faith.

We bring to you authors who are at the forefront of spiritual thought and experience. While each has something different to say, they all say it in a voice that you can hear.

Our books are designed to welcome you and then to engage, stimulate and inspire. We judge our success not only by whether or not our books are beautiful and commercially successful, but by whether or not they make a difference in your life.

We at Jewish Lights take great care to produce beautiful books that present meaningful spiritual content in a form that reflects the art of making high quality books. Therefore, we want to acknowledge those who contributed to the production of this book.

Stuart M. Matlins, Publisher

PRODUCTION
Marian B. Wallace & Bridgett Taylor

EDITORIAL
Sandra Korinchak, Emily Wichland,
Martha McKinney & Amanda Dupuis

BOOK DESIGN
Glenn Suokko, Woodstock, Vermont

TYPESETTING
Reuben Kantor, QEP Design, Jamaica Plain, Massachusetts

JACKET & TEXT PRINTING AND BINDING
Lake Book, Melrose Park, Illinois

Spirituality

The Women's Torah Commentary: *New Insights from Women Rabbis on the 54 Weekly Torah Portions* Ed. by *Rabbi Elyse Goldstein*

For the first time, women rabbis provide a commentary on the entire Torah. More than 25 years after the first woman was ordained a rabbi in America, women have an impressive group of spiritual role models that they never had before. Here, in a week-by-week format, these inspiring teachers bring their rich perspectives to bear on the biblical text. A perfect gift for others, or for yourself. 6 x 9, 496 pp, HC, ISBN 1-58023-076-8 **$34.95**

Bringing the Psalms to Life
How to Understand and Use the Book of Psalms by *Rabbi Daniel F. Polish*

Here, the most beloved—and least understood—of the books in the Bible comes alive. This simultaneously insightful and practical guide shows how the psalms address a myriad of spiritual issues in our lives: feeling abandoned, overcoming illness, dealing with anger, and more. 6 x 9, 208 pp, HC, ISBN 1-58023-077-6 **$21.95**

Stepping Stones to Jewish Spiritual Living: *Walking the Path*
Morning, Noon, and Night by *Rabbi James L. Mirel* & *Karen Bonnell Werth*

Transforms our daily routine into sacred acts of mindfulness. Chapters are arranged according to the cycle of each day. "A wonderful, practical, and inspiring guidebook to gently bring the riches of Jewish practice into our busy, everyday lives. Highly recommended." —*Rabbi David A. Cooper.* 6 x 9, 240 pp, Quality PB, ISBN 1-58023-074-1 **$16.95**; HC, ISBN 1-58023-003-2 **$21.95**

Parenting As a Spiritual Journey:
Deepening Ordinary & Extraordinary Events into Sacred Occasions
by Rabbi Nancy Fuchs-Kreimer 6 x 9, 224 pp, Quality PB, ISBN 1-58023-016-4 **$16.95**

The Year Mom Got Religion: *One Woman's Midlife Journey into Judaism*
by Lee Meyerhoff Hendler 6 x 9, 208 pp, Quality PB, ISBN 1-58023-070-9 **$15.95**; HC, ISBN 1-58023-000-8 **$19.95**

Moses—The Prince, the Prophet: *His Life, Legend & Message for Our Lives*
by Rabbi Levi Meier, Ph.D. 6 x 9, 224 pp, Quality PB, ISBN 1-58023-069-5 **$16.95**; HC, ISBN 1-58023-013-X **$23.95**

Ancient Secrets: *Using the Stories of the Bible to Improve Our Everyday Lives*
by Rabbi Levi Meier, Ph.D. 5½ x 8½, 288 pp, Quality PB, ISBN 1-58023-064-4 **$16.95**

Or phone, fax or mail to: **JEWISH LIGHTS Publishing**
Sunset Farm Offices, Route 4 • P.O. Box 237 • Woodstock, Vermont 05091
Tel: (802) 457-4000 • Fax: (802) 457-4004 • www.jewishlights.com
Credit card orders: **(800) 962-4544** (9AM–5PM ET Monday–Friday)
Generous discounts on quantity orders. SATISFACTION GUARANTEED. Prices subject to change.

Spirituality—The Kushner Series

Honey from the Rock, Special Anniversary Edition
An Introduction to Jewish Mysticism
by *Lawrence Kushner*

An insightful and absorbing introduction to the ten gates of Jewish mysticism and how it applies to daily life. "The easiest introduction to Jewish mysticism you can read."
6 x 9, 176 pp, Quality PB, ISBN 1-58023-073-3 **$15.95**

Eyes Remade for Wonder
The Way of Jewish Mysticism and Sacred Living
A Lawrence Kushner Reader

Intro. by *Thomas Moore*

Whether you are new to Kushner or a devoted fan, you'll find inspiration here. With samplings from each of Kushner's works, and a generous amount of new material, this book is to be read and reread, each time discovering deeper layers of meaning in our lives.
6 x 9, 240 pp, Quality PB, ISBN 1-58023-042-3 **$16.95**; HC, ISBN 1-58023-014-8 **$23.95**

Invisible Lines of Connection
Sacred Stories of the Ordinary
by *Lawrence Kushner* **AWARD WINNER!**

Through his everyday encounters with family, friends, colleagues and strangers, Kushner takes us deeply into our lives, finding flashes of spiritual insight in the process.
6 x 9, 160 pp, Quality PB, ISBN 1-879045-98-2 **$15.95**; HC, ISBN 1-879045-52-4 **$21.95**

The Book of Letters
A Mystical Hebrew Alphabet **AWARD WINNER!**
by Lawrence Kushner
Popular HC Edition, 6 x 9, 80 pp, 2-color text, ISBN 1-879045-00-1 **$24.95**; *Deluxe Gift Edition*, 9 x 12, 80 pp, HC, 2-color text, ornamentation, slipcase, ISBN 1-879045-01-X **$79.95**; *Collector's Limited Edition*, 9 x 12, 80 pp, HC, gold-embossed pages, hand-assembled slipcase. With silkscreened print. Limited to 500 signed and numbered copies, ISBN 1-879045-04-4 **$349.00**

The Book of Words
Talking Spiritual Life, Living Spiritual Talk **AWARD WINNER!**
by Lawrence Kushner   6 x 9, 160 pp, Quality PB, 2-color text, ISBN 1-58023-020-2 **$16.95**; 152 pp, HC, ISBN 1-879045-35-4 **$21.95**

God Was in This Place & I, i Did Not Know
Finding Self, Spirituality and Ultimate Meaning
by Lawrence Kushner   6 x 9, 192 pp, Quality PB, ISBN 1-879045-33-8 **$16.95**

The River of Light: *Jewish Mystical Awareness* **SPECIAL ANNIVERSARY EDITION**
by Lawrence Kushner   6 x 9, 192 pp, Quality PB, ISBN 1-58023-096-2 **$16.95**

Spirituality

My People's Prayer Book: *Traditional Prayers, Modern Commentaries*
Ed. by *Dr. Lawrence A. Hoffman*

This momentous, critically-acclaimed series is truly a people's prayer book, one that provides a diverse and exciting commentary to the traditional liturgy. It will help modern men and women find new wisdom and guidance in Jewish prayer, and bring liturgy into their lives. Each book includes Hebrew text, modern translation, and commentaries *from all perspectives* of the Jewish world. Vol. 1—*The Sh'ma and Its Blessings,* 7 x 10, 168 pp, HC, ISBN 1-879045-79-6 **$23.95**
Vol. 2—*The Amidah,* 7 x 10, 240 pp, HC, ISBN 1-879045-80-X **$23.95**
Vol. 3—*P'sukei D'zimrah* (Morning Psalms), 7 x 10, 240 pp, HC, ISBN 1-879045-81-8 **$23.95**
Vol. 4—*Seder K'riat Hatorah* (The Torah Service), 7 x 10, 264 pp, ISBN 1-879045-82-6 **$23.95**

Voices from Genesis: *Guiding Us through the Stages of Life*
by *Dr. Norman J. Cohen*

In a brilliant blending of modern *midrash* (finding contemporary meaning from biblical texts) and the life stages of Erik Erikson's developmental psychology, the characters of Genesis come alive to give us insights for our own journeys. 6 x 9, 192 pp, HC, ISBN 1-879045-75-3 **$21.95**

God Whispers: *Stories of the Soul, Lessons of the Heart*
by Rabbi Karyn D. Kedar 6 x 9, 176 pp, Quality PB, ISBN 1-58023-088-1 **$15.95**

Being God's Partner: *How to Find the Hidden Link Between Spirituality and Your Work*
by Rabbi Jeffrey K. Salkin; Intro. by Norman Lear **AWARD WINNER!**
6 x 9, 192 pp, Quality PB, ISBN 1-879045-65-6 **$16.95**; HC, ISBN 1-879045-37-0 **$19.95**

ReVisions: *Seeing Torah through a Feminist Lens* **AWARD WINNER!**
by Rabbi Elyse Goldstein 5½ x 8½, 208 pp, HC, ISBN 1-58023-047-4 **$19.95**

Soul Judaism: *Dancing with God into a New Era*
by Rabbi Wayne Dosick 5½ x 8½, 304 pp, Quality PB, ISBN 1-58023-053-9 **$16.95**

Finding Joy: *A Practical Spiritual Guide to Happiness* **AWARD WINNER!**
by Rabbi Dannel I. Schwartz with Mark Hass
6 x 9, 192 pp, Quality PB, ISBN 1-58023-009-1 **$14.95**; HC, ISBN 1-879045-53-2 **$19.95**

The Empty Chair: *Finding Hope and Joy—*
Timeless Wisdom from a Hasidic Master, Rebbe Nachman of Breslov **AWARD WINNER!**
Adapted by Moshe Mykoff and the Breslov Research Institute
4 x 6, 128 pp, Deluxe PB, 2-color text, ISBN 1-879045-67-2 **$9.95**

The Gentle Weapon: *Prayers for Everyday and Not-So-Everyday Moments*
Adapted from the Wisdom of Rebbe Nachman of Breslov by Moshe Mykoff and
S. C. Mizrahi, with the Breslov Research Institute
4 x 6, 144 pp, Deluxe PB, 2-color text, ISBN 1-58023-022-9 **$9.95**

"Who Is a Jew?" *Conversations, Not Conclusions* by Meryl Hyman
6 x 9, 272 pp, Quality PB, ISBN 1-58023-052-0 **$16.95**; HC, ISBN 1-879045-76-1 **$23.95**

Jewish Meditation

Discovering Jewish Meditation
Instruction & Guidance for Learning an Ancient Spiritual Practice
by *Nan Fink Gefen*

Gives readers of any level of understanding the tools to learn the practice of Jewish meditation on your own, starting you on the path to a deep spiritual and personal connection to God and to greater insight about your life. 6 x 9, 208 pp, Quality PB, ISBN 1-58023-067-9 **$16.95**

Meditation from the Heart of Judaism: *Today's Teachers Share Their Practices, Techniques, and Faith*
Ed. by *Avram Davis*

A "how-to" guide for both beginning and experienced meditators, drawing on the wisdom of 22 masters of meditation who explain why and how they meditate. A detailed compendium of the experts' "best practices" offers advice and starting points. 6 x 9, 256 pp, Quality PB, ISBN 1-58023-049-0 **$16.95**; HC, ISBN 1-879045-77-X **$21.95**

The Way of Flame
A Guide to the Forgotten Mystical Tradition of Jewish Meditation
by *Avram Davis* 4½ x 8, 176 pp, Quality PB, ISBN 1-58023-060-1 **$15.95**

Entering the Temple of Dreams: *Jewish Prayers, Movements, and Meditations for the End of the Day* by *Tamar Frankiel* and *Judy Greenfeld*
Nighttime spirituality is much more than bedtime prayers! Here, you'll uncover deeper meaning to familiar nighttime prayers—and learn to combine the prayers with movements and meditations to enhance your physical and psychological well-being.
7 x 10, 192 pp, Illus., Quality PB, ISBN 1-58023-079-2 **$16.95**

Minding the Temple of the Soul: *Balancing Body, Mind, and Spirit through Traditional Jewish Prayer, Movement, and Meditation*
by *Tamar Frankiel* and *Judy Greenfeld*
This new spiritual approach to physical health introduces readers to a spiritual tradition that affirms the body and enables them to reconceive their bodies in a more positive light. Focuses on traditional Jewish prayers, with exercises, movements, and meditations. 7 x 10, 184 pp, Quality PB, Illus., ISBN 1-879045-64-8 **$16.95**; Audiotape of the Blessings, Movements and Meditations (60-min. cassette), JN01 **$9.95**; Videotape of the Movements and Meditations (46-min. VHS), S507 **$20.00**

Spirituality & More

These Are the Words: *A Vocabulary of Jewish Spiritual Life*
by *Arthur Green*

What are the most essential ideas, concepts and terms that an educated person needs to know about Judaism? From *Adonai* (My Lord) to *zekhut* (merit), this enlightening and entertaining journey through Judaism teaches us the 149 core Hebrew words that constitute the basic vocabulary of Jewish spiritual life. 6 x 9, 304 pp, HC, ISBN 1-58023-024-5 **$21.95**

The Enneagram and Kabbalah: *Reading Your Soul*
by *Rabbi Howard A. Addison*

Combines two of the most powerful maps of consciousness known to humanity—The Tree of Life (the *Sefirot*) from the Jewish mystical tradition of *Kabbalah*, and the nine-pointed Enneagram—and shows how, together, they can provide a powerful tool for self-knowledge, critique, and transformation. 6 x 9, 176 pp, Quality PB, ISBN 1-58023-001-6 **$15.95**

Embracing the Covenant
Converts to Judaism Talk About Why & How
Ed. and with Intros. by *Rabbi Allan L. Berkowitz* and *Patti Moskovitz*

Through personal experiences of 20 converts to Judaism, this book illuminates reasons for converting, the quest for a satisfying spirituality, the appeal of the Jewish tradition and how conversion has changed lives—the convert's, and the lives of those close to them.
6 x 9, 192 pp, Quality PB, ISBN 1-879045-50-8 **$15.95**

Shared Dreams: *Martin Luther King, Jr. and the Jewish Community*
by Rabbi Marc Schneier; Preface by Martin Luther King III
6 x 9, 240 pp, HC, ISBN 1-58023-062-8 **$24.95**

Mystery Midrash: *An Anthology of Jewish Mystery & Detective Fiction*
Ed. by Lawrence W. Raphael; Preface by Joel Siegel, ABC's *Good Morning America*
6 x 9, 304 pp, Quality PB, ISBN 1-58023-055-5 **$16.95**

The Jewish Gardening Cookbook: *Growing Plants & Cooking for Holidays & Festivals*
by Michael Brown 6 x 9, 224 pp, HC, Illus., ISBN 1-58023-004-0 **$21.95**

Wandering Stars: *An Anthology of Jewish Fantasy & Science Fiction* Ed. by Jack Dann; Intro. by Isaac Asimov 6 x 9, 272 pp, Quality PB, ISBN 1-58023-005-9 **$16.95**

More Wandering Stars
An Anthology of Outstanding Stories of Jewish Fantasy and Science Fiction
Ed. by Jack Dann; Intro. by Isaac Asimov 6 x 9, 192 pp, Quality PB, ISBN 1-58023-063-6 **$16.95**

A Heart of Wisdom: *Making the Jewish Journey from Midlife through the Elder Years*
Ed. by Susan Berrin; Foreword by Harold Kushner
6 x 9, 384 pp, Quality PB, ISBN 1-58023-051-2 **$18.95**; HC, ISBN 1-879045-73-7 **$24.95**

Sacred Intentions: *Daily Inspiration to Strengthen the Spirit, Based on Jewish Wisdom*
by Rabbi Kerry M. Olitzky and Rabbi Lori Forman
4½ x 6½, 448 pp, Quality PB, ISBN 1-58023-061-X **$15.95**

Healing/Wellness/Recovery

Jewish Pastoral Care
A Practical Handbook from Traditional and Contemporary Sources
Ed. by *Rabbi Dayle A. Friedman*

This innovative resource builds on the classic foundations of pastoral care, enriching it with uniquely Jewish traditions and wisdom. Gives today's Jewish pastoral counselors practical guidelines based in the Jewish tradition. 6 x 9, 352 pp, HC, ISBN 1-58023-078-4 **$35.00**

Healing of Soul, Healing of Body
Spiritual Leaders Unfold the Strength & Solace in Psalms
Ed. by *Rabbi Simkha Y. Weintraub, CSW,* for The National Center for Jewish Healing

A source of solace for those who are facing illness, as well as those who care for them. Provides a wellspring of strength with inspiring introductions and commentaries by eminent spiritual leaders reflecting all Jewish movements. 6 x 9, 128 pp, Quality PB, Illus., 2-color text, ISBN 1-879045-31-1 **$14.95**

Self, Struggle & Change: *Family Conflict Stories in Genesis and Their Healing Insights for Our Lives*
by *Dr. Norman J. Cohen*

How do I find wholeness in my life and in my family's life? Here a modern master of biblical interpretation brings us greater understanding of the ancient text and of ourselves in this intriguing re-telling of conflict between husband and wife, father and son, brothers and sisters. 6 x 9, 224 pp, Quality PB, ISBN 1-879045-66-4 **$16.95**; HC, ISBN 1-879045-19-2 **$21.95**

    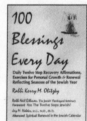

Twelve Jewish Steps to Recovery: *A Personal Guide to Turning from Alcoholism & Other Addictions . . . Drugs, Food, Gambling, Sex . . .* by Rabbi Kerry M. Olitzky & Stuart A. Copans, M.D. Preface by Abraham J. Twerski, M.D.; Intro. by Rabbi Sheldon Zimmerman; "Getting Help"by JACS Foundation 6 x 9, 144 pp, Quality PB, ISBN 1-879045-09-5 **$13.95**

One Hundred Blessings Every Day: *Daily Twelve Step Recovery Affirmations, Exercises for Personal Growth & Renewal Reflecting Seasons of the Jewish Year* by Rabbi Kerry M. Olitzky, with selected meditations prepared by Rabbi James Stone Goodman, Danny Siegel, and Gordon Tucker. Foreword by Rabbi Neil Gillman, The Jewish Theological Seminary of America; Afterword by Dr. Jay Holder, Director, Exodus Treatment Center 4½ x 6½, 432 pp, Quality PB, ISBN 1-879045-30-3 **$14.95**

Recovery from Codependence: *A Jewish Twelve Steps Guide to Healing Your Soul* by Rabbi Kerry M. Olitzky; Foreword by Marc Galanter, M.D., Director, Division of Alcoholism & Drug Abuse, NYU Medical Center; Afterword by Harriet Rossetto, Director, Gateways Beit T'shuvah 6 x 9, 160 pp, Quality PB, ISBN 1-879045-32-X **$13.95**; HC, ISBN 1-879045-27-3 **$21.95**

Renewed Each Day: *Daily Twelve Step Recovery Meditations Based on the Bible* by Rabbi Kerry M. Olitzky & Aaron Z. *Vol. I: Genesis & Exodus*; Intro. by Rabbi Michael A. Signer; Afterword by JACS Foundation. *Vol. II: Leviticus, Numbers and Deuteronomy*; Intro. by Sharon M. Strassfeld; Afterword by Rabbi Harold M. Schulweis
Vol. I: 6 x 9, 224 pp, Quality PB, ISBN 1-879045-12-5 **$14.95**
Vol. II: 6 x 9, 280 pp, Quality PB, ISBN 1-879045-13-3 **$14.95**

Children's Spirituality

In Our Image
God's First Creatures
by *Nancy Sohn Swartz*
Full-color illus. by *Melanie Hall*

For ages
4 & up

NONDENOMINATIONAL, NONSECTARIAN

A playful new twist on the Creation story—from the perspective of the animals. Celebrates the interconnectedness of nature and the harmony of all living things. "The vibrantly colored illustrations nearly leap off the page in this delightful interpretation." —*School Library Journal*

"A message all children should hear, presented in words and pictures that children will find irresistible." —*Rabbi Harold Kushner*, author of *When Bad Things Happen to Good People*

9 x 12, 32 pp, HC, Full-color illus., ISBN 1-879045-99-0 **$16.95**

God's Paintbrush

For ages
4 & up

by *Sandy Eisenberg Sasso*; Full-color illus. by *Annette Compton*
MULTICULTURAL, NONDENOMINATIONAL, NONSECTARIAN

Invites children of all faiths and backgrounds to encounter God openly in their own lives. Wonderfully interactive; provides questions adult and child can explore together at the end of each episode. "An excellent way to honor the imaginative breadth and depth of the spiritual life of the young." —*Dr. Robert Coles*, Harvard University
11 x 8½, 32 pp, HC, Full-color illus., ISBN 1-879045-22-2 **$16.95**

Also available: A Teacher's Guide: **A Guide for Jewish & Christian Educators and Parents**
8½ x 11, 32 pp, PB, ISBN 1-879045-57-5 **$6.95**

God's Paintbrush Celebration Kit 9½ x 12, HC, Includes 5 sessions/40 full-color Activity Sheets and Teacher Folder with complete instructions, ISBN 1-58023-050-4 **$21.95**

In God's Name

For ages
4 & up

by *Sandy Eisenberg Sasso*; Full-color illus. by *Phoebe Stone*
MULTICULTURAL, NONDENOMINATIONAL, NONSECTARIAN

Like an ancient myth in its poetic text and vibrant illustrations, this award-winning modern fable about the search for God's name celebrates the diversity and, at the same time, the unity of all the people of the world. "What a lovely, healing book!" —*Madeleine L'Engle*
9 x 12, 32 pp, HC, Full-color illus., ISBN 1-879045-26-5 **$16.95**

What Is God's Name? (A Board Book)

For ages
0–4

An abridged board book version of the award-winning *In God's Name*.
5 x 5, 24 pp, Board, Full-color illus., ISBN 1-893361-10-1 **$7.95**

Children's Spirituality

God Said Amen

by *Sandy Eisenberg Sasso*
Full-color illus. by *Avi Katz*

For ages
4 & up

MULTICULTURAL, NONDENOMINATIONAL, NONSECTARIAN

A warm and inspiring tale of two kingdoms: Midnight Kingdom is overflowing with water but has no oil to light its lamps; Desert Kingdom is blessed with oil but has no water to grow its gardens. The kingdoms' rulers ask God for help but are too stubborn to ask each other. It takes a minstrel, a pair of royal riding-birds and their young keepers, and a simple act of kindness to show that they need only reach out to each other to find God's answer to their prayers.

9 x 12, 32 pp, HC, Full-color illus., ISBN 1-58023-080-6 **$16.95**

For Heaven's Sake

by *Sandy Eisenberg Sasso*; Full-color illus. by *Kathryn Kunz Finney*

For ages
4 & up

MULTICULTURAL, NONDENOMINATIONAL, NONSECTARIAN

Everyone talked about heaven: "Thank heavens." "Heaven forbid." "For heaven's sake, Isaiah." But no one would say what heaven was or how to find it. So Isaiah decides to find out, by seeking answers from many different people. "This book is a reminder of how well Sandy Sasso knows the minds of children. But it may surprise—and delight—readers to find how well she knows us grown-ups too." —*Maria Harris*, National Consultant in Religious Education, and author of *Teaching and Religious Imagination* 9 x 12, 32 pp, HC, Full-color illus., ISBN 1-58023-054-7 **$16.95**

But God Remembered: Stories of Women from Creation to the Promised Land

by *Sandy Eisenberg Sasso*; Full-color illus. by *Bethanne Andersen*

For ages
8 & up

NONDENOMINATIONAL, NONSECTARIAN

A fascinating collection of four different stories of women only briefly mentioned in biblical tradition and religious texts. Award-winning author Sasso vibrantly brings to life courageous and strong women from ancient tradition; all teach important values through their actions and faith. "Exquisite. . . . A book of beauty, strength and spirituality." —*Association of Bible Teachers* 9 x 12, 32 pp, HC, Full-color illus., ISBN 1-879045-43-5 **$16.95**

God in Between

by *Sandy Eisenberg Sasso*; Full-color illus. by *Sally Sweetland*

For ages
4 & up

MULTICULTURAL, NONDENOMINATIONAL, NONSECTARIAN

If you wanted to find God, where would you look? A magical, mythical tale that teaches that God can be found where we are: within all of us and the relationships between us. "This happy and wondrous book takes our children on a sweet and holy journey into God's presence." —*Rabbi Wayne Dosick, Ph.D.*, author of *Golden Rules* and *Soul Judaism*
9 x 12, 32 pp, HC, Full-color illus., ISBN 1-879045-86-9 **$16.95**

Children's Spirituality

A Prayer for the Earth
The Story of Naamah, Noah's Wife
by *Sandy Eisenberg Sasso*
Full-color illus. by *Bethanne Andersen*

For ages
4 & up

NONDENOMINATIONAL, NONSECTARIAN

This new story, based on an ancient text, opens readers' religious imaginations to new ideas about the well-known story of the Flood. When God tells Noah to bring the animals of the world onto the ark, God also calls on Naamah, Noah's wife, to save each plant on Earth.

"A lovely tale. . . . Children of all ages should be drawn to this parable for our times."
—*Tomie dePaola*, artist/author of books for children
9 x 12, 32 pp, HC, Full-color illus., ISBN 1-879045-60-5 **$16.95**

The 11th Commandment: Wisdom from Our Children
by *The Children of America*
MULTICULTURAL, NONDENOMINATIONAL, NONSECTARIAN

For all ages

"If there were an Eleventh Commandment, what would it be?" Children of many religious denominations across America answer this question—in their own drawings and words. "A rare book of spiritual celebration for all people, of all ages, for all time."—*Bookviews*
8 x 10, 48 pp, HC, Full-color illus., ISBN 1-879045-46-X **$16.95**

Sharing Blessings: Children's Stories for Exploring the Spirit of the Jewish Holidays
by *Rahel Musleah* and *Rabbi Michael Klayman*
Full-color illus. by *Mary O'Keefe Young*

For ages
6 & up

What is the spiritual message of each of the Jewish holidays? How do we teach it to our children? Many books tell children about the historical significance and customs of the holidays. Now, through engaging, creative stories about one family's preparation, *Sharing Blessings* explores ways to get into the *spirit* of 13 different holidays. "Lighthearted, and yet thorough—allows all Jewish parents (even those with very little Jewish education) to introduce the spirit of our cherished holiday traditions." —*Shari Lewis*, creator and star of PBS' *Lamb Chop's Play-Along*
8½ x 11, 64 pp, HC, Full-color illus., ISBN 1-879045-71-0 **$18.95**

The Book of Miracles
A Young Person's Guide to Jewish Spiritual Awareness
by *Lawrence Kushner*

For ages
9 & up

From the miracle at the Red Sea to the miracle of waking up this morning, this intriguing book introduces kids to a way of everyday spiritual thinking to last a lifetime. Kushner, whose award-winning books have brought spirituality to life for countless adults, now shows young people how to use Judaism as a foundation on which to build their lives. "A well-written, easy to understand, very lovely guide to Jewish spirituality. I recommend it to all teens as a good read." —*Kimberly Kirberger*, co-author, *Chicken Soup for the Teenage Soul* 6 x 9, 96 pp, HC, 2-color illus., ISBN 1-879045-78-8 **$16.95**

Life Cycle & Holidays

How to Be a Perfect Stranger, In 2 Volumes
A Guide to Etiquette in Other People's Religious Ceremonies

Ed. by *Stuart M. Matlins* & *Arthur J. Magida* **AWARD WINNER!**

What will happen? What do I do? What do I wear? What do I say? What should I avoid doing, wearing, saying? What are their basic beliefs? Should I bring a gift? In question-and-answer format, *How to Be a Perfect Stranger* explains the rituals and celebrations of America's major religions/denominations, helping an interested guest to feel comfortable, participate to the fullest extent possible, and avoid violating anyone's religious principles. It is not a guide to theology, nor is it presented from the perspective of any particular faith.
Vol. 1: *America's Largest Faiths*, 6 x 9, 432 pp, HC, ISBN 1-879045-39-7 **$24.95**
Vol. 2: *Other Faiths in America*, 6 x 9, 416 pp, HC, ISBN 1-879045-63-X **$24.95**

Putting God on the Guest List, 2nd Ed.
How to Reclaim the Spiritual Meaning of Your Child's Bar or Bat Mitzvah

by *Rabbi Jeffrey K. Salkin* **AWARD WINNER!**

The expanded, updated, revised edition of today's most influential book (over 60,000 copies in print) about finding core spiritual values in American Jewry's most misunderstood ceremony.
6 x 9, 224 pp, Quality PB, ISBN 1-879045-59-1 **$16.95**; HC, ISBN 1-879045-58-3 **$24.95**

For Kids—Putting God on Your Guest List
How to Claim the Spiritual Meaning of Your Bar or Bat Mitzvah
by Rabbi Jeffrey K. Salkin 6 x 9, 144 pp, Quality PB, ISBN 1-58023-015-6 **$14.95**

Bar/Bat Mitzvah Basics
A Practical Family Guide to Coming of Age Together
Ed. by Cantor Helen Leneman 6 x 9, 240 pp, Quality PB, ISBN 1-879045-54-0 **$16.95**;
HC, ISBN 1-879045-51-6 **$24.95**

The New Jewish Baby Book AWARD WINNER!
Names, Ceremonies, & Customs—A Guide for Today's Families
by Anita Diamant 6 x 9, 336 pp, Quality PB, ISBN 1-879045-28-1 **$16.95**

Hanukkah: The Art of Jewish Living
by Dr. Ron Wolfson 7 x 9, 192 pp, Quality PB, Illus., ISBN 1-879045-97-4 **$16.95**

The Shabbat Seder: The Art of Jewish Living
by Dr. Ron Wolfson 7 x 9, 272 pp, Quality PB, Illus., ISBN 1-879045-90-7 **$16.95**
Also available are these helpful companions to *The Shabbat Seder*: Booklet of the Blessings and Songs, ISBN 1-879045-91-5 **$5.00**; Audiocassette of the Blessings, DN03 **$6.00**; Teacher's Guide, ISBN 1-879045-92-3 **$4.95**

The Passover Seder: The Art of Jewish Living
by Dr. Ron Wolfson 7 x 9, 352 pp, Quality PB, Illus., ISBN 1-879045-93-1 **$16.95**
Also available are these helpful companions to *The Passover Seder*: Passover Workbook, ISBN 1-879045-94-X **$6.95**; Audiocassette of the Blessings, DN04 **$6.00**; Teacher's Guide, ISBN 1-879045-95-8 **$4.95**

Life Cycle

Jewish Paths toward Healing and Wholeness
A Personal Guide to Dealing with Suffering
by *Rabbi Kerry M. Olitzky*; Foreword by *Debbie Friedman*

"Why me?" Why do we suffer? How can we heal? Grounded in the spiritual traditions of Judaism, this book provides healing rituals, psalms and prayers that help readers initiate a dialogue with God, to guide them along the complicated path of healing and wholeness.
6 x 9, 192 pp, Quality PB, ISBN 1-58023-068-7 **$15.95**

Mourning & Mitzvah: *A Guided Journal for Walking the Mourner's Path through Grief to Healing*
by *Anne Brener, L.C.S.W.*; Foreword by *Rabbi Jack Riemer*; Intro. by *Rabbi William Cutter*

For those who mourn a death, for those who would help them, for those who face a loss of any kind, Brener teaches us the power and strength available to us in the fully experienced mourning process. 7½ x 9, 288 pp, Quality PB, ISBN 1-879045-23-0 **$19.95**

Tears of Sorrow, Seeds of Hope
A Jewish Spiritual Companion for Infertility and Pregnancy Loss
by *Rabbi Nina Beth Cardin*

A spiritual companion that enables us to mourn infertility, a lost pregnancy, or a stillbirth within the prayers, rituals, and meditations of Judaism. By drawing on the texts of tradition, it creates readings and rites of mourning, and through them provides a wellspring of compassion, solace—and hope. 6 x 9, 192 pp, HC, ISBN 1-58023-017-2 **$19.95**

Lifecycles
V. 1: *Jewish Women on Life Passages & Personal Milestones* AWARD WINNER!
Ed. and with Intros. by Rabbi Debra Orenstein
V. 2: *Jewish Women on Biblical Themes in Contemporary Life* AWARD WINNER!
Ed. and with Intros. by Rabbi Debra Orenstein and Rabbi Jane Rachel Litman
V. 1: 6 x 9, 480 pp, Quality PB, ISBN 1-58023-018-0 **$19.95**; HC, ISBN 1-879045-14-1 **$24.95**
V. 2: 6 x 9, 464 pp, Quality PB, ISBN 1-58023-019-9 **$19.95**; HC, ISBN 1-879045-15-X **$24.95**

Grief in Our Seasons: *A Mourner's Kaddish Companion*
by Rabbi Kerry M. Olitzky 4½ x 6½, 448 pp, Quality PB, ISBN 1-879045-55-9 **$15.95**

A Time to Mourn, A Time to Comfort: *A Guide to Jewish Bereavement and Comfort*
by Dr. Ron Wolfson 7 x 9, 336 pp, Quality PB, ISBN 1-879045-96-6 **$16.95**

When a Grandparent Dies
A Kid's Own Remembering Workbook for Dealing with Shiva and the Year Beyond
by Nechama Liss-Levinson, Ph.D.
8 x 10, 48 pp, HC, Illus., 2-color text, ISBN 1-879045-44-3 **$15.95**

So That Your Values Live On: *Ethical Wills & How to Prepare Them*
Ed. by Rabbi Jack Riemer & Professor Nathaniel Stampfer
6 x 9, 272 pp, Quality PB, ISBN 1-879045-34-6 **$17.95**

Theology/Philosophy

Torah of the Earth: *Exploring 4,000 Years of Ecology in Jewish Thought*
In 2 Volumes Ed. by *Rabbi Arthur Waskow*
Major new resource offering us an invaluable key to understanding the intersection of ecology and Judaism. Leading scholars provide us with a guided tour of ecological thought from four major Jewish viewpoints. Vol. 1: *Biblical Israel & Rabbinic Judaism,* 6 x 9, 272 pp, Quality PB, ISBN 1-58023-086-5 **$19.95**; Vol. 2: *Zionism & Eco-Judaism,* 6 x 9, 336 pp, Quality PB, ISBN 1-58023-087-3 **$19.95**

Broken Tablets: *Restoring the Ten Commandments and Ourselves*
Ed. by *Rabbi Rachel S. Mikva*; Intro. by *Rabbi Lawrence Kushner*;
Afterword by *Rabbi Arnold Jacob Wolf* AWARD WINNER!
Twelve outstanding spiritual leaders each share profound and personal thoughts about these biblical commands and why they have such a special hold on us.
6 x 9, 192 pp, HC, ISBN 1-58023-066-0 **$21.95**

Evolving Halakhah: *A Progressive Approach to Traditional Jewish Law*
by *Rabbi Dr. Moshe Zemer*
Innovative and provocative, this book affirms the system of traditional Jewish law, *halakhah,* as flexible enough to accommodate the changing realities of each generation. It shows that the traditional framework for understanding the Torah's commandments can be the living heart of Jewish life for all Jews. 6 x 9, 480 pp, HC, ISBN 1-58023-002-4 **$40.00**

God & the Big Bang
Discovering Harmony Between Science & Spirituality AWARD WINNER!
by Daniel C. Matt
6 x 9, 216 pp, Quality PB, ISBN 1-879045-89-3 **$16.95**; HC, ISBN 1-879045-48-6 **$21.95**

Israel—A Spiritual Travel Guide AWARD WINNER!
A Companion for the Modern Jewish Pilgrim
by Rabbi Lawrence A. Hoffman 4¾ x 10, 256 pp, Quality PB, ISBN 1-879045-56-7 **$18.95**

Godwrestling—Round 2: *Ancient Wisdom, Future Paths* AWARD WINNER!
by Rabbi Arthur Waskow
6 x 9, 352 pp, Quality PB, ISBN 1-879045-72-9 **$18.95**; HC, ISBN 1-879045-45-1 **$23.95**

Ecology & the Jewish Spirit: *Where Nature & the Sacred Meet* Ed. and with Intros.
by Ellen Bernstein 6 x 9, 288 pp, Quality PB, ISBN 1-58023-082-2 **$16.95**;
HC, ISBN 1-879045-88-5 **$23.95**

Israel: *An Echo of Eternity* by Abraham Joshua Heschel; New Intro. by
Dr. Susannah Heschel 5½ x 8, 272 pp, Quality PB, ISBN 1-879045-70-2 **$18.95**

The Earth Is the Lord's: *The Inner World of the Jew in Eastern Europe*
by Abraham Joshua Heschel 5½ x 8, 112 pp, Quality PB, ISBN 1-879045-42-7 **$13.95**

A Passion for Truth: *Despair and Hope in Hasidism* by Abraham Joshua Heschel
5½ x 8, 352 pp, Quality PB, ISBN 1-879045-41-9 **$18.95**

Theology/Philosophy

A Heart of Many Rooms
Celebrating the Many Voices within Judaism
by *Dr. David Hartman* **AWARD WINNER!**

Named a *Publishers Weekly* "Best Book of the Year." Addresses the spiritual and theological questions that face all Jews and all people today. From the perspective of traditional Judaism, Hartman shows that commitment to both Jewish tradition and to pluralism can create understanding between people of different religious convictions.
6 x 9, 352 pp, HC, ISBN 1-58023-048-2 **$24.95**

A Living Covenant: *The Innovative Spirit in Traditional Judaism*
by *Dr. David Hartman* **AWARD WINNER!**

Winner, National Jewish Book Award. Hartman reveals a Judaism grounded in covenant—a relational framework—informed by the metaphor of marital love rather than that of parent-child dependency. 6 x 9, 368 pp, Quality PB, ISBN 1-58023-011-3 **$18.95**

The Death of Death: *Resurrection and Immortality in Jewish Thought*
by *Dr. Neil Gillman* **AWARD WINNER!**

Does death end life, or is it the passage from one stage of life to another? This National Jewish Book Award Finalist explores the original and compelling argument that Judaism, a religion often thought to pay little attention to the afterlife, not only offers us rich ideas on the subject—but delivers a deathblow to death itself. 6 x 9, 336 pp, Quality PB, ISBN 1-58023-081-4 **$18.95**; HC, ISBN 1-879045-61-3 **$23.95**

Aspects of Rabbinic Theology by Solomon Schechter; New Intro. by Dr. Neil Gillman
6 x 9, 448 pp, Quality PB, ISBN 1-879045-24-9 **$19.95**

The Last Trial: *On the Legends and Lore of the Command to Abraham to Offer Isaac as a Sacrifice* by Shalom Spiegel; New Intro. by Judah Goldin
6 x 9, 208 pp, Quality PB, ISBN 1-879045-29-X **$17.95**

Judaism and Modern Man: *An Interpretation of Jewish Religion* by Will Herberg; New Intro. by Dr. Neil Gillman 5½ x 8½, 336 pp, Quality PB, ISBN 1-879045-87-7 **$18.95**

Seeking the Path to Life **AWARD WINNER!**
Theological Meditations on God and the Nature of People, Love, Life and Death
by Rabbi Ira F. Stone
6 x 9, 160 pp, Quality PB, ISBN 1-879045-47-8 **$14.95**; HC, ISBN 1-879045-17-6 **$19.95**

The Spirit of Renewal: *Finding Faith after the Holocaust* **AWARD WINNER!**
by Rabbi Edward Feld
6 x 9, 224 pp, Quality PB, ISBN 1-879045-40-0 **$16.95**

Tormented Master: *The Life and Spiritual Quest of Rabbi Nahman of Bratslav*
by Dr. Arthur Green
6 x 9, 416 pp, Quality PB, ISBN 1-879045-11-7 **$18.95**

Your Word Is Fire: *The Hasidic Masters on Contemplative Prayer*
Ed. and Trans. with a New Introduction by Dr. Arthur Green and Dr. Barry W. Holtz
6 x 9, 160 pp, Quality PB, ISBN 1-879045-25-7 **$14.95**

The Way Into... Series

A major 14-volume series to be completed over the next several years, *The Way Into...* provides an accessible and usable "guided tour" of the Jewish faith, its people, its history and beliefs—in total, an introduction to Judaism for adults that will enable them to understand and interact with sacred texts. Each volume is written by a major modern scholar and teacher, and is organized around an important concept of Judaism.

The Way Into... will enable all readers to achieve a real sense of Jewish cultural literacy through guided study. Forthcoming volumes include:

The Way Into Torah

by *Dr. Norman J. Cohen*

What is "Torah"? What are the different approaches to studying Torah? What are the different levels of understanding Torah? For whom is the study intended? Explores the origins and development of Torah, why it should be studied and how to do it.
6 x 9, 160 pp, HC, ISBN 1-58023-028-8 **$21.95**

The Way Into Jewish Prayer

by *Dr. Lawrence A. Hoffman*

Opens the door to 3,000 years of the Jewish way to God by making available all you need to feel at home in Jewish worship. Provides basic definitions of the terms you need to know as well as thoughtful analysis of the depth that lies beneath Jewish prayer.
6 x 9, 224 pp, HC, ISBN 1-58023-027-X **$21.95**

The Way Into Jewish Mystical Tradition

by *Rabbi Lawrence Kushner*

Explains the principles of Jewish mystical thinking, their religious and spiritual significance, and how they relate to our lives. A book that allows us to experience and understand the Jewish mystical approach to our place in the world.
6 x 9, 176 pp, HC, ISBN 1-58023-029-6 **$21.95**

The Way Into Encountering God in Judaism

by *Dr. Neil Gillman*

Explains how Jews have encountered God throughout history—and today—by exploring the many metaphors for God in Jewish tradition. Explores the Jewish tradition's passionate but also conflicting ways of relating to God as Creator, relational partner, and a force in history and nature.
6 x 9, 176 pp, HC, ISBN 1-58023-025-3 **$21.95**